Architecture & Landscape

An approach for improvement of social relations in public spaces after COVID-19 quarantine period

Interdisciplinary Design Universe

Ali Khiabanian – Hadi Gahramani

© All Rights Reserved

All rights reserved. No part of this book may be reproduced or transmitted in any form or by any means, electronic or mechanical, including photocopying and recording, or by any information storage and retrieval system, without permission in writing from the author.

Title: Architecture & Landscape
Authors: Ali Khiabanian, Hadi Adine Ghahramani

Translator (from Persian): R. Kafouri
Editor: Dourna Kiavar

Cover design: Ali Khiabanian

ISBN: **978-1942912613**
Publisher: **Supreme Art**

Prepare for Publishing: Asan Nashr,
www.ASANASHR.com

Table of Content

Shades Garden	11	Rainbow Skirt	133
Stone & Trees Pavilion	19	Bio-Gravity Pavilion	140
The Pavilion of Bones	23	ReUnity Pavilion	146
Solid Waves pavilion	28	Phoenix Garden 1	151
Familiar House	34	Phoenix Garden 2	159
Desert City	38	Music Pavilion	168
Workshop design process	47	Project of Neda Sadeghinahr	173
Pattern and Mirror Garden	48	Dovecote	180
Iranian Garden	57	Pattern Pavilion	189
Project of Nasim Beidaghdar	67	Lotus Pavilion	196
Helix	75	Wicker Pavilion	202
Hill Pavilion	82	Project of Nasim Tabrizi	207
A Place for Gathering	88	Temporary Forest Residence in Arasbaran	212
Project of Soheyla Asi	93	Land rise pavilion	221
Forum Pavilion	99	Haoma pavilion	229
Organic product sales pavilion	106	Project of Maryam Torabi	236
Pendulous Pavilion	114	Lookout	246
Green Trench	126	Bloom pavilion	254

About the book

After beginning of the quarantine in Iran, the Interdisciplinary Design Universe continued its activities virtually, like other offices. It was initially seemed difficult. We should codify a new system especially for the workshops and training courses. Fortunately, the students may communicate with their teachers through Telegram or WhatsApp applications and ask their questions. In this period, some institutes and architectures planned their lectures in Instagram. But, I and the IDU group were thinking about a more detailed project. Reviewing the project IDU architects and our apprehensions to promote quality of architecture in Iran and consulting with the students of the previous courses, we decided to virtually hold an architecture workshop and publish the selected works in a book.

The main idea of the workshop was codified as below

We want to spend more time with each other after the quarantine and hold social activities, ceremonies and religious customs with more vivacity after termination of the quarantine deprived us from visiting our friends and relatives. Therefore, we began to analyze different urban spaces of Iran especially its parks. Unfortunately, Iranian cities have not sufficient urban spaces. The buildings are constructed beside each other and there is very little vacancy in the downtowns. Even, there is not appropriate space for religious customs. It may be stated that collective spaces such as squares, city halls, parks, etc. was not important in the recent decades. Accordingly, the Interdisciplinary Design Universe "IDU Architects" presented several conceptual designs to promote quality of urban spaces to Tabriz Municipality. Unfortunately, the plans and ideas were not welcomed. But this workshop and reception of 19 young architects helped development of these ideas and project.

Ali Khiabanian

Conceptual design to promote the quality of Imam Khomeini street

Conceptual designs to promote the quality of urban spaces

Golden Trees

Conceptual design to promote quality of Beheshti Square
Tabriz, Iran
Interdisciplinary Design Universe "IDUArchitects"

Shades garden

IDU Architects

The shades garden is a project offered to promote quality of parks of Tabriz to the municipality. This project is a set of structures in different dimensions designed based on Iranian-Islamic pictures and using the parametric technique. The small pictures are placed in the base of the structure and they become big and transform gradually. Thickness of the pictures, especially in upper parts, creates various shades through movement of the sun. Shade of the polygons becomes small and big, transform, and even is omitted. Therefore, this project was named as "Shades Garden".

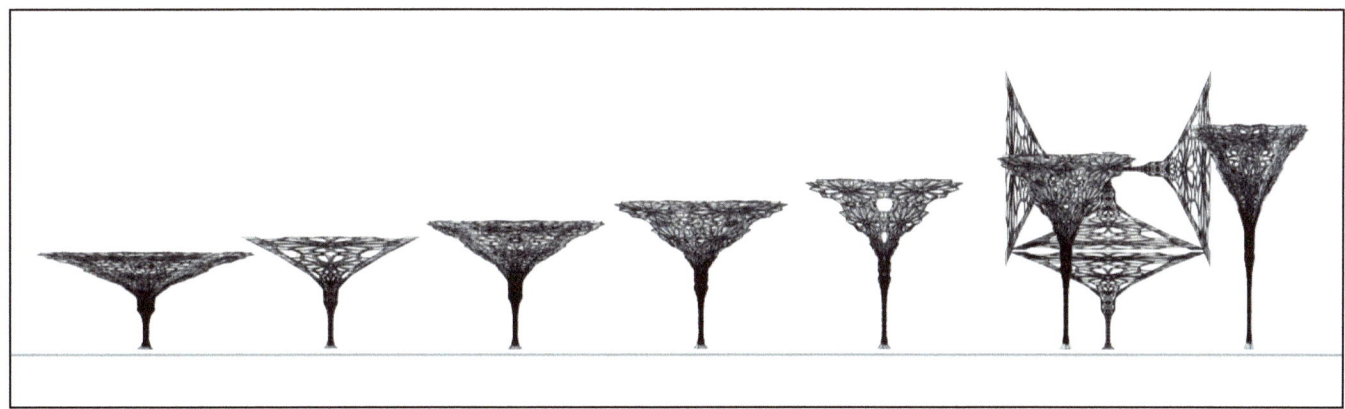

Site plan

Facade of garden

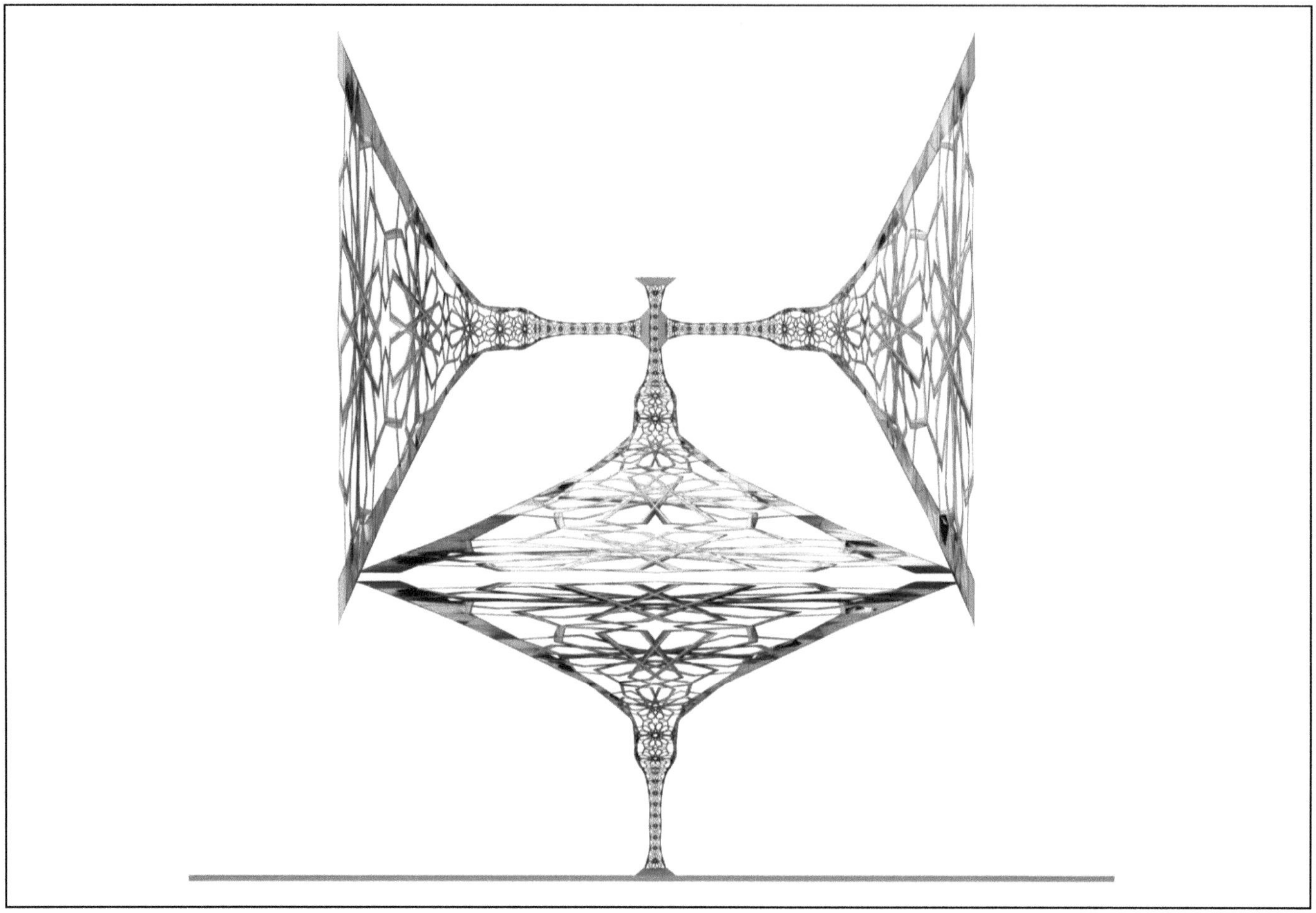

facade of garden

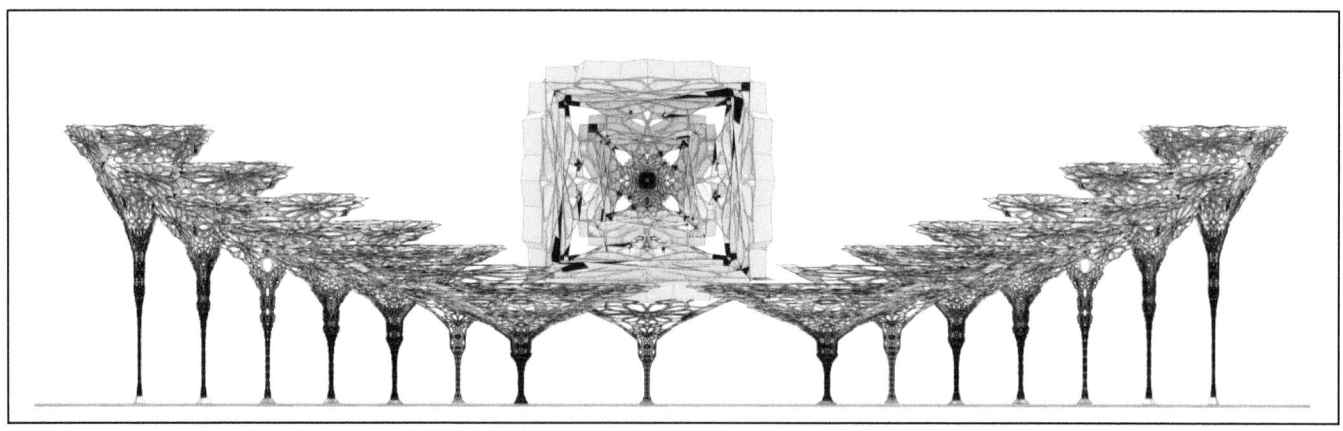

Projects of Hadi Adine Ghahramani

Looking back a century or a century, we can say that after humans have focused their minds on the design of cities in general, everything will be fine. Cities are generally a healthier, more fun, and more beautiful environment. More than half of the world's population now lives in cities, and by 2050, about 6.4 billion people will be living in cities. Rapid population growth, industrialization, climate change, water pollution, and the preservation, renewal, and expansion of urban water infrastructure are just some of the unprecedented challenges facing management and urban water systems. The term city coincidence is used for cities that grow randomly. Of course, this place is usually reasonable and a defensible place, on a hill or island, or somewhere near an extractable source or a crossroads of two modes of transport. Today we consider the city as a living thing and therefore We define the city as a place for innovation, social cohesion, creativity, and cultural flourishing. The principles of smart cities provide a framework for supporting sustainable development professionals, and therefore can be considered to prevent future crises by considering frameworks.

Our general view in this workshop was collective and practical ideas for future cities and improving human life in different situations, and this factor has caused various spatial definitions of urban spaces by students and colleagues, so that using these patterns can be used to understand the concepts mentioned. The general face was observed in living environments. But not managing the high population density with the slightest change in the situation can pose a threat to resources - water, energy, food - and have a profound effect on human health and well-being, the environment, and the economy, so try to collect these ideas. Under the guise of a variety of ideas, these works can be combined to provide the authorities and those involved with the initiative to promote urban spaces.

Stone & Trees Pavilion

Talesh forest, Mazandaran, Iran

In this project, considering a natural space and defining it as a platform for collective activities, an environment has been provided for public gatherings and traditional ceremonies, so that we can use this space to have a favorable and suitable environment for people's harmony with nature.

The Pavilion of Bones

Takhti, Tehran, Iran

Today's cities, by ignoring nature, have caused a lot of inconsistencies in people's life manners, so considering the city as a living being, I have designed a multi-functional space for users. A place to revive the performance of this place as a one of main bone of city.

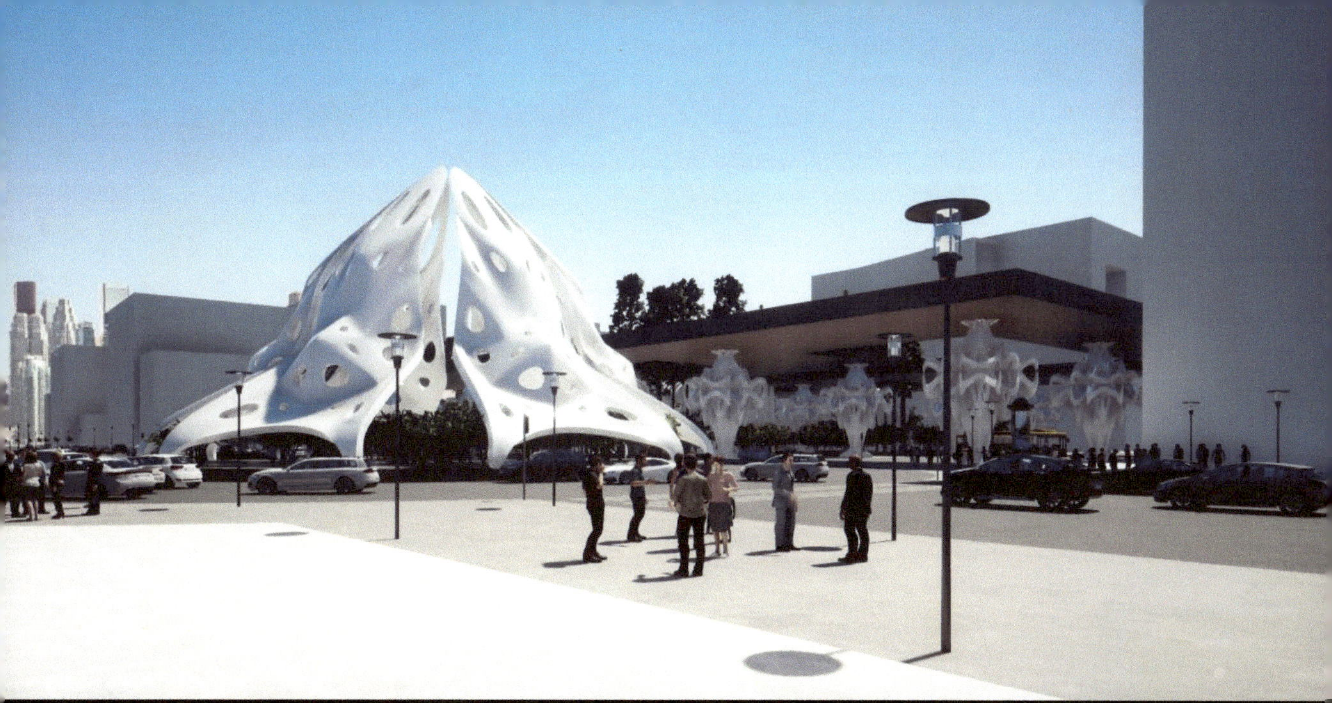
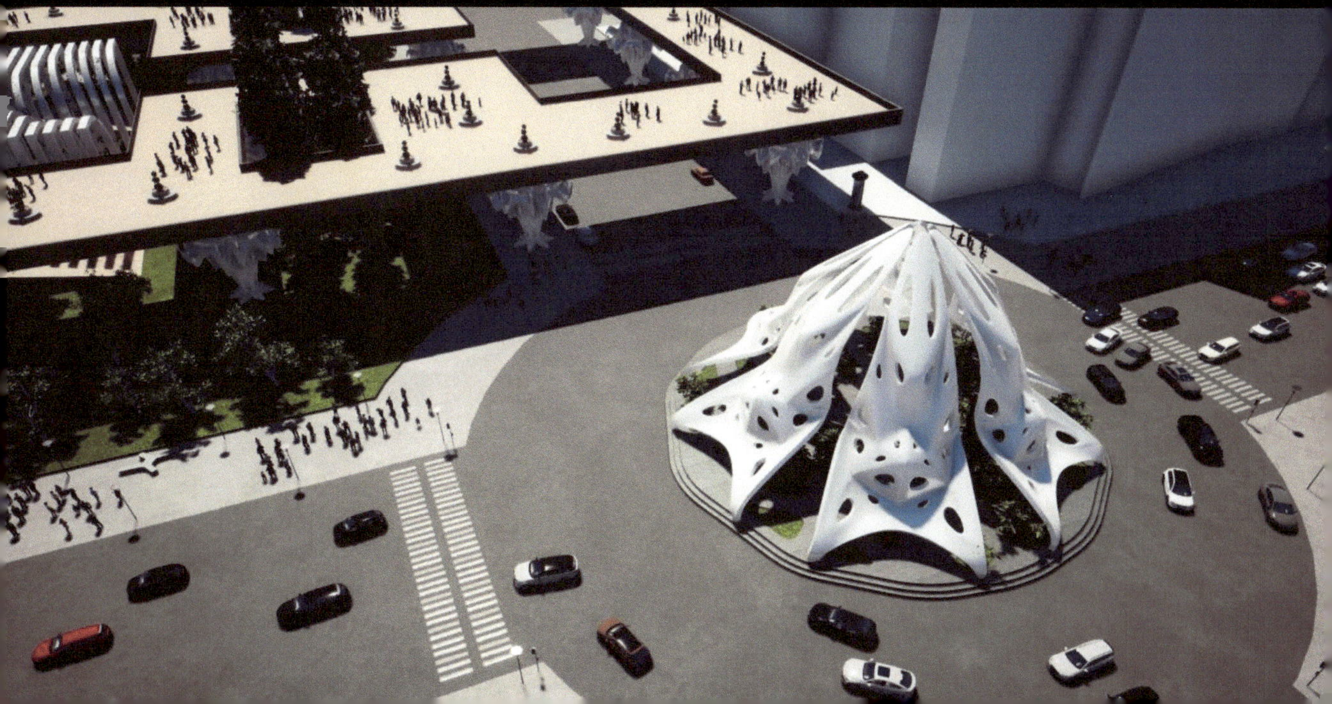

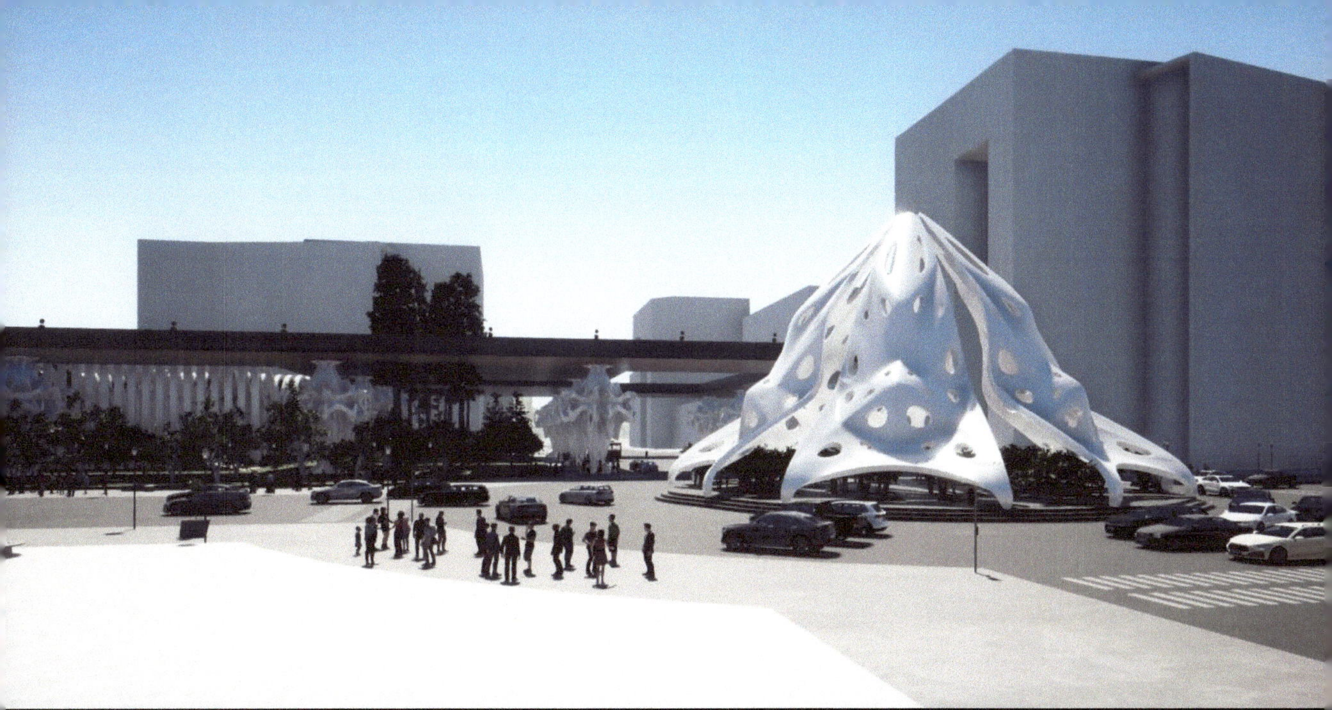

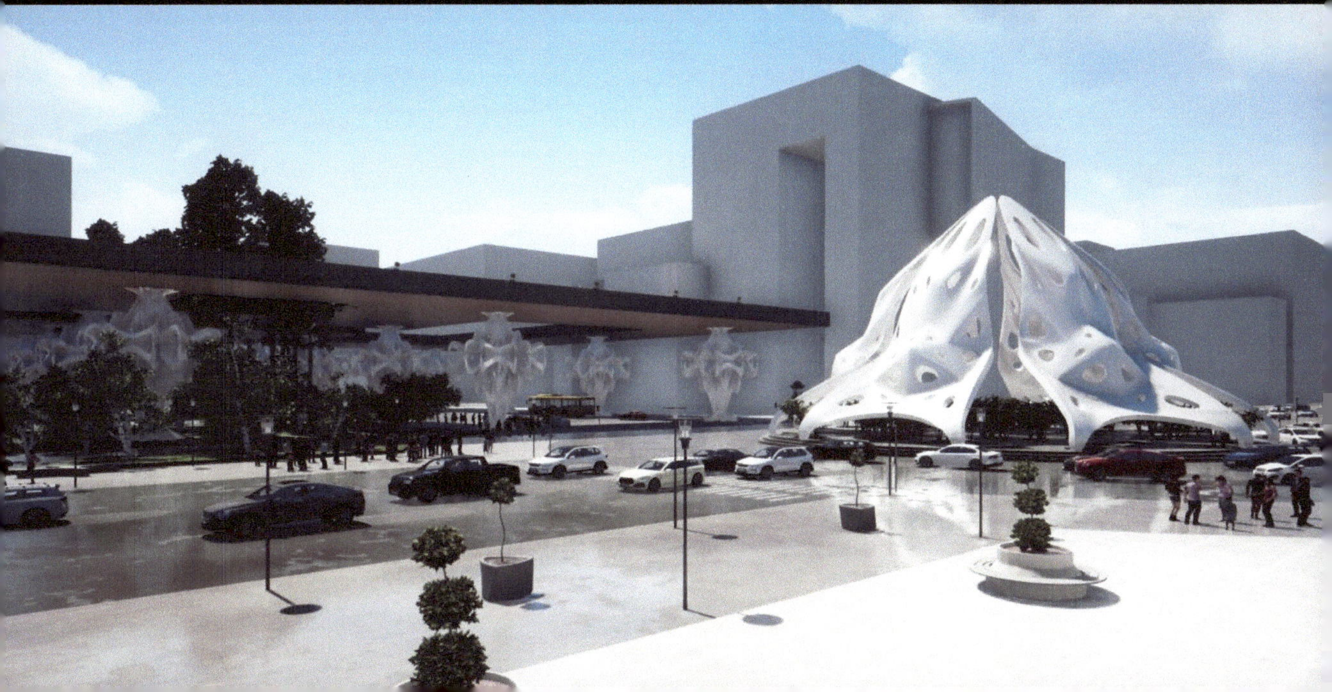

Solid Waves pavilion

Bandar Anzali, Mazandaran, Iran

The sea and waves, as the boundaries which have diminished in value over time, have been and are a natural and imaginative space. In this project, considering the behavior of the waves and the environment of this area, try to design an attractive place to present urban art works and programs. In this way, a new usage will be defined for this place.

30

32

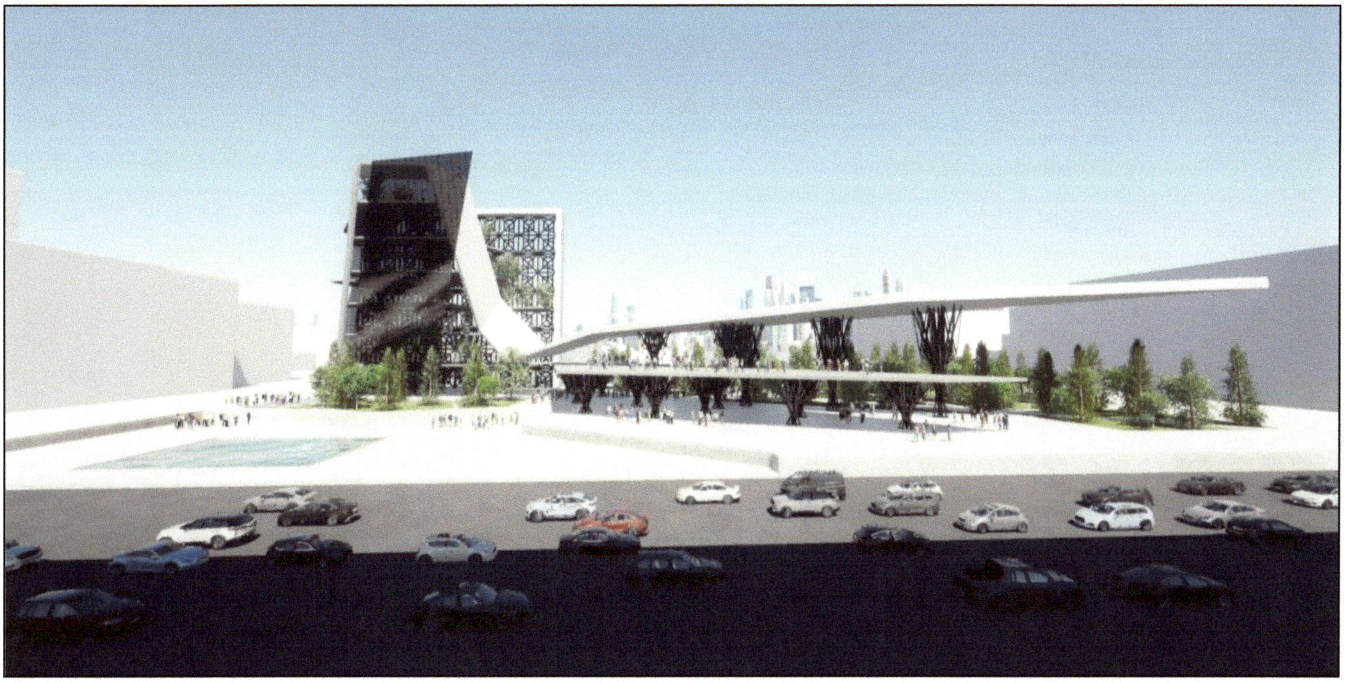

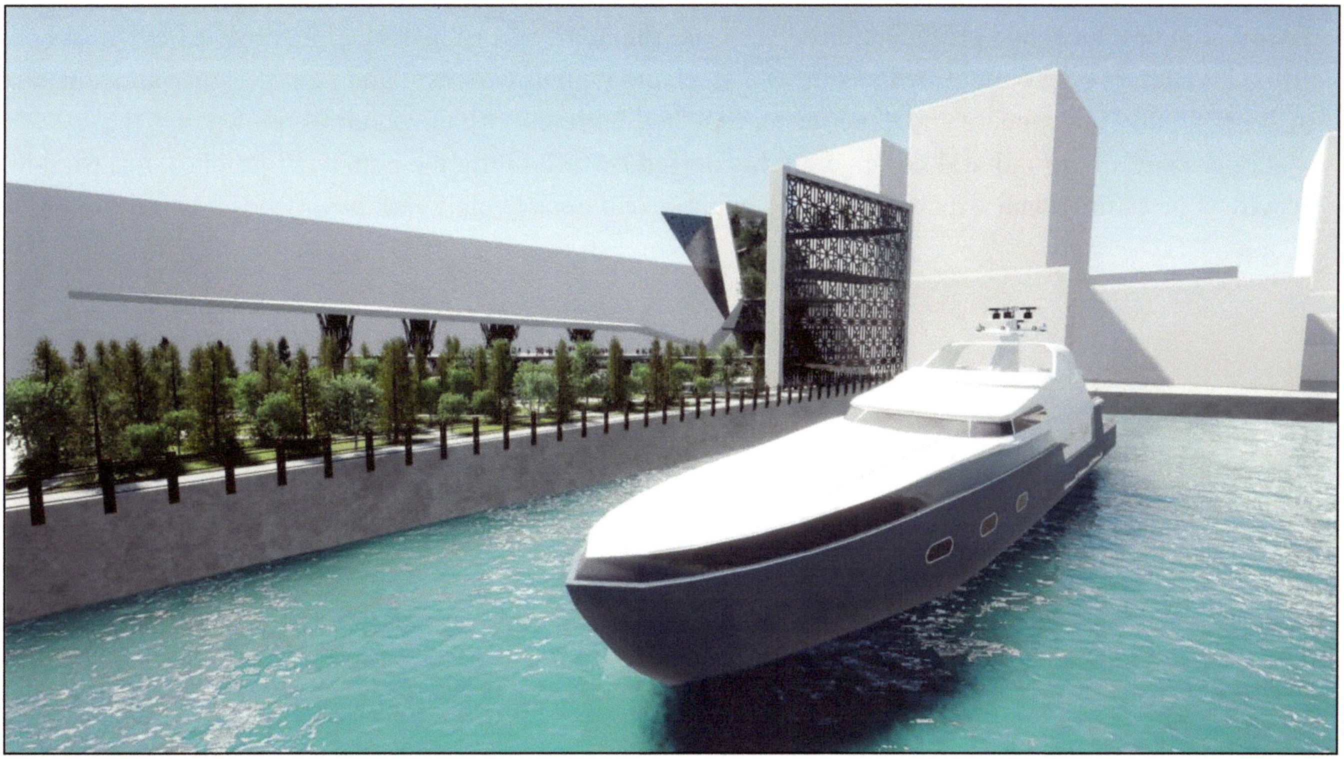

Familiar House

Sadr Alley, Tabriz, Iran

The old houses, local and original architecture, are the main part of historical memory of cities. When urban dwellers were not confined to iron and steel and by using the soil and stones, water and sun, also by long-standing awareness and experience, they had built and organized cities. Nowadays these spaces are part of our cultural heritage. In this design by redefining the pattern of porches, has tried to provide a new functional structure which is suitable and coordinated with new needs and culture of people.

36

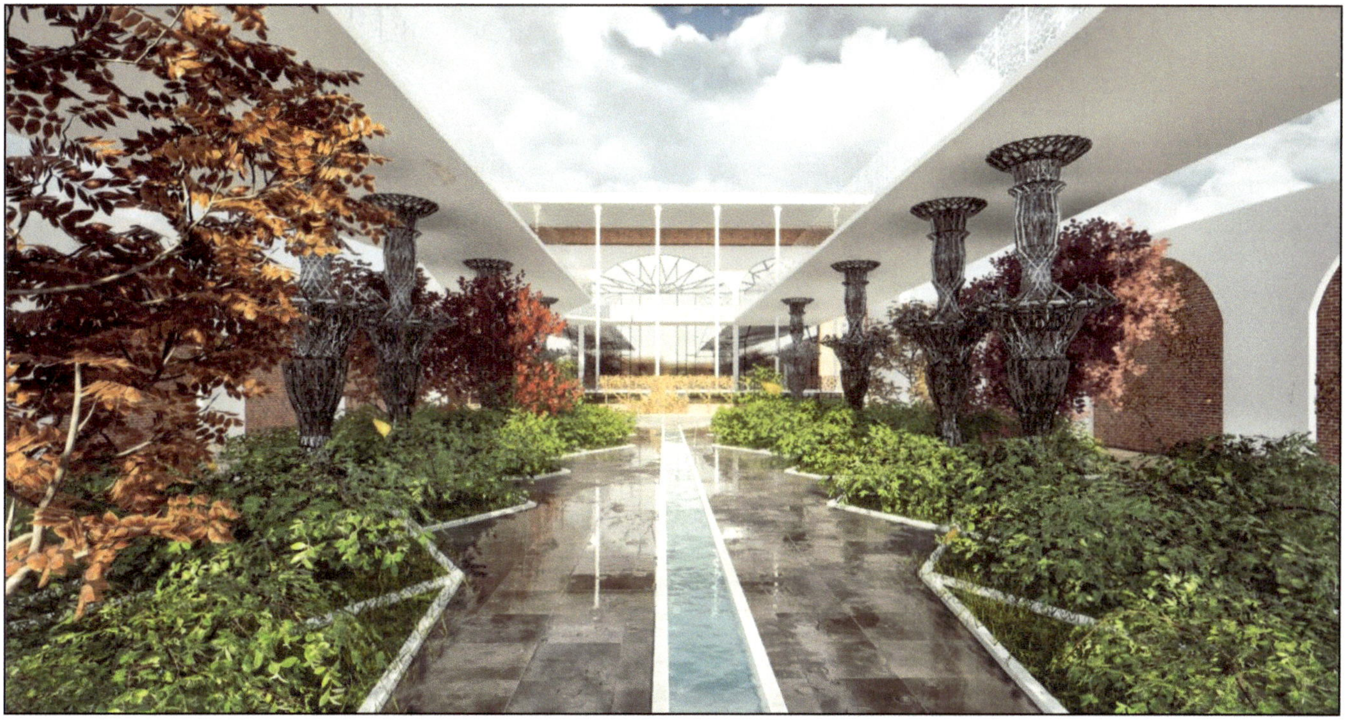

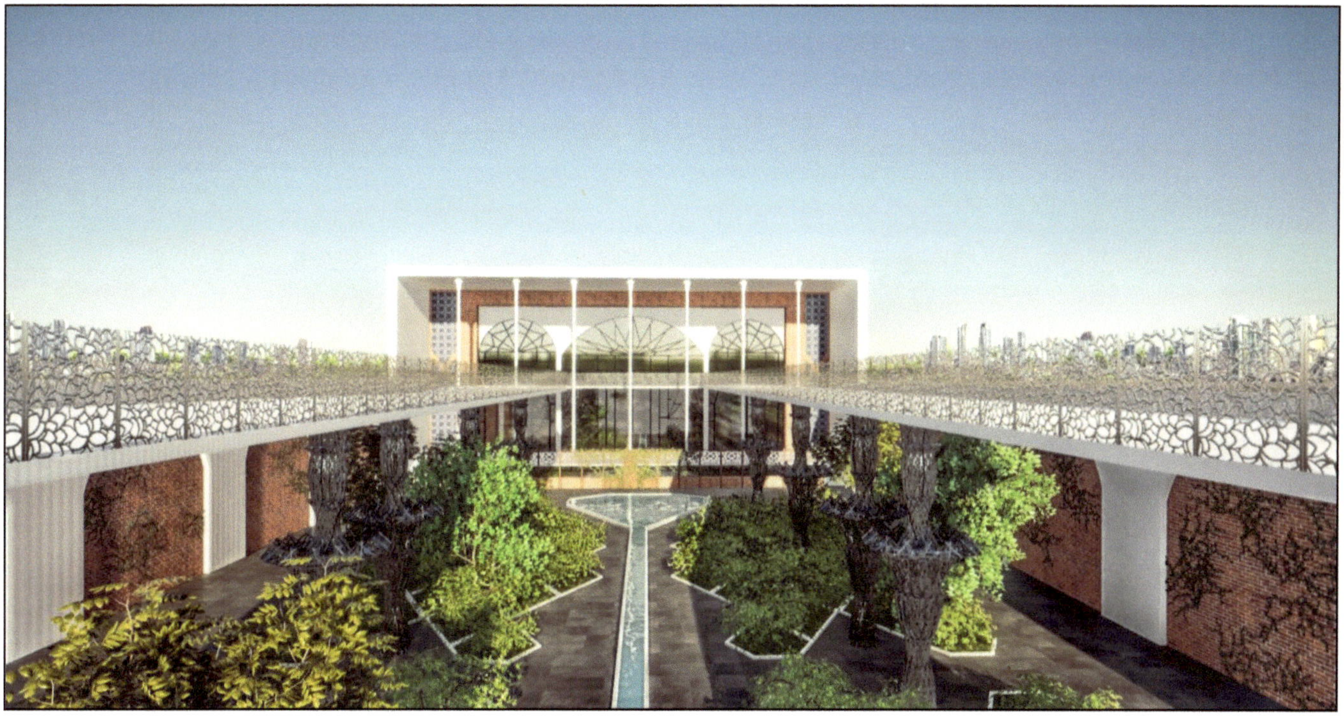

Desert City

The architecture expo in the heart of the desert inspired by thirsty cracked soil

Yazd, Iran

The desert is considered as one of the most virgin natural spaces in the world, and human being always try to adapt their environment. A space called Desert City has been proposed to use this space to create a sustainable environment inspired by plant texture and Earth's manner with natural factors.

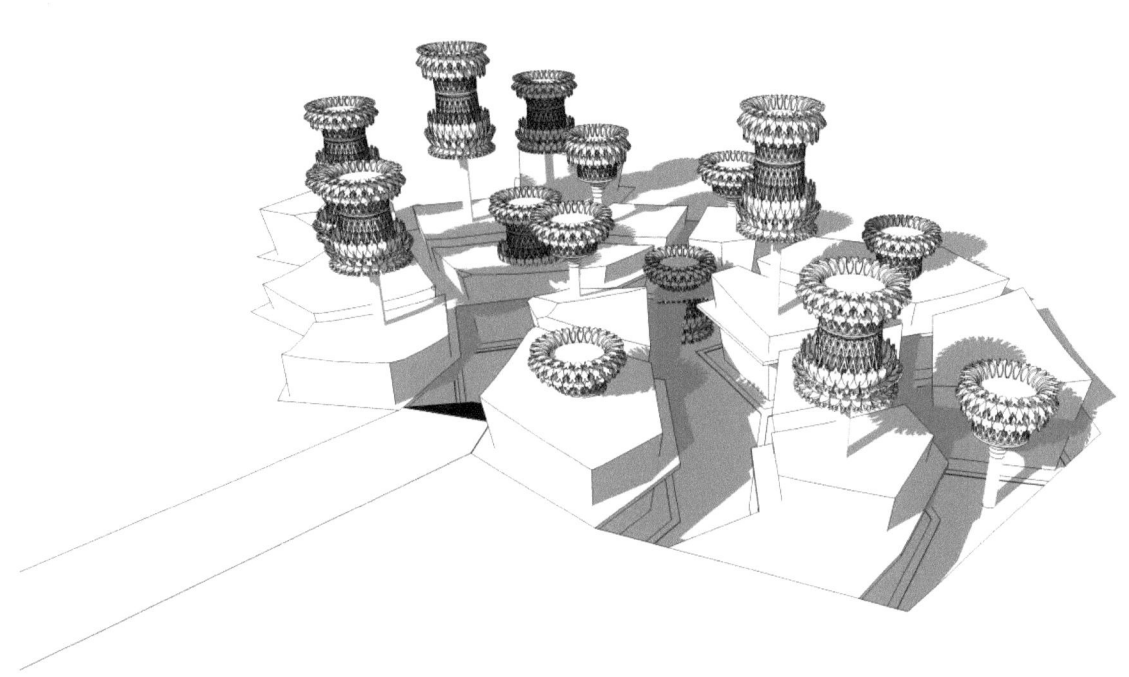

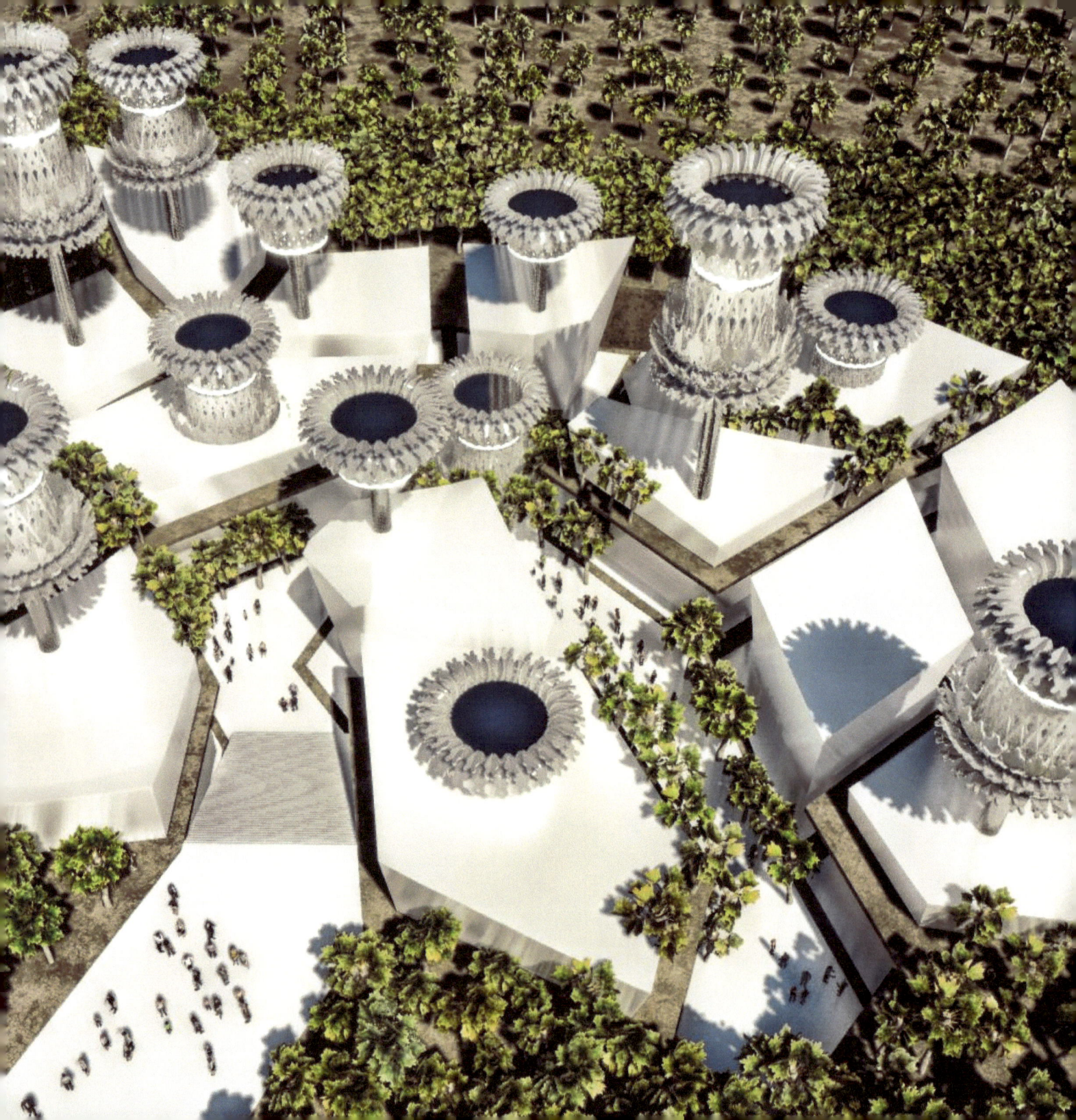

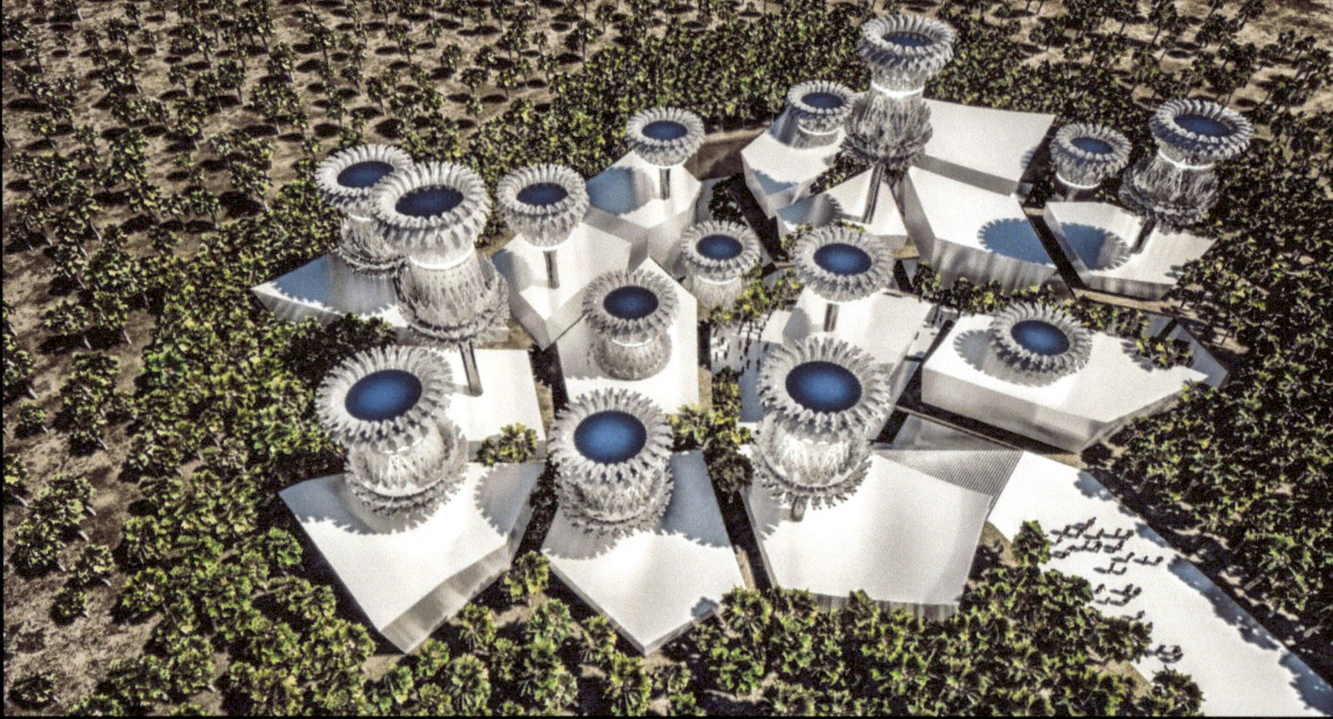

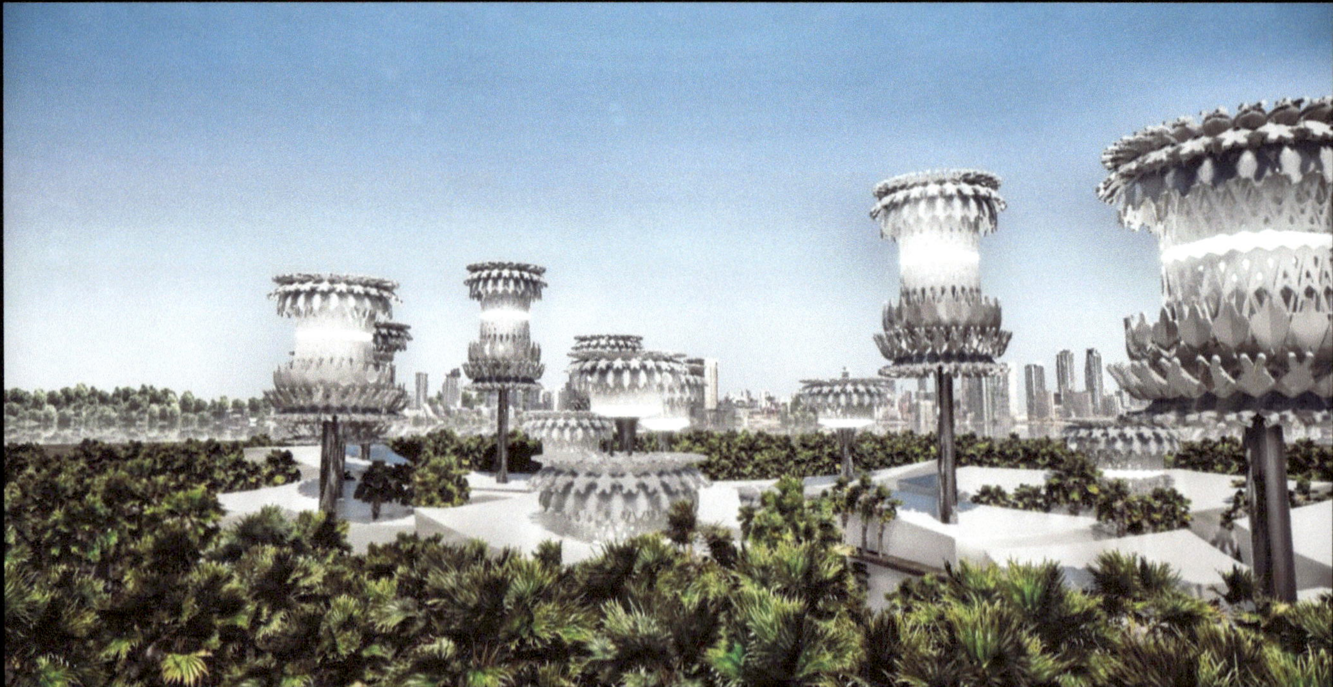

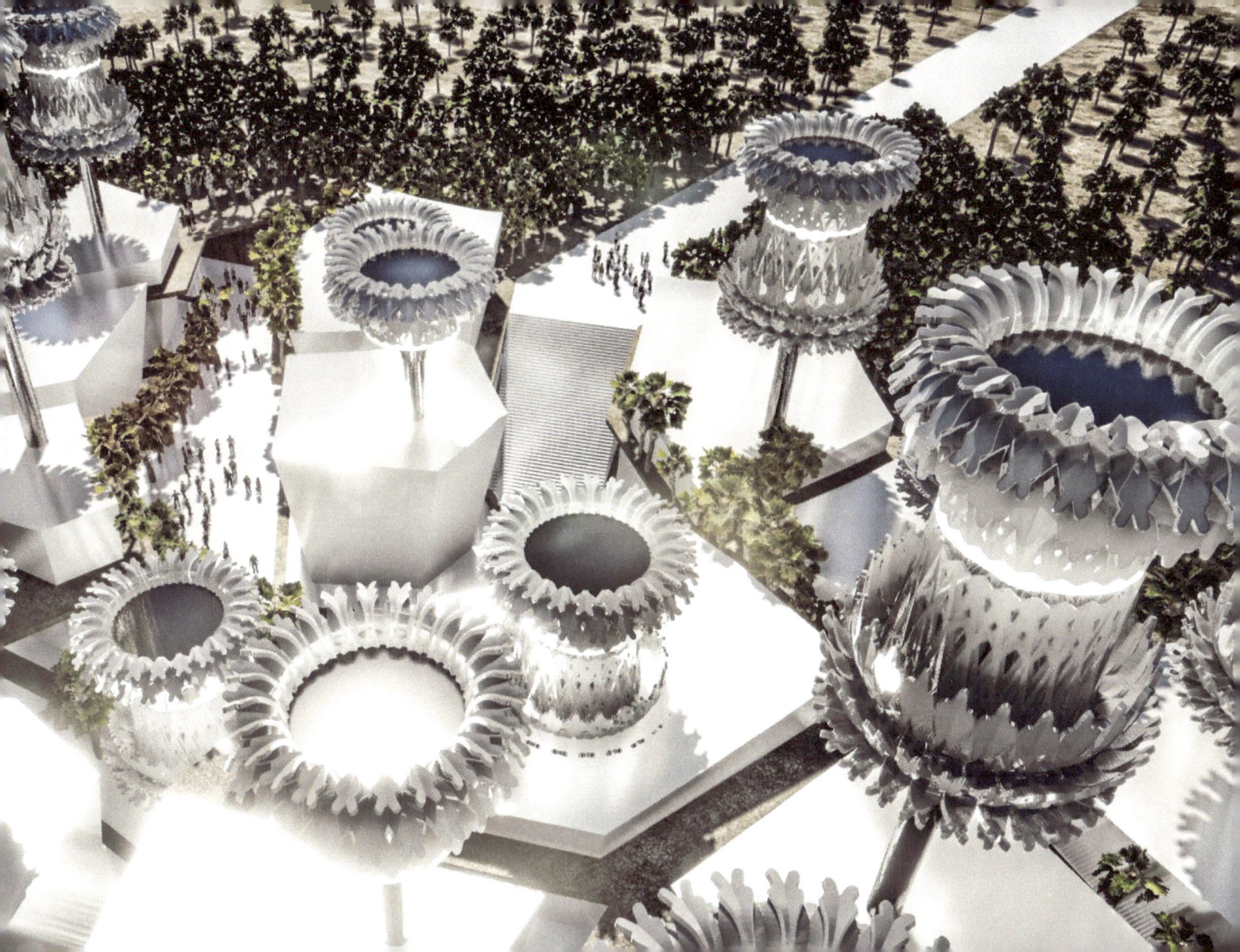

Selected Projects of Workshop

Workshop design process

- To talk about theories
- To study of 3Ds MAX software
- To technically study the modifiers- software- 3Ds Max software. The participants of the project design were only permitted to use these modifiers.
- To verify the ideas and concepts of the participants
- To correct the project and primary plans
- To review the trainings and complete the 3D models by the instructors of the workshop
- To present the final plan and select the projects
- To render the selected projects

Pattern and Mirror Garden
Arezoo Hosseinzadehazad

Pattern and mirror garden which follows Iranian garden structures in a completely ordered and simple space tries to create the sense of garden and attract addresses. The horizontal elements are the prominent ingredients directing the addressees' sight. This element is inspired by tree structure and made using Karbandi geometry which simultaneously includes the structure and architectural decorations in the dome structure and is a sever function of geometry. Karbandi is done on the arch and dome standing over pillars in corners. In this project, tree structure is used to place the Karbandies on a pillar.

In Iranian architecture, water is a symbol of light and life and reflexes the images as a mirror. To express this, shallow pools were designed under the columns. Presence of this element in the first stage frames the addresses' sight and then creates a dynamic and unique space during the day through creating regular geometrical shadows in the floor. This space is an integration of inside and outside and reminds roofed columned spaces of Iranian architecture.

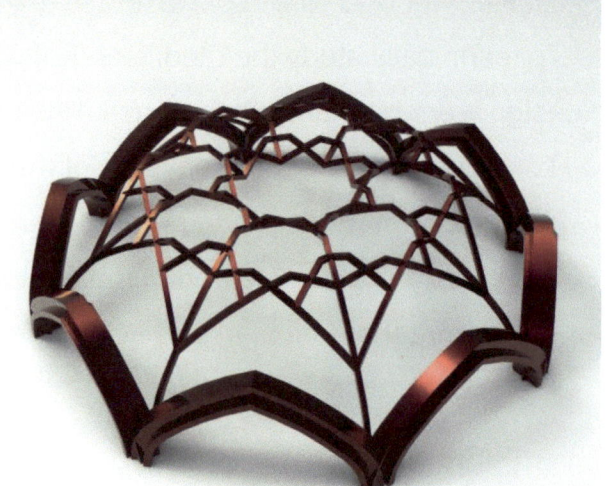
Karbandi Structure

Triangle modeling

Circle array

Pulling the lower levels out

Taper

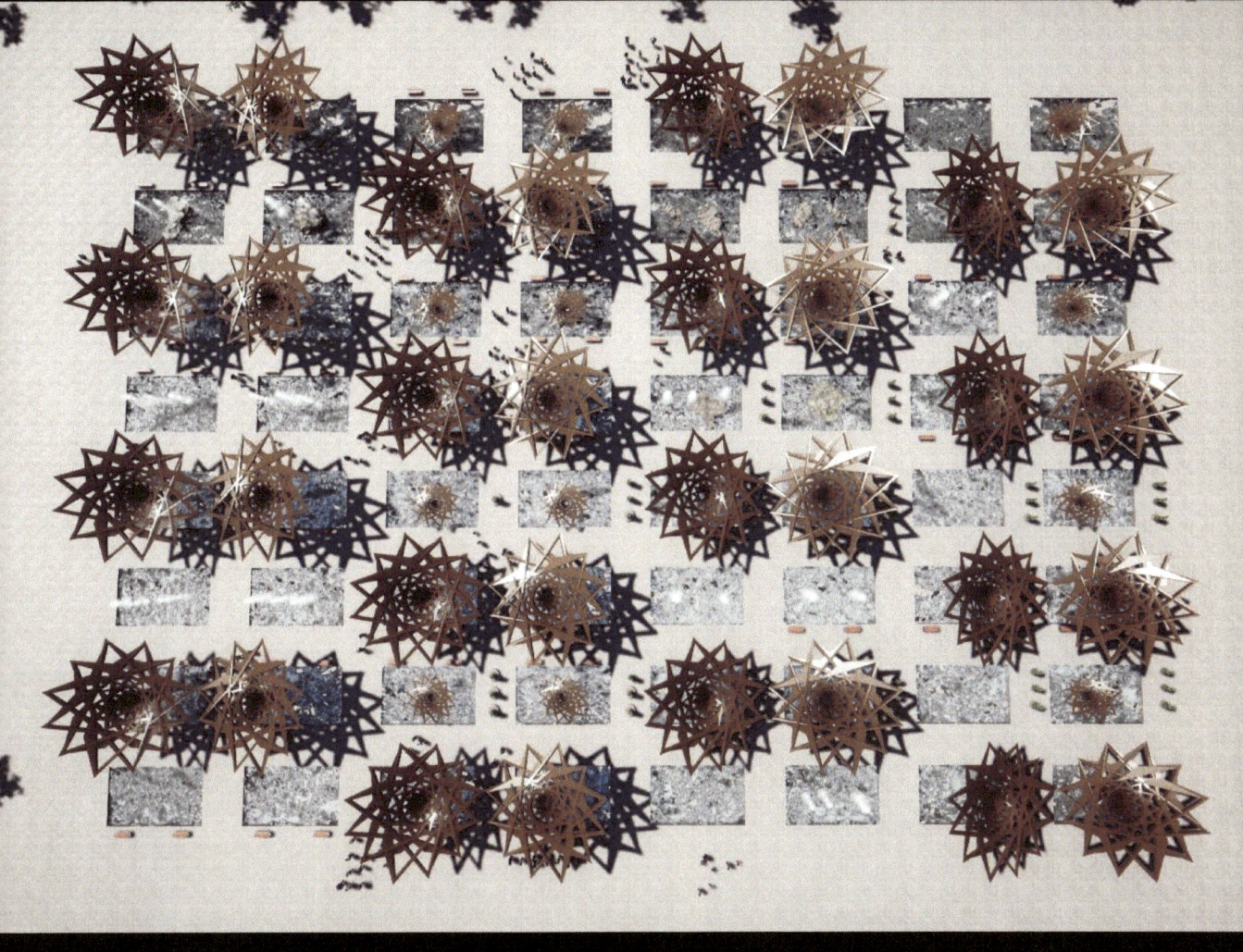

Site plan

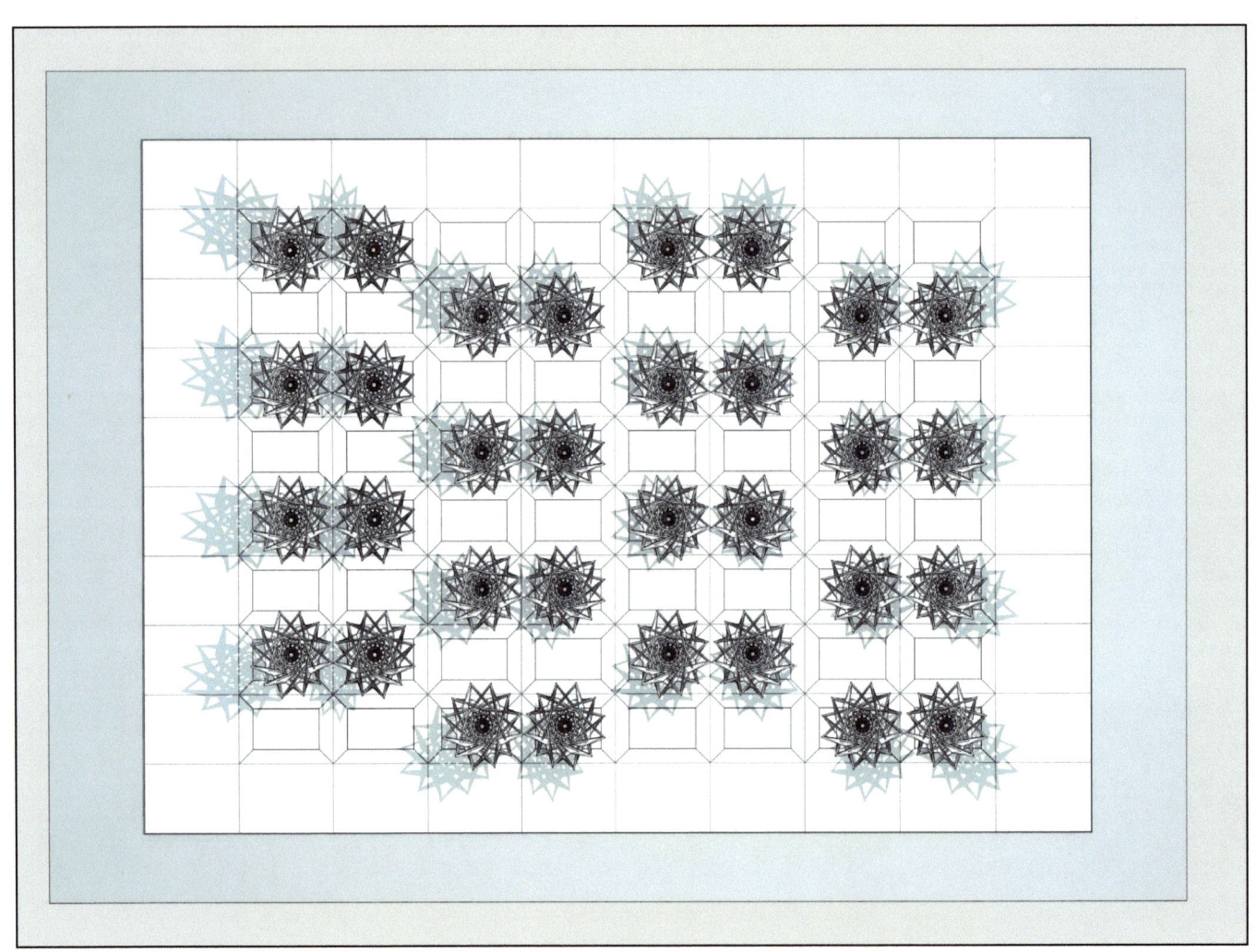

Site plan

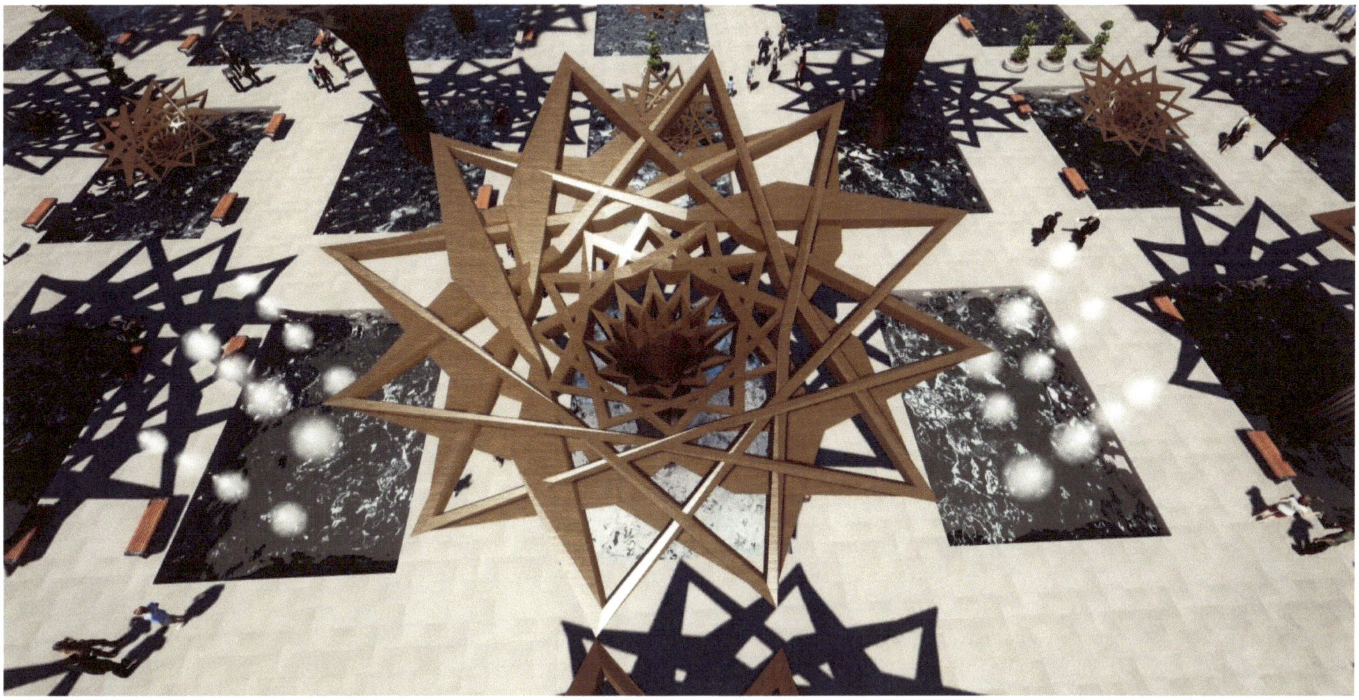

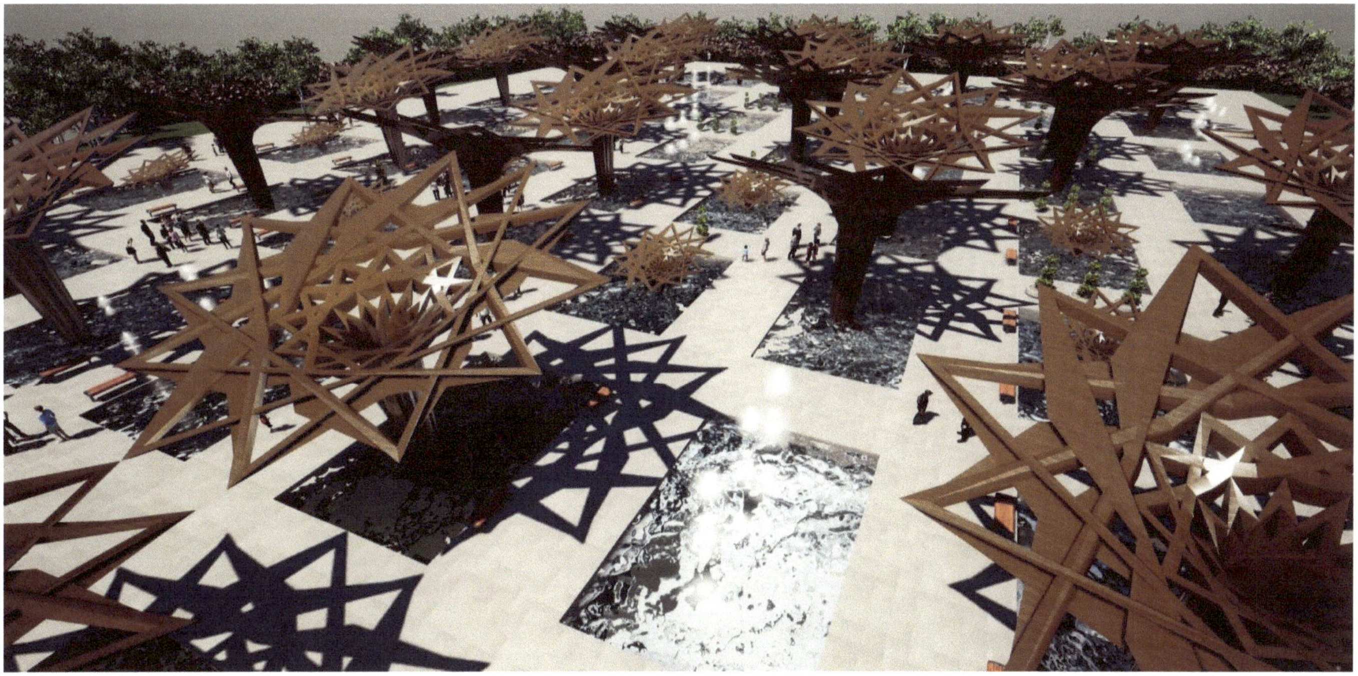

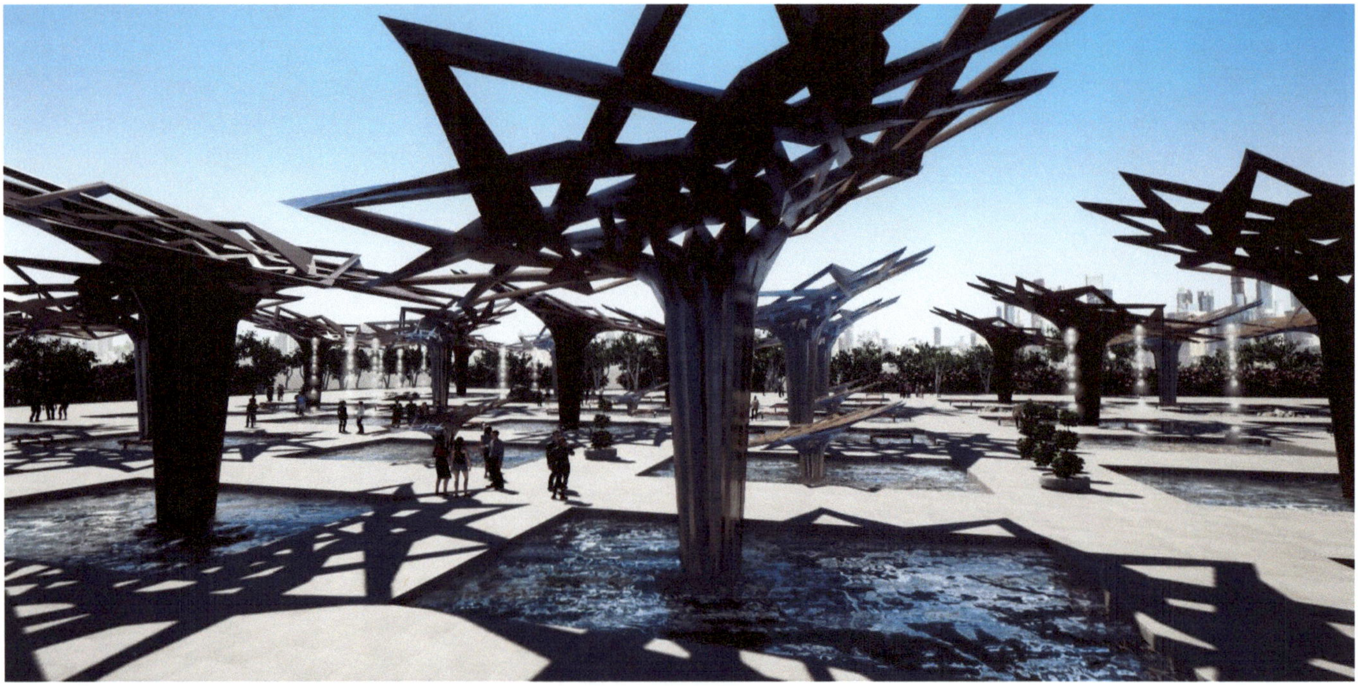

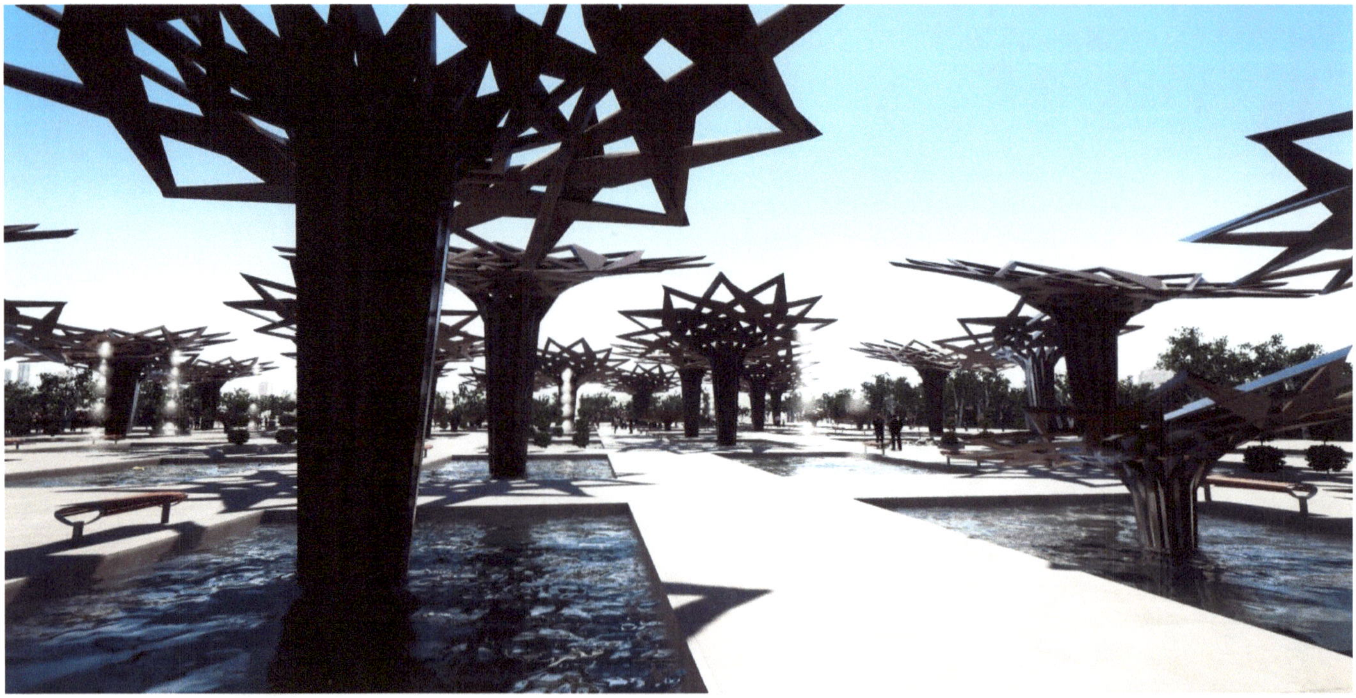

55

Iranian Garden

Arezoo Hosseinzadehazad

The Iranian garden is a heaven parable and one of the important works of Iranian architecture which creates an effective space through intelligent combination of the architectural elements and art. Regular geometry, centrality and symmetry, natural elements, and artificial elements are of the distinguishing features of this structure. In the Iranian garden, centrality is formed via interference of two vertical and horizontal axels and is mainly manifested by a pond or pavilion. The main axles are created by terracing, trees, and ponds. In this plan, it is emphasized considering variable purposes, different materials and symbolic element of tree.

The designed volumes of the site have been inspired of trees and dome geometry. When you stand beneath the dome, it will be automatically seen as nested circles. This idea has been used to design the main structure in form of a set of spiral circles. In dome, unity is formed of multiplicity but this is reverse in this element indicating to growth and zenith.

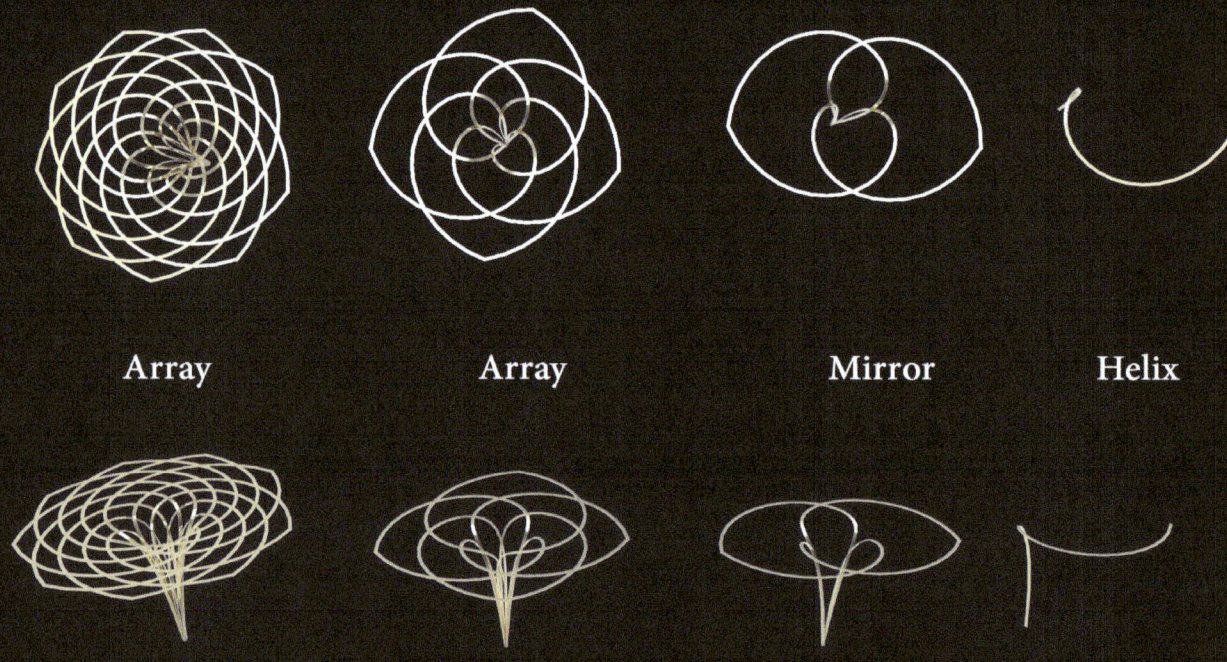

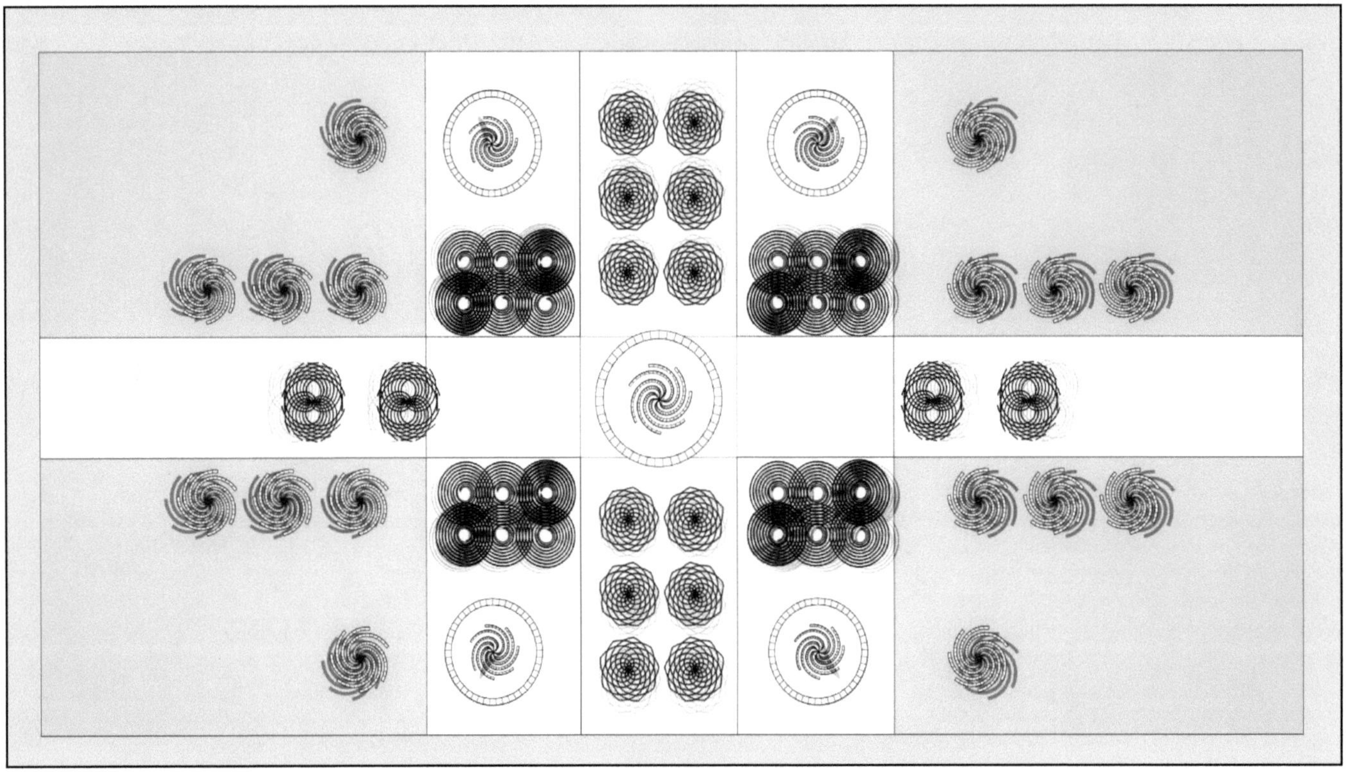

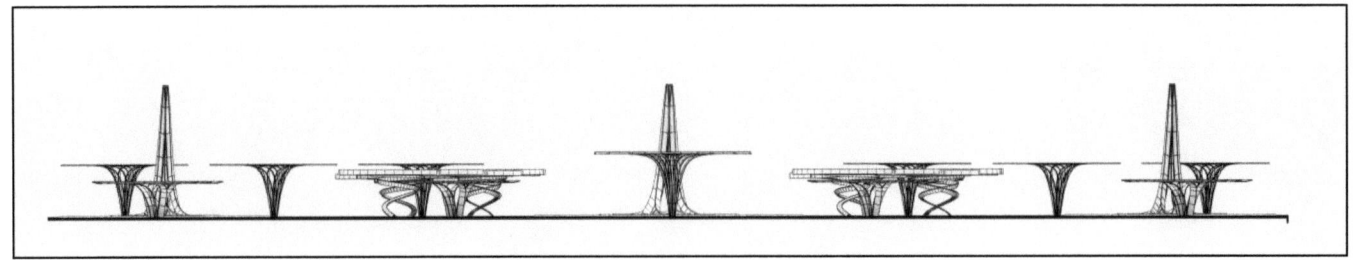

Site plan

Facade of site plan

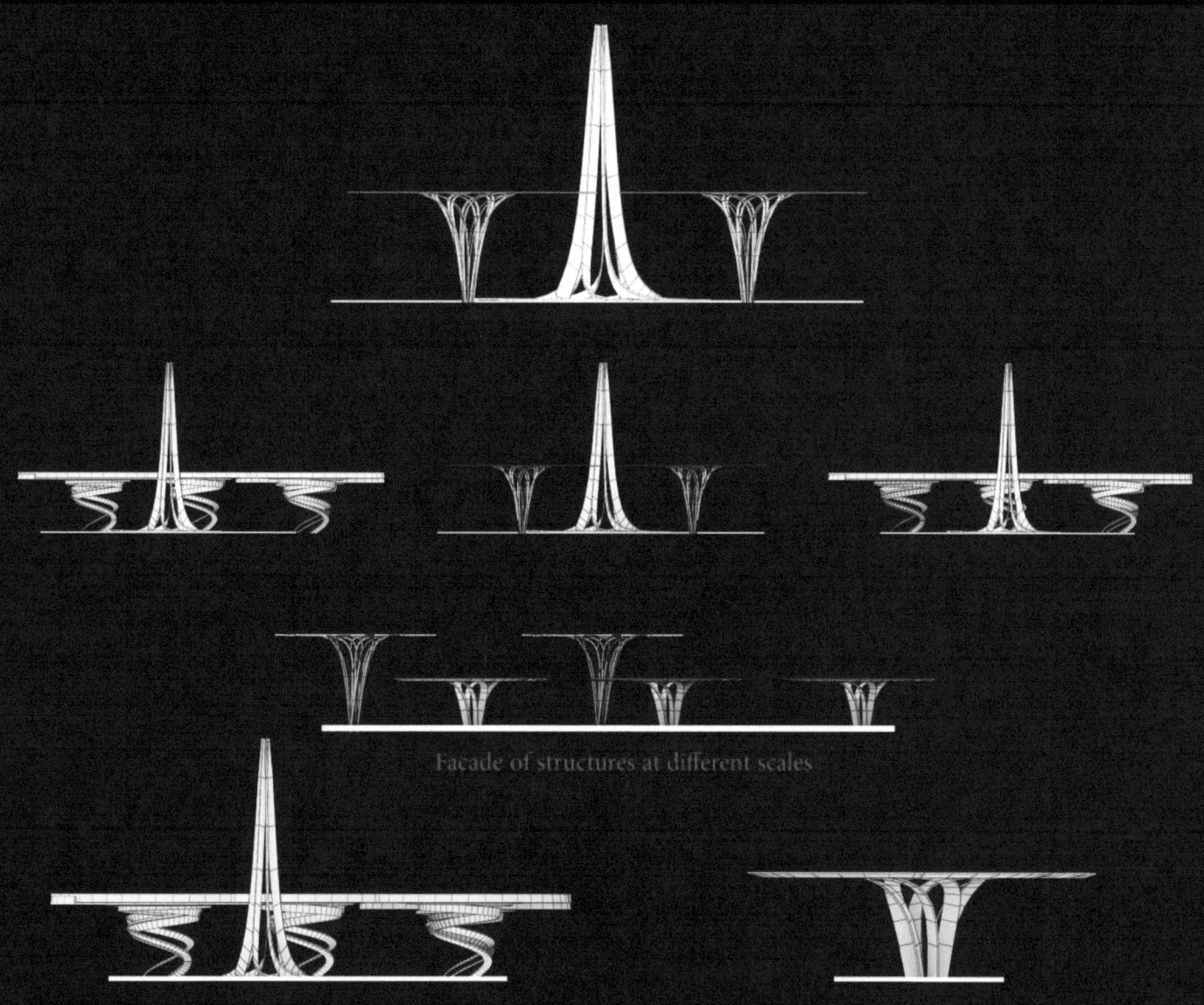

Facade of structures at different scales

62

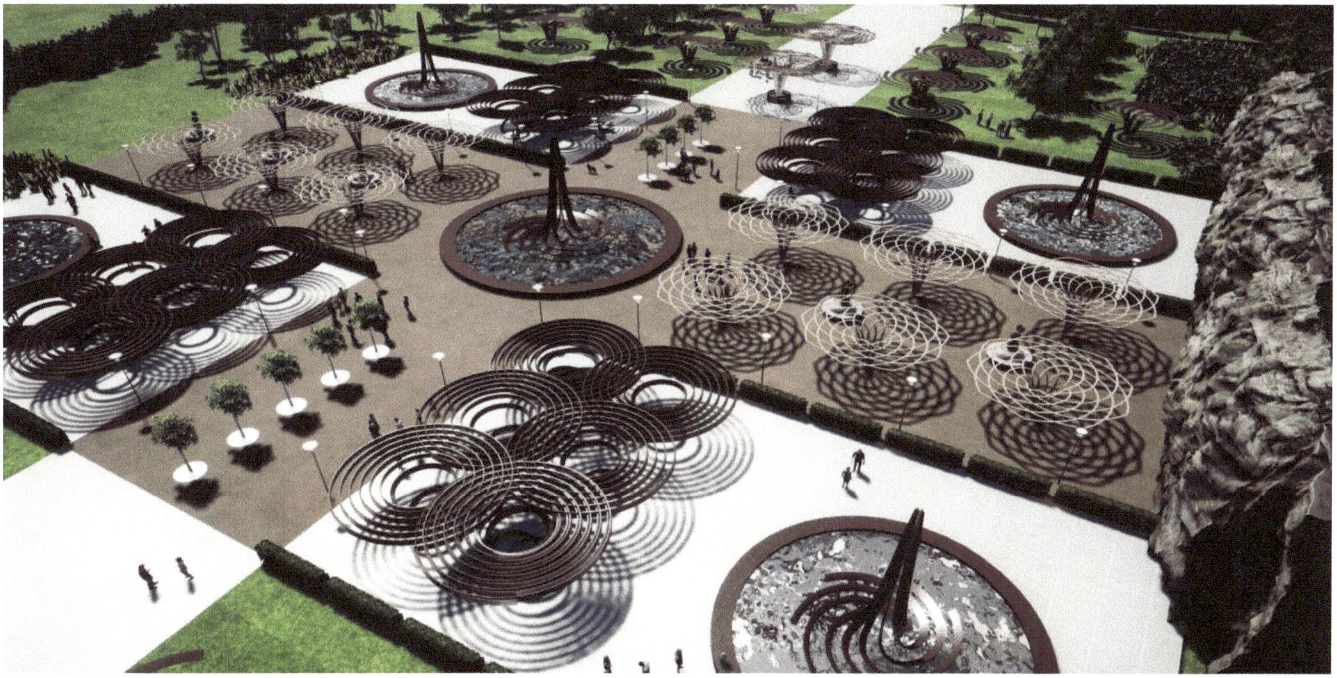

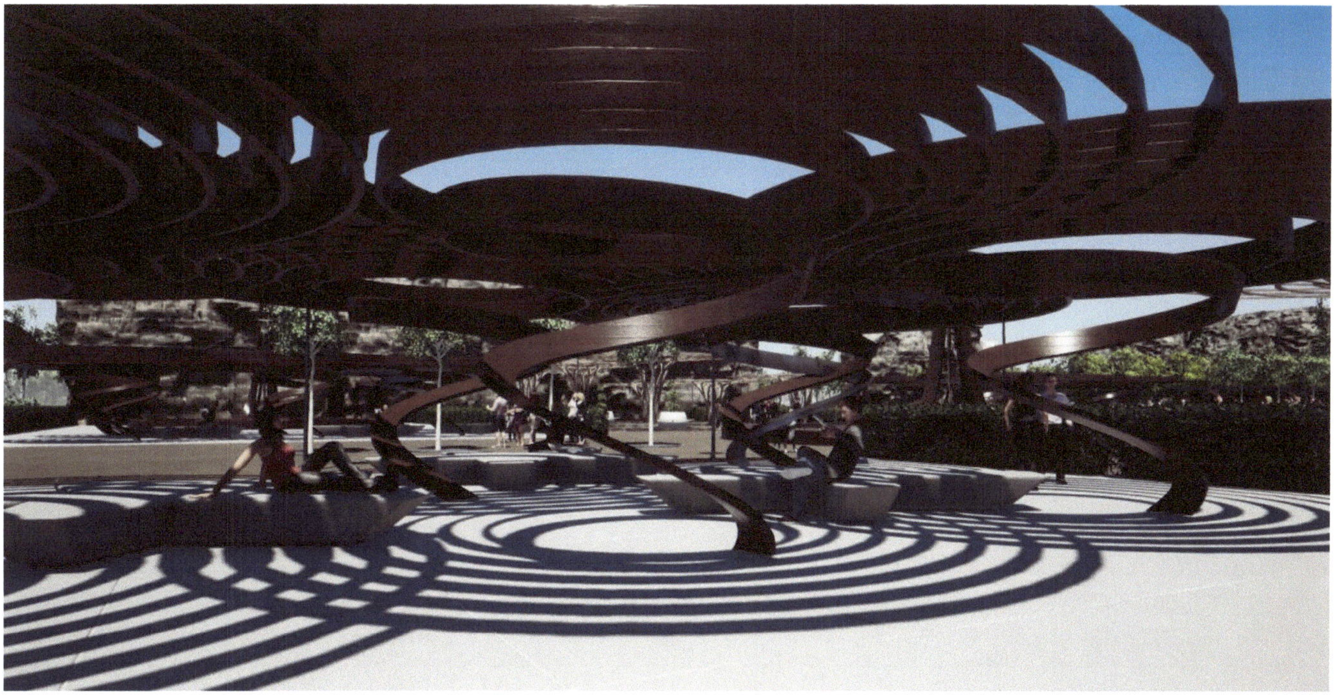

Project description

Nasim Beidaghdar

The workshop is mainly designed to gather people after the coronavirus. A group of the participants designed a single volume or a centralist structure where people enter and may stay there temporarily. However, my main goal focused on the merging of movement and sitting. Accordingly, I designed a path through repeating and changing of the main structure, a path where the people may move, sit on wood surfaces, lie down, watch the sky, and enjoy play of light and colored glasses. In my opinion, we need to move, run and walk, lie down, and mediate after some months of quarantine and staying home. Such a plan which may be potentially executed in different lands and dimensions may enhance spatial quality of parks and urban green spaces.

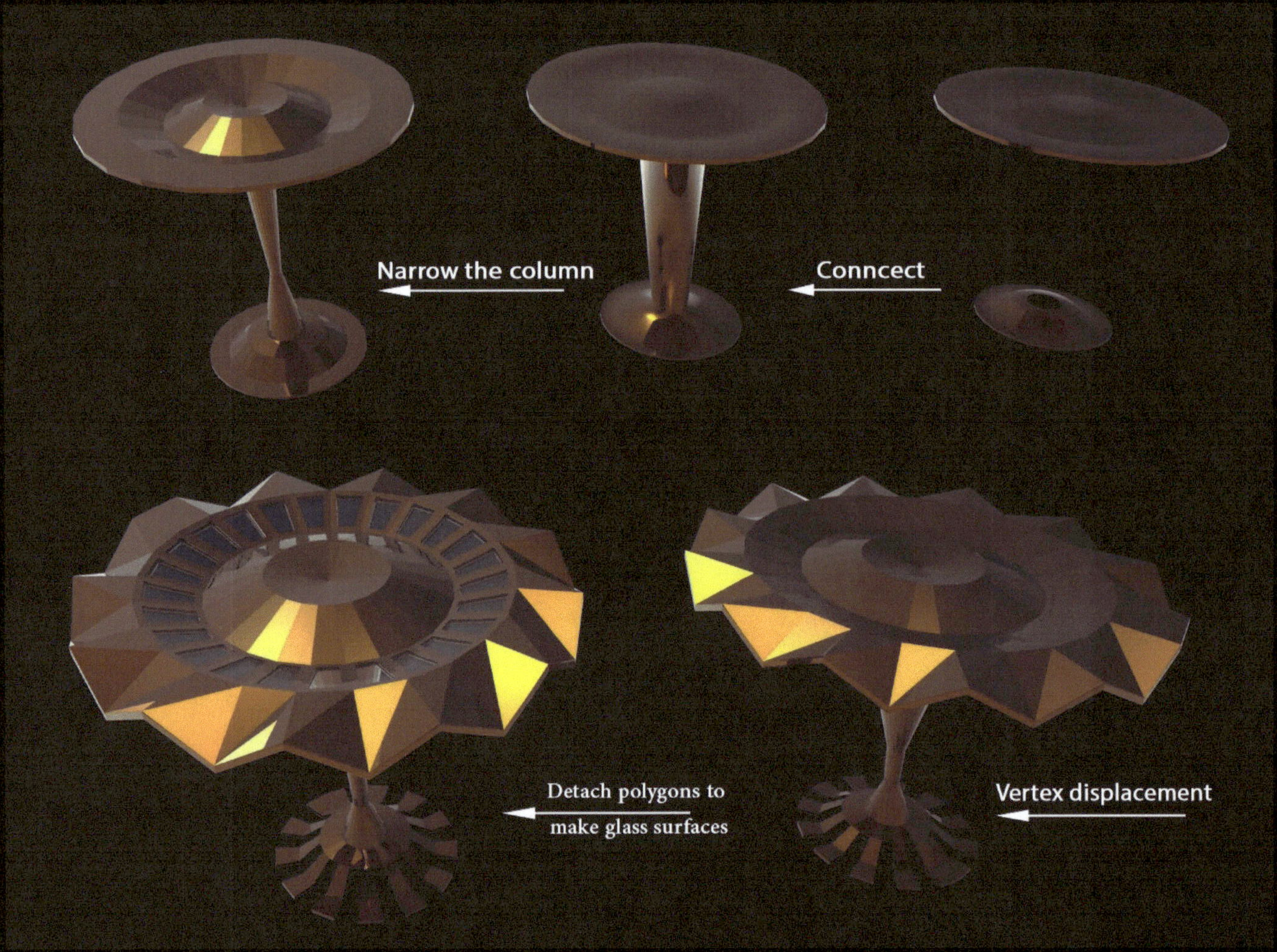

Narrow the column ← Conncect ←

Detach polygons to make glass surfaces ← Vertex displacement ←

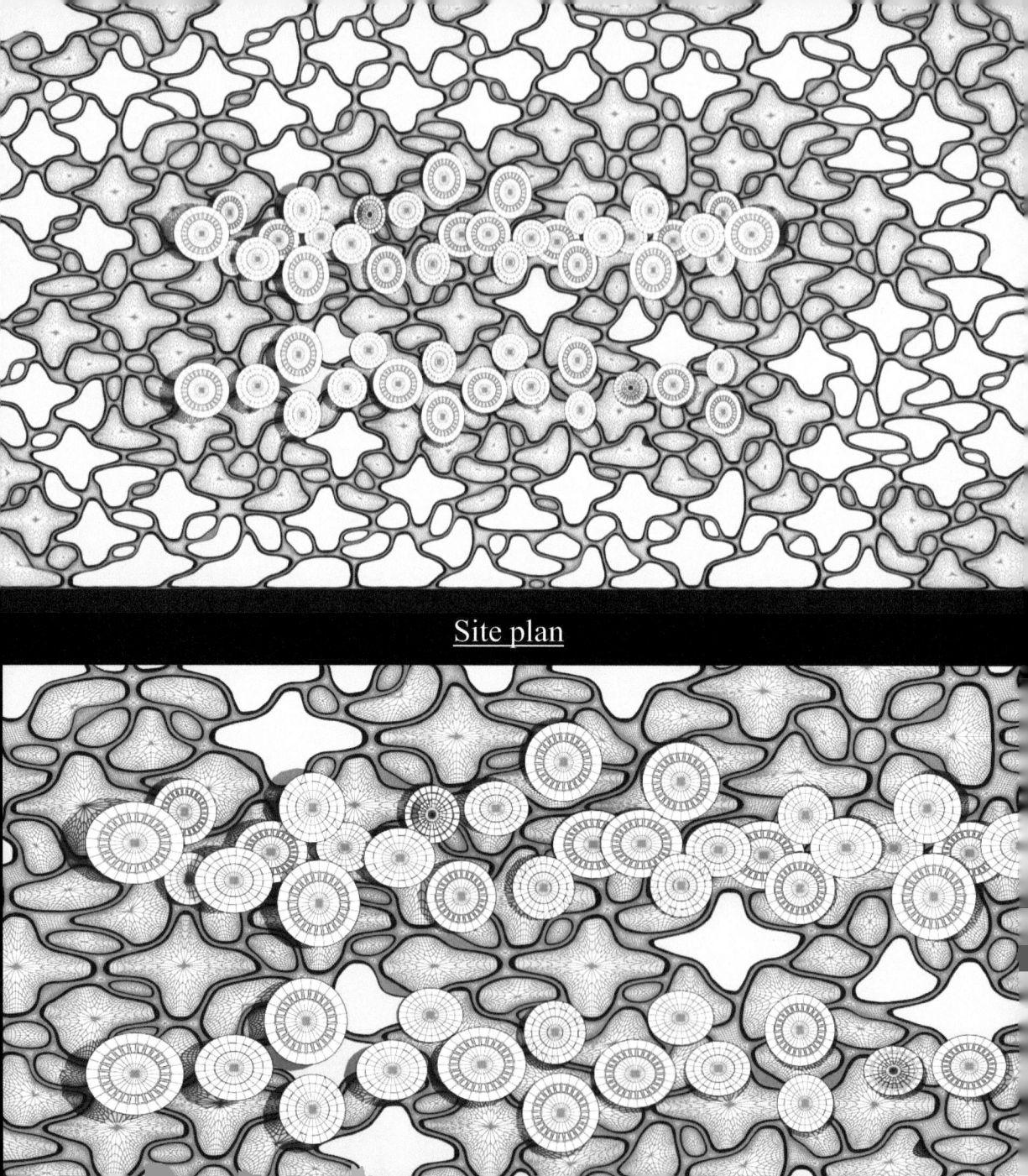

Site plan

71

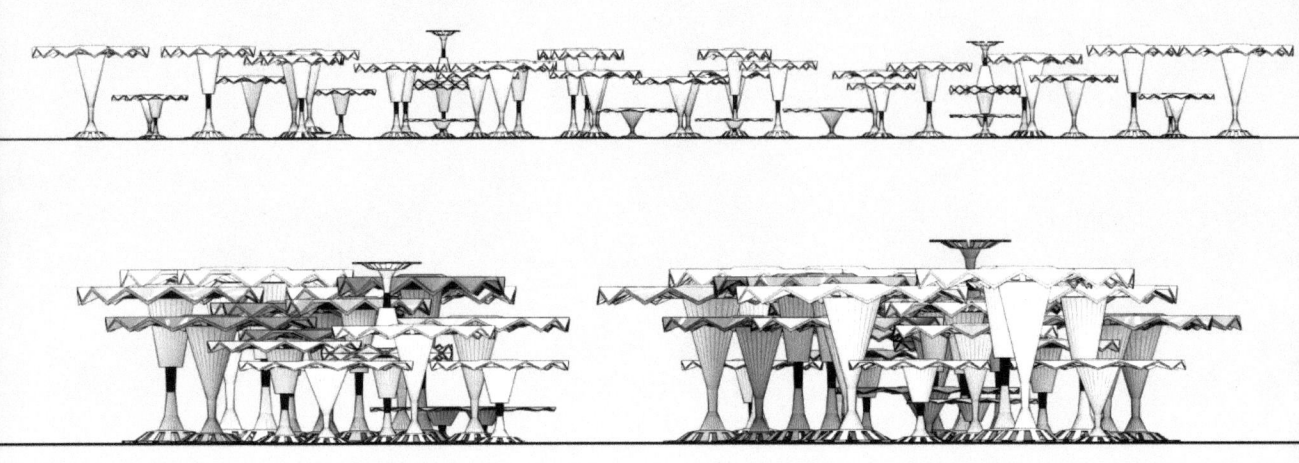

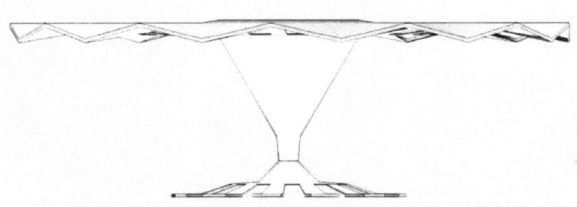

Facade of structures at different scales

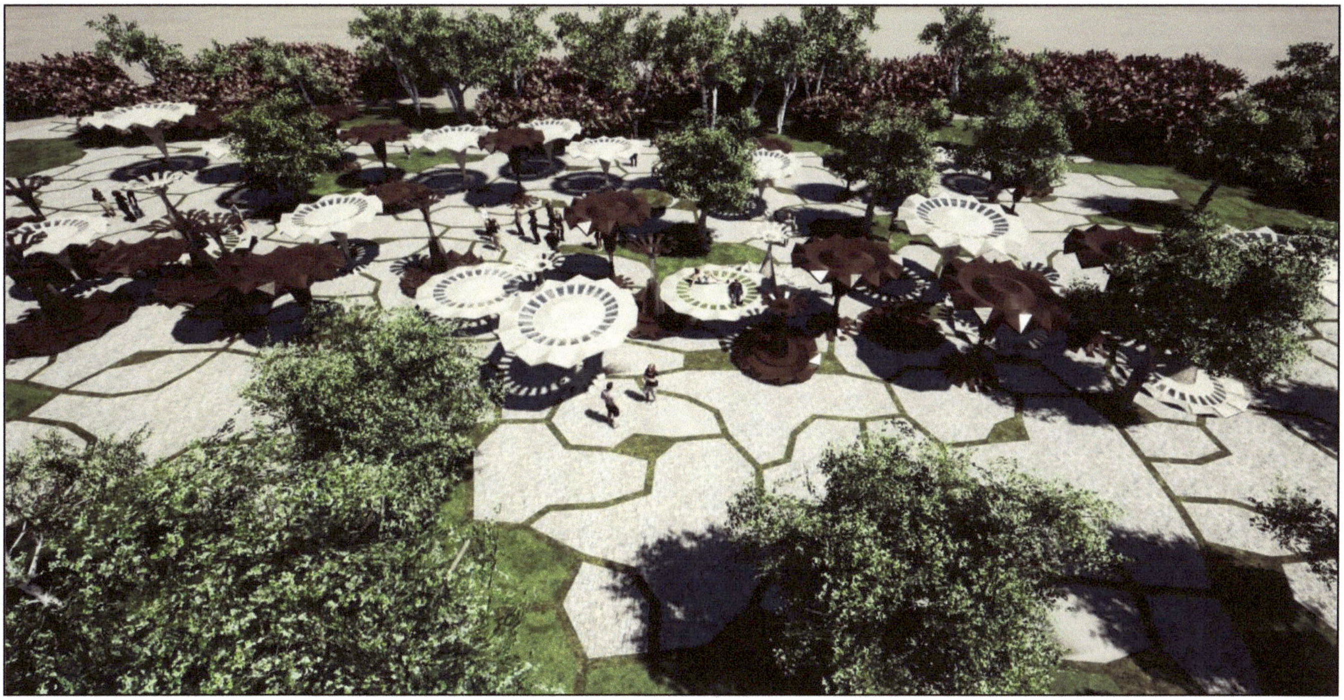

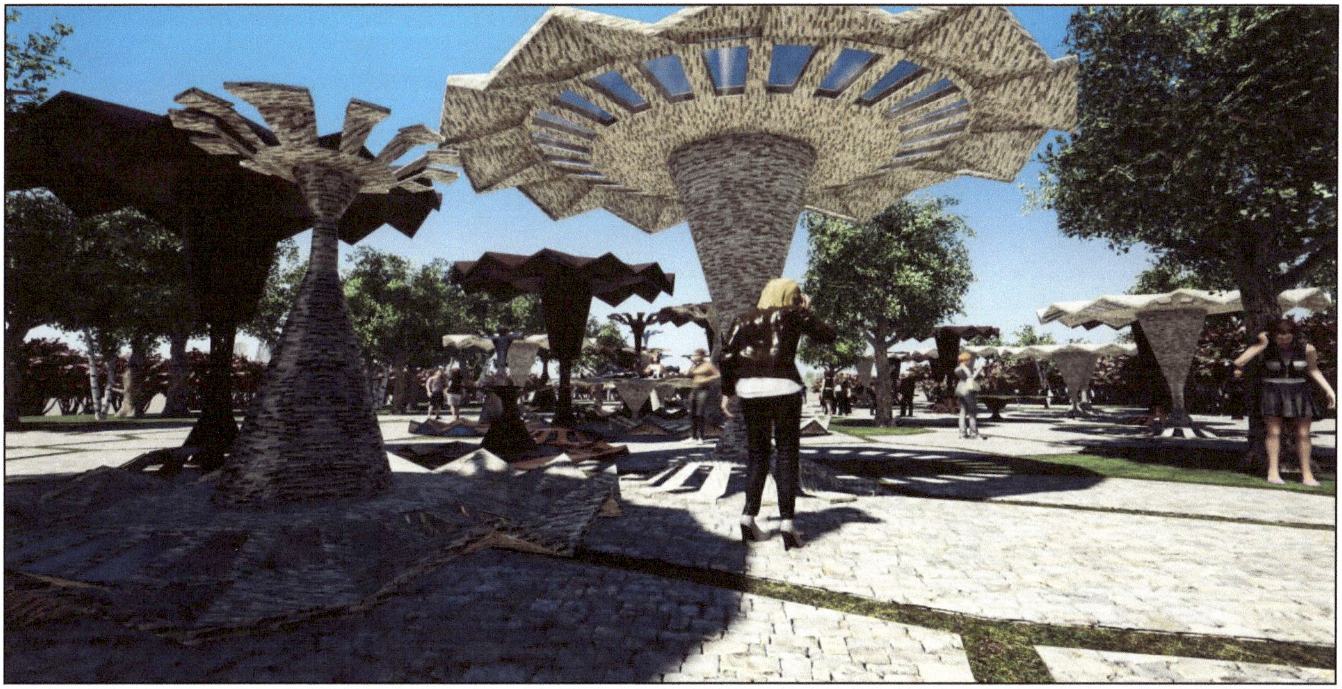

Helix
Parinaz Yeganeh

    Helix is one of the important and complex forms in 3Ds Max software. When this line is drawn, it expands in three coordinate directions, twists and moves up. The created structure may be changed in space through changing the parameters and a creative and dynamic space may be created through repeating and symmetrizing the main form. According to my experiences about helix which were obtained in the workshop, I drawn a spline based on it and arrayed and symmetrized it according to the design process of the next page. Scattering of this flexible structure and its curved shadows create a place to have a different experience of the space.

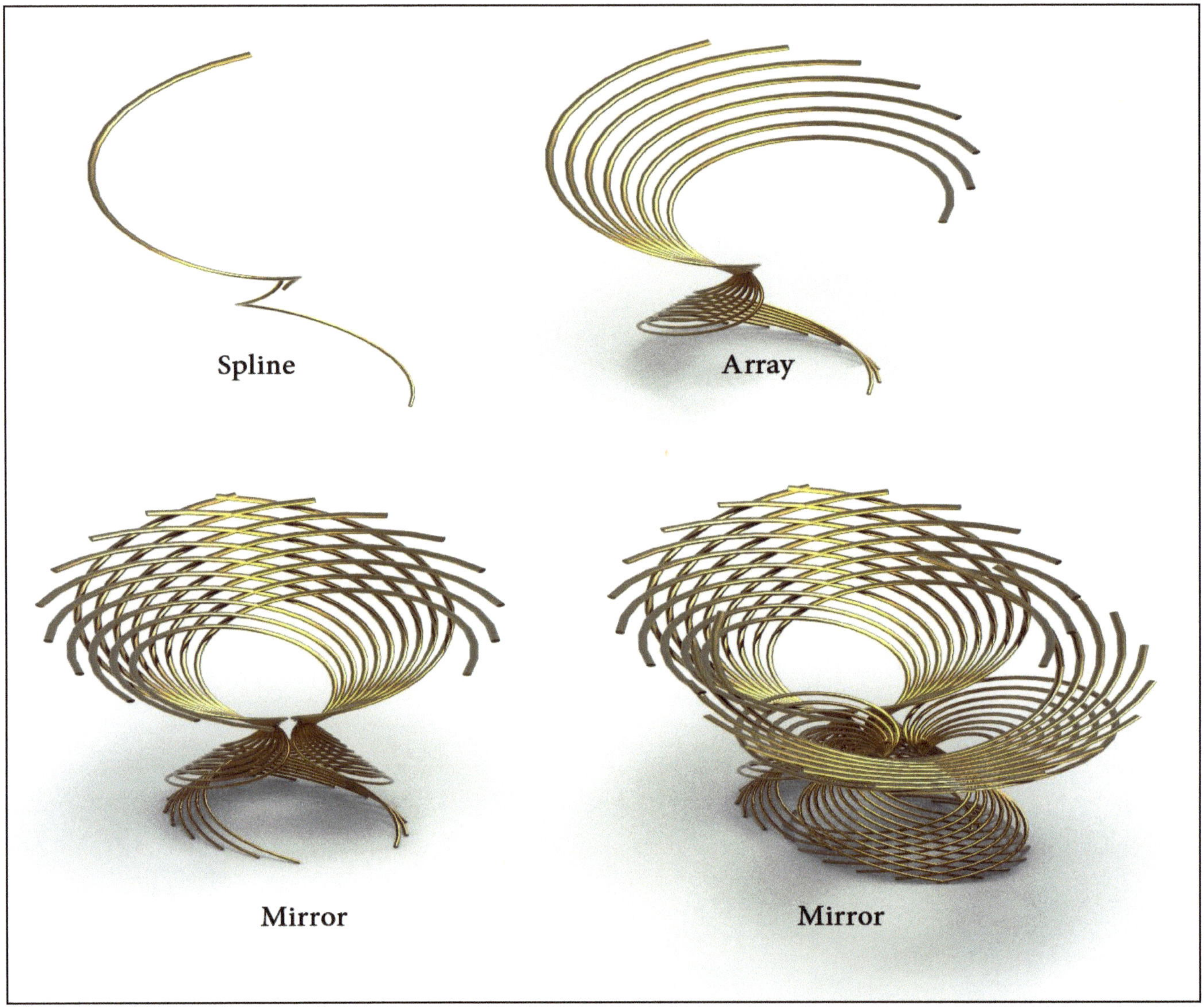

Spline

Array

Mirror

Mirror

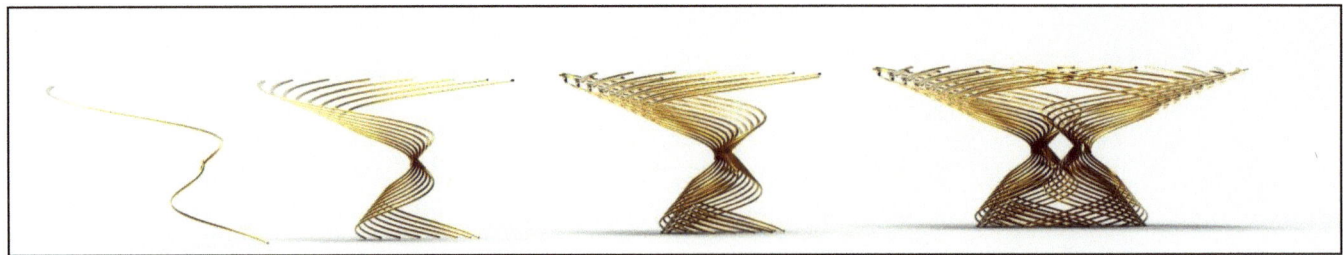

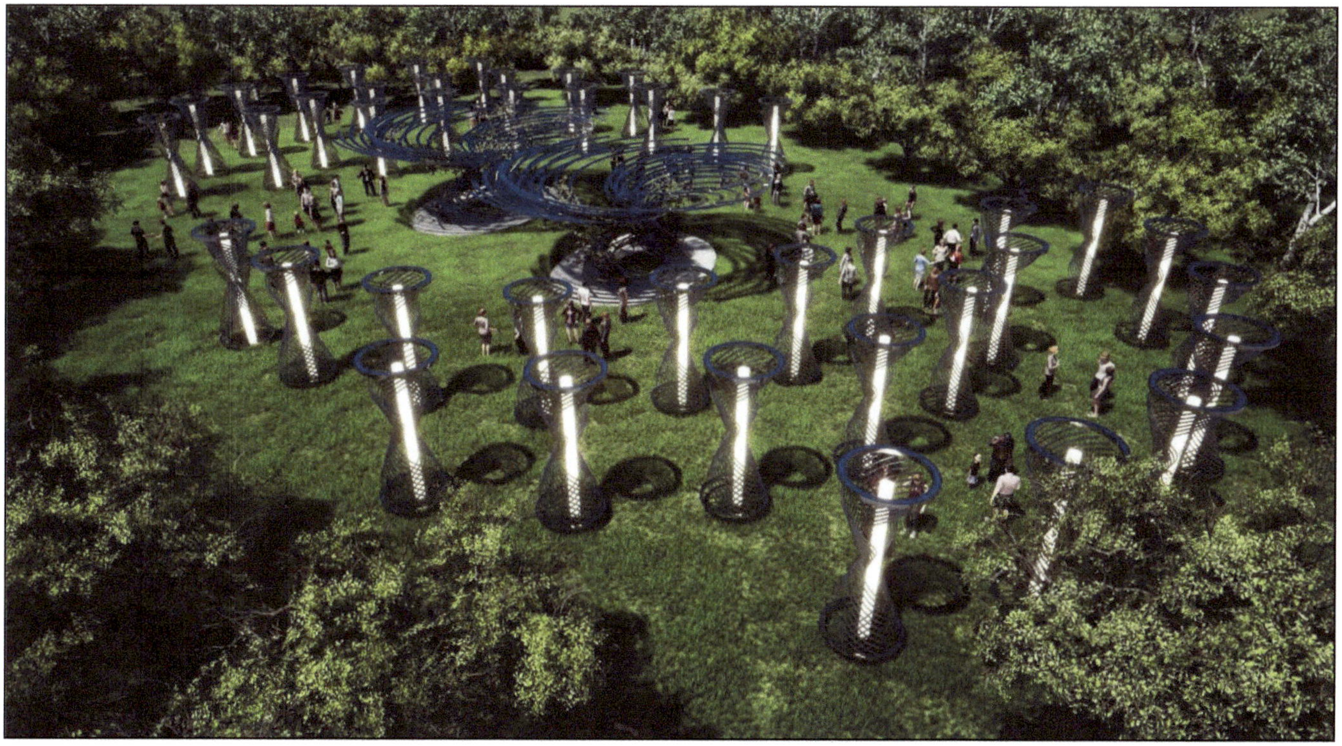

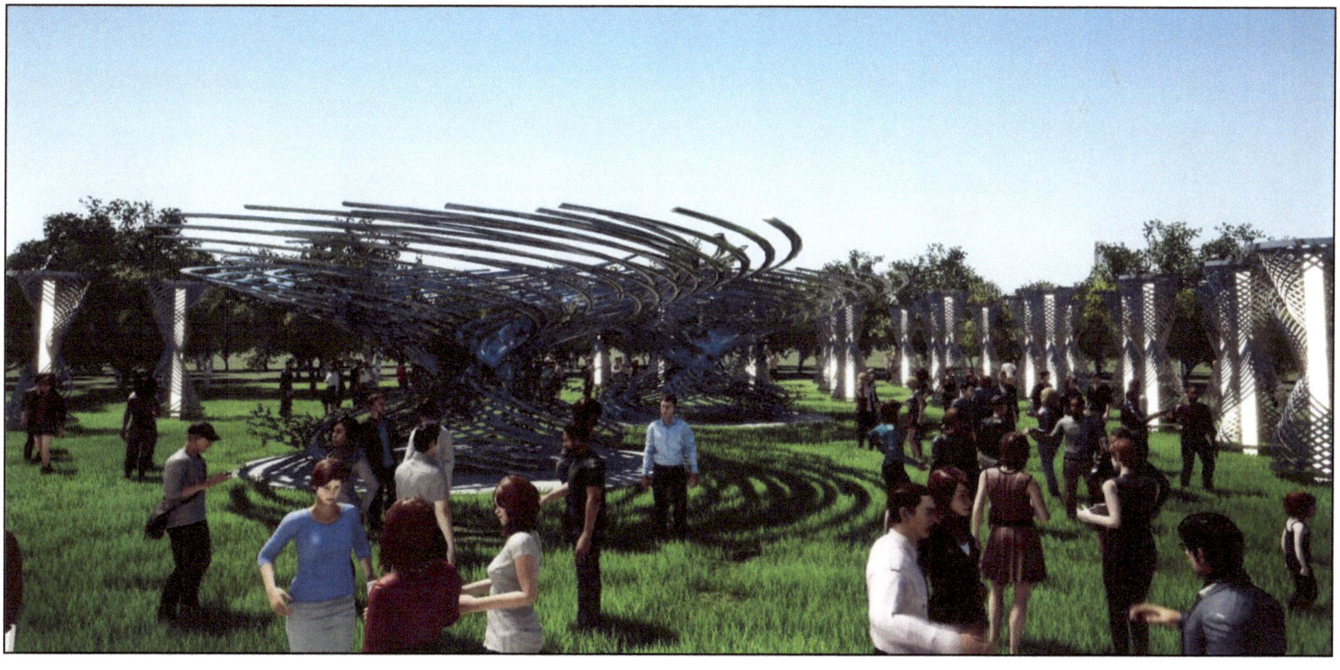

80

81

Hill Pavilion

Parinaz Yeganeh

After months of quarantine, we will surely miss the nature, mountains and plains and probably decide to have a long travel to nature. It is not possible for all especially citizens of big cities. Therefore, Hill Pavilion is a response to eagers of citizens to hill climbing and get away from urban crowded spaces. Shallow pools and big shadow of the pavilion create an ideal space for gathering of people and different groups in warm summers.
This 11-meter high structure is covered with grass and may be executed in different dimensions and districts. City parks are generally leveled and there is not any height difference there. This project changes the skyline, expands our perspective through changing the height and lessens the strait of apartments and towers.

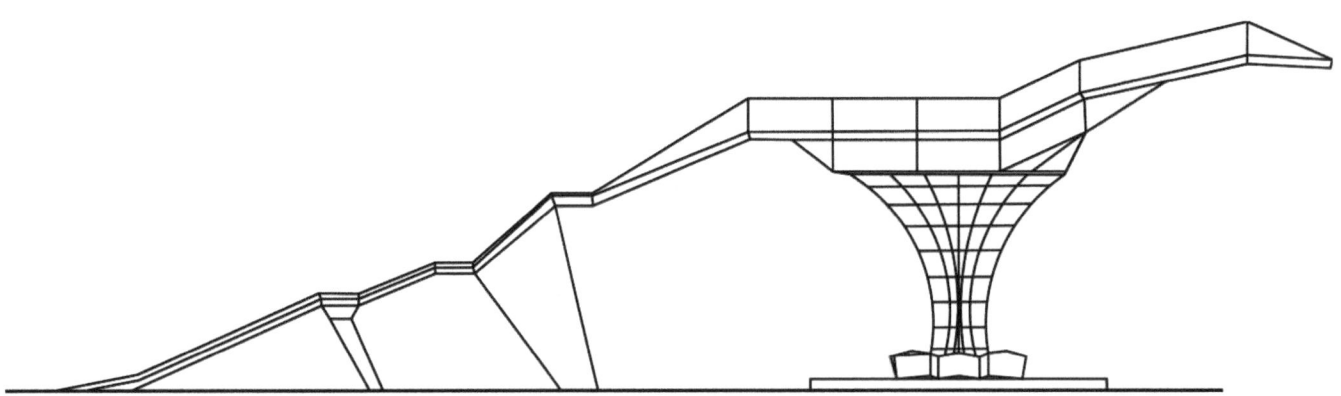

Design Process

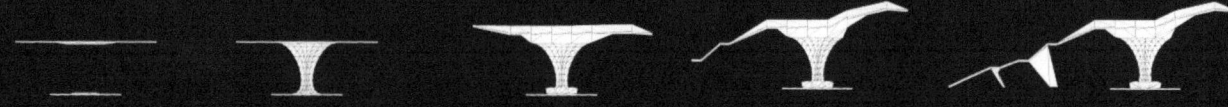

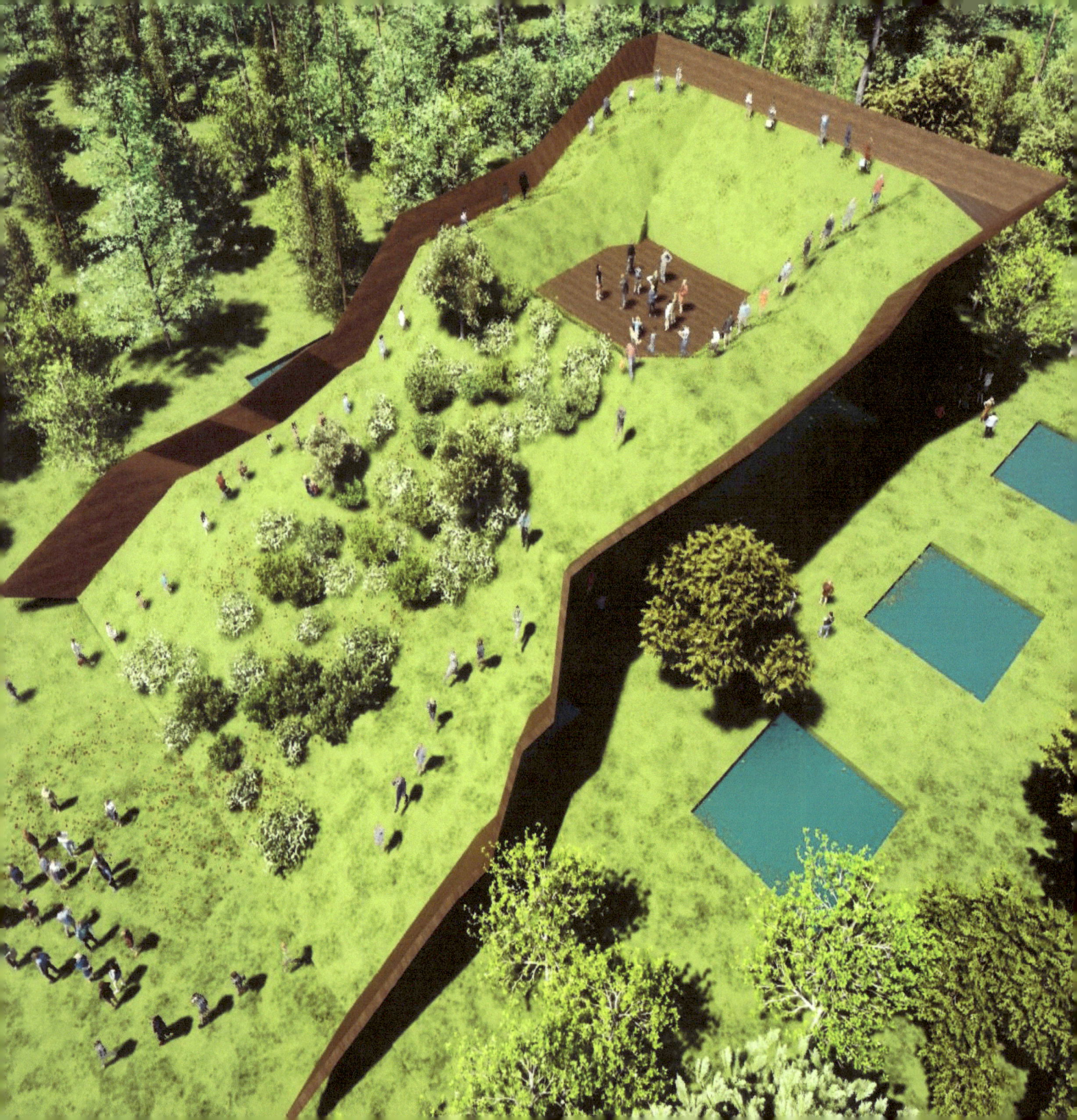

85

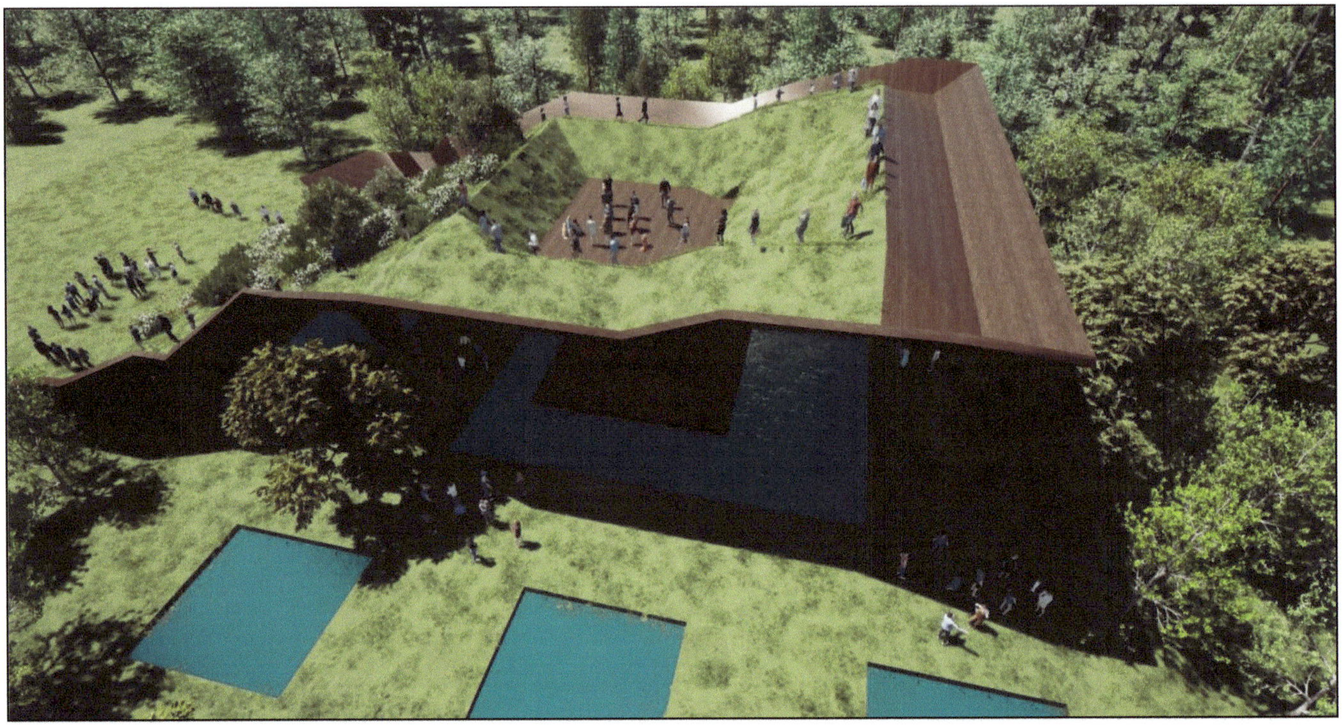

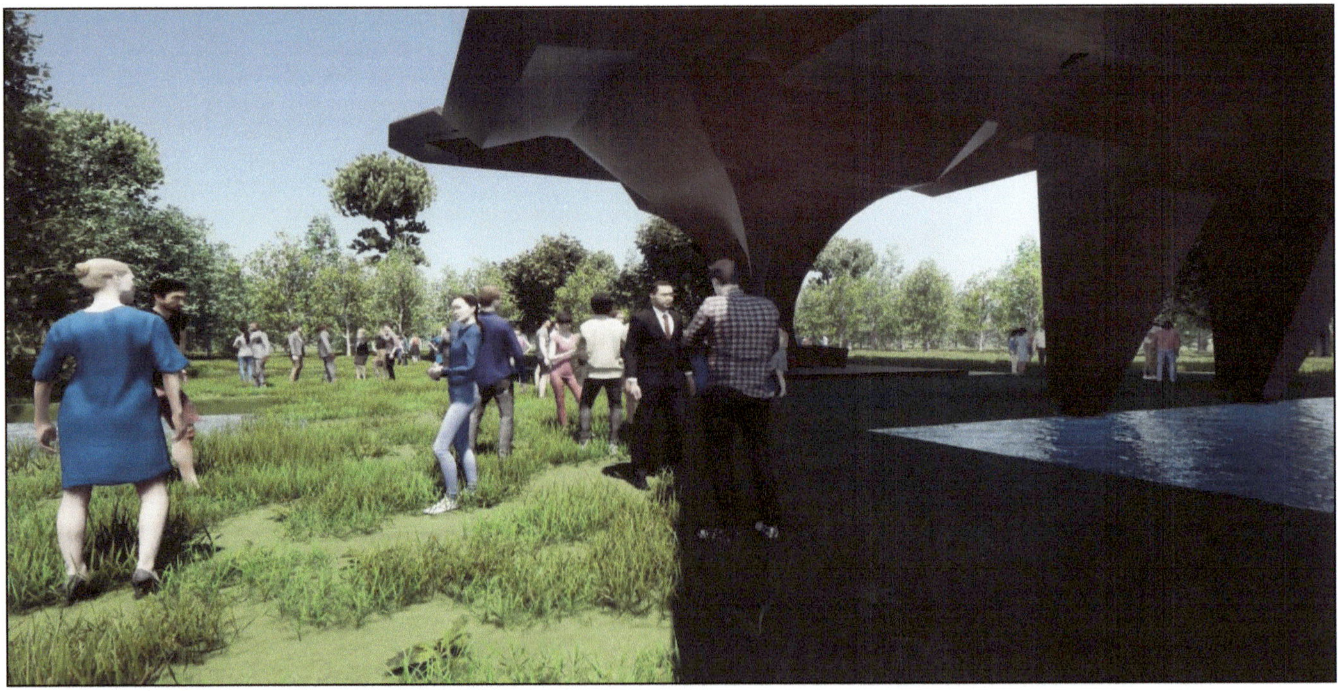

A Place for Gathering

Soheyla Asi

One of most popular subjects in the world nowadays is the wish list of after quarantine period of COVID-19 virus. The importance of social distance is mentioned by different ways to all people around world. However, it was hard to get used to these rules, but people are now more sensitive and conscious about them.

So now socialists and psychologists are worry about the influence of this period on people and they are trying to suggest new ways and activities for after quarantine period. It is clear that some of pervious social activates and relations must be revised. The role of semi open public spaces will be so effective in this period.

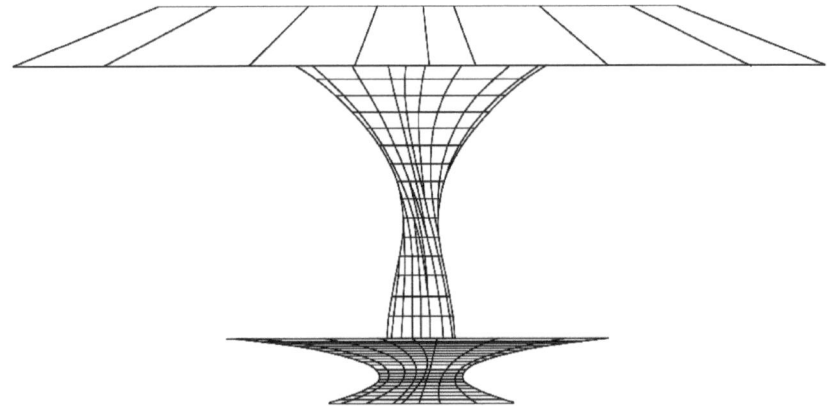

This idea is the main concept of this design. A place which is trying to gather people in appropriate distances to become more social in public spaces. The central pool as a symbol of purity with two structure raised to the sky play an important role in inviting people. A place for ceremonies and different fairs. In addition to the attractiveness of the space, it allows people to sit away from the central crowded

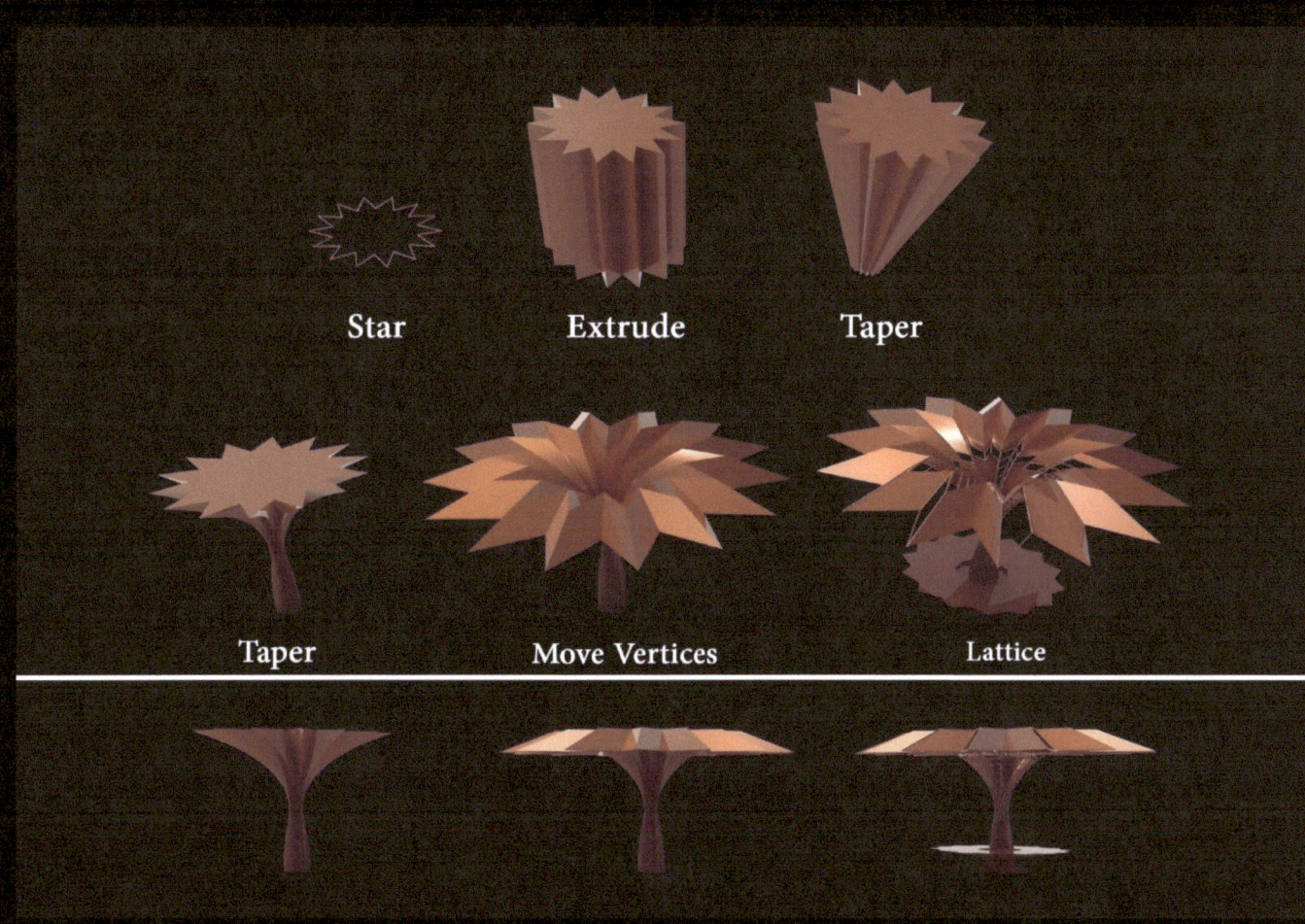

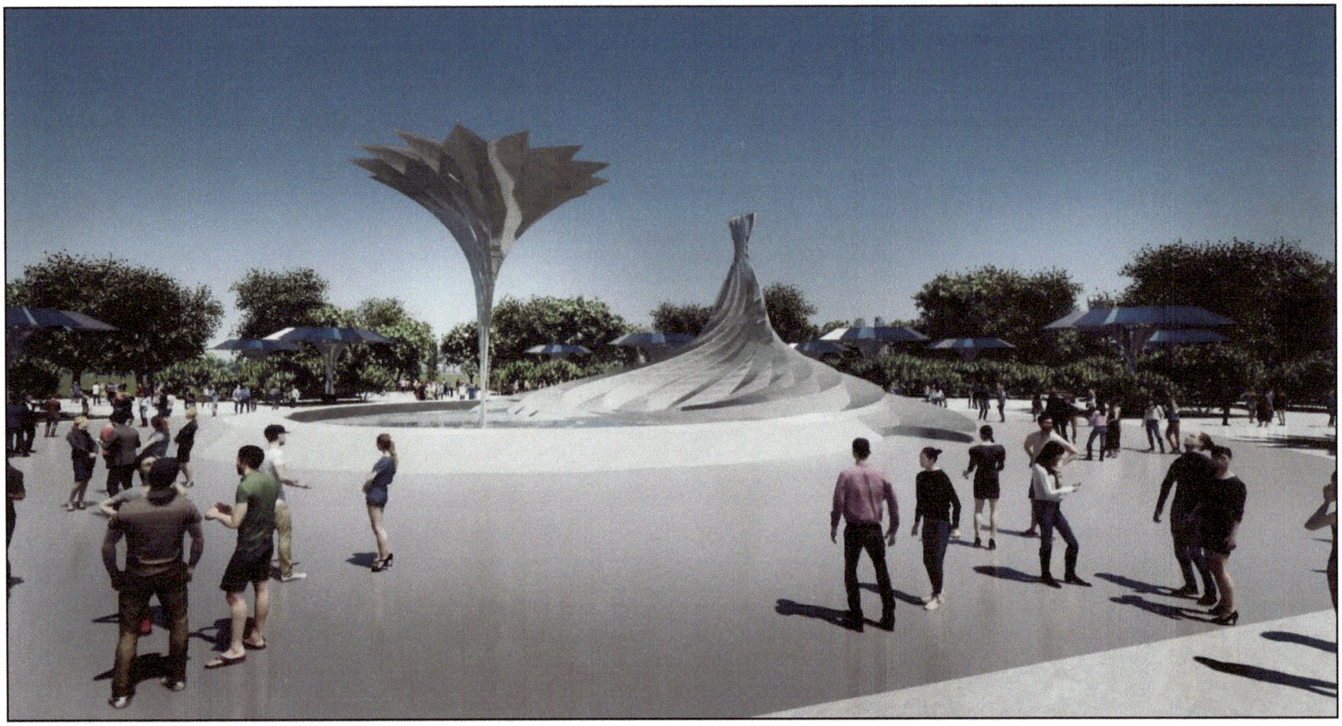

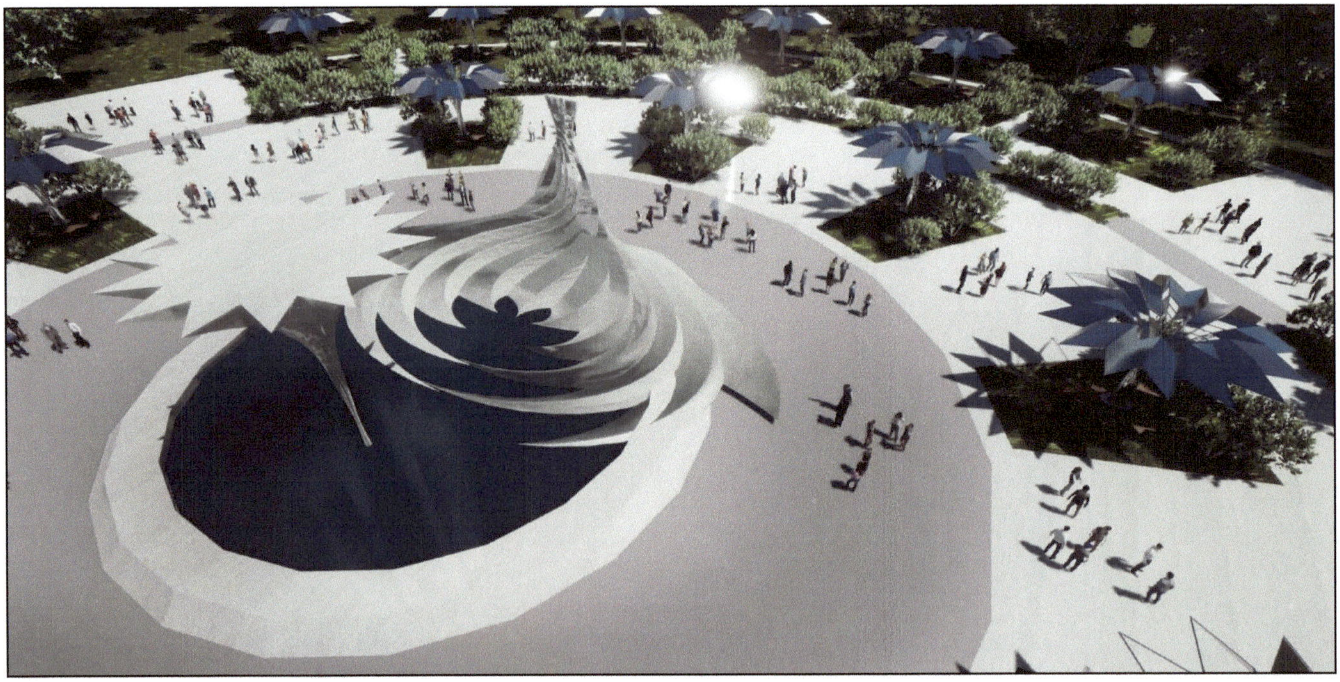

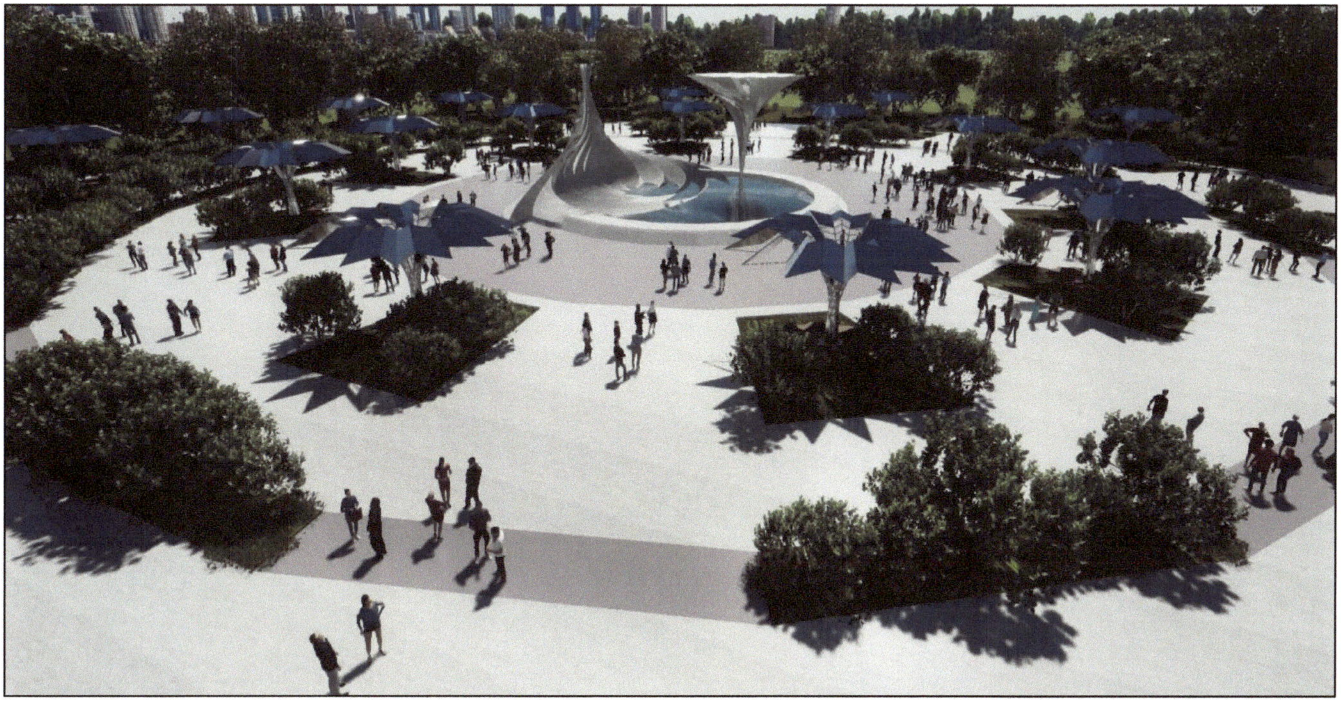

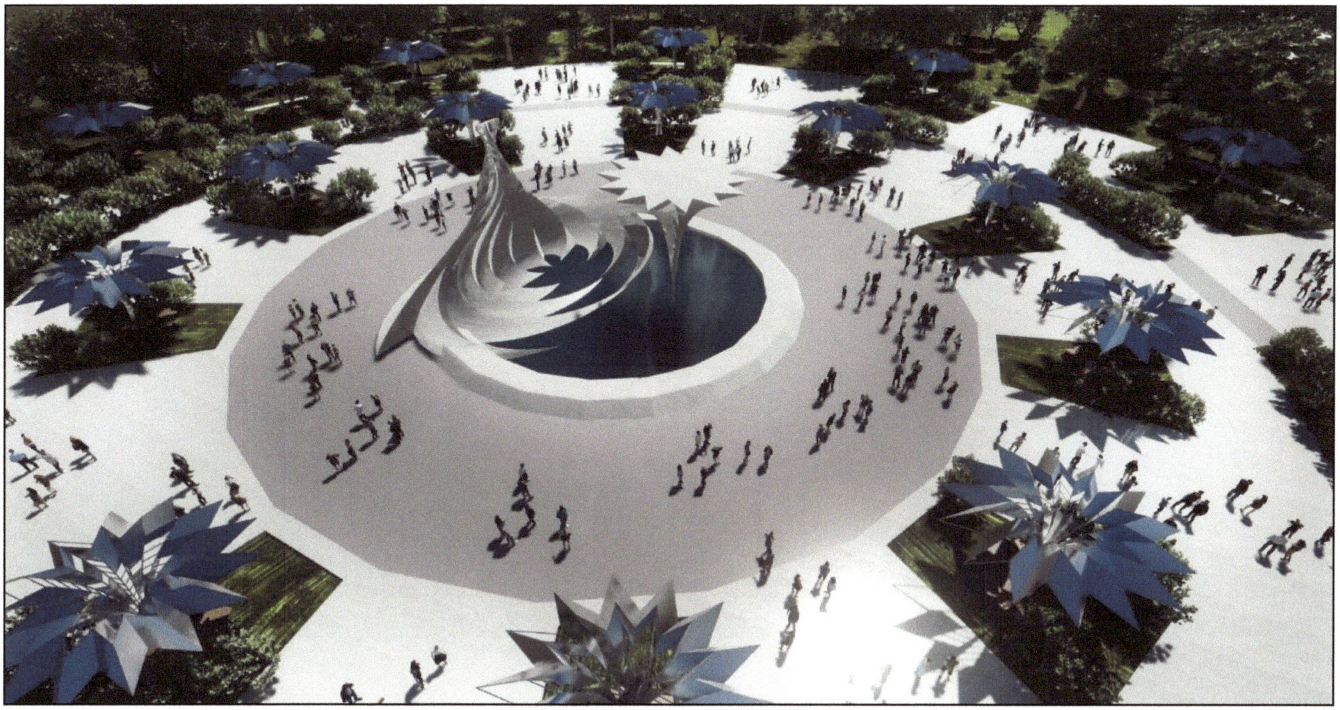

92

Project description

Soheyla Asi

Unlike the previous project, which was centrally organized, this design has been randomly distributed on the site. In fact, the site is not specified for this project. Just two structures were designed which are suitable and flexible for any public space in city.

In the first structure, wood, metal and Plexiglas materials have been used and the second structure is made of woven metal rods which allows ivy plants to grow and rise.

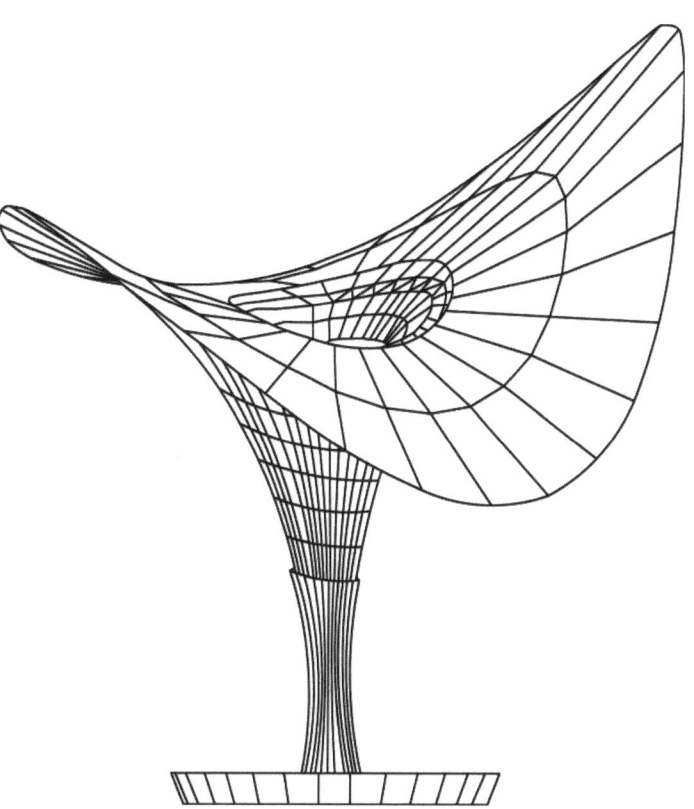

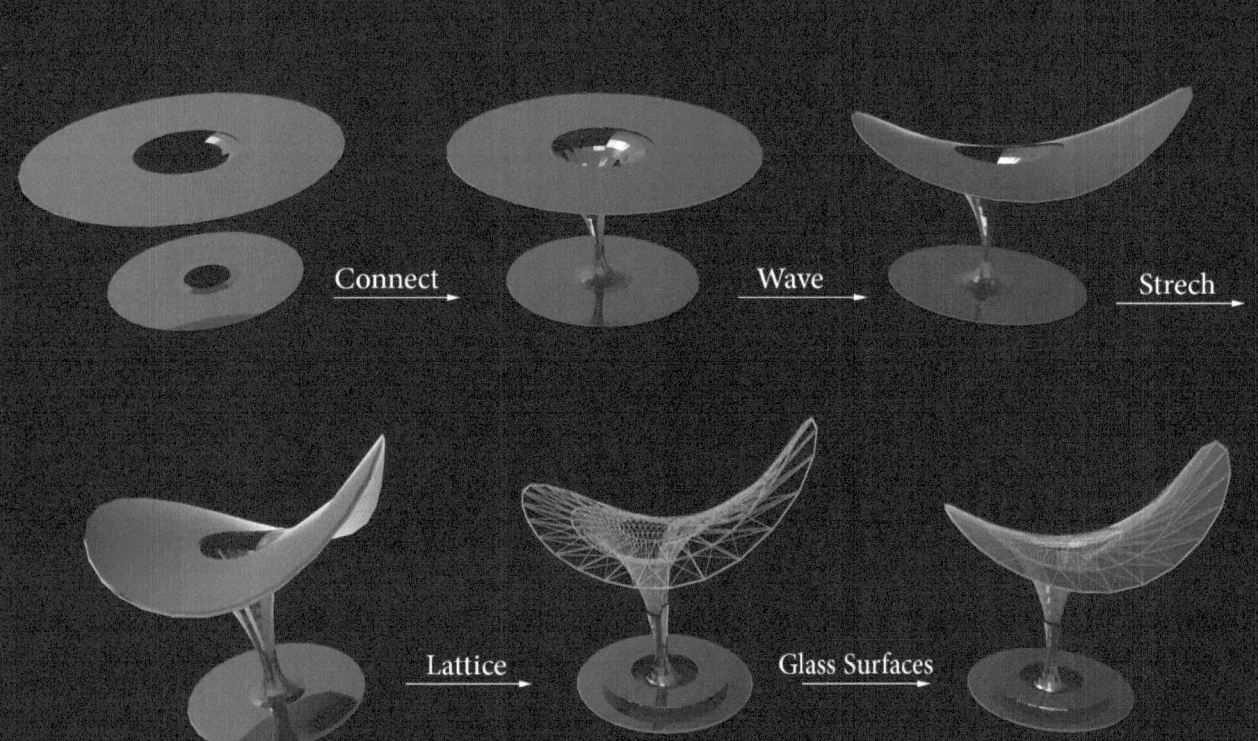

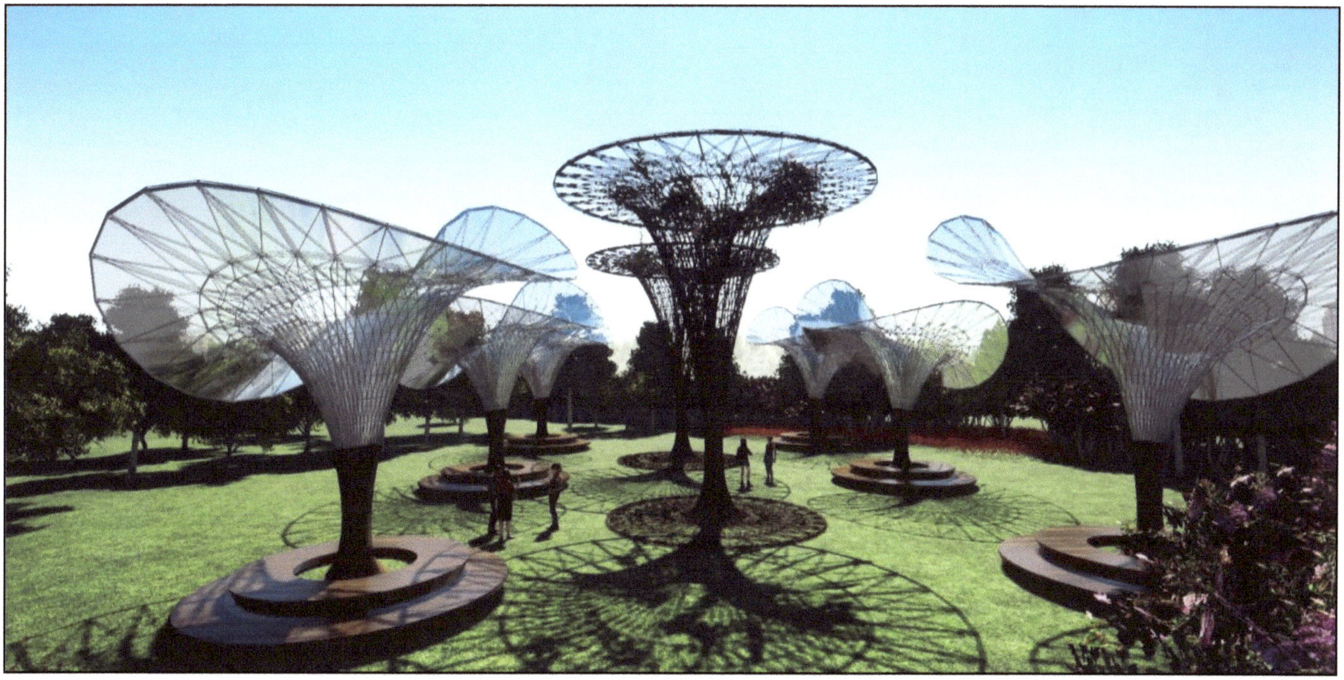

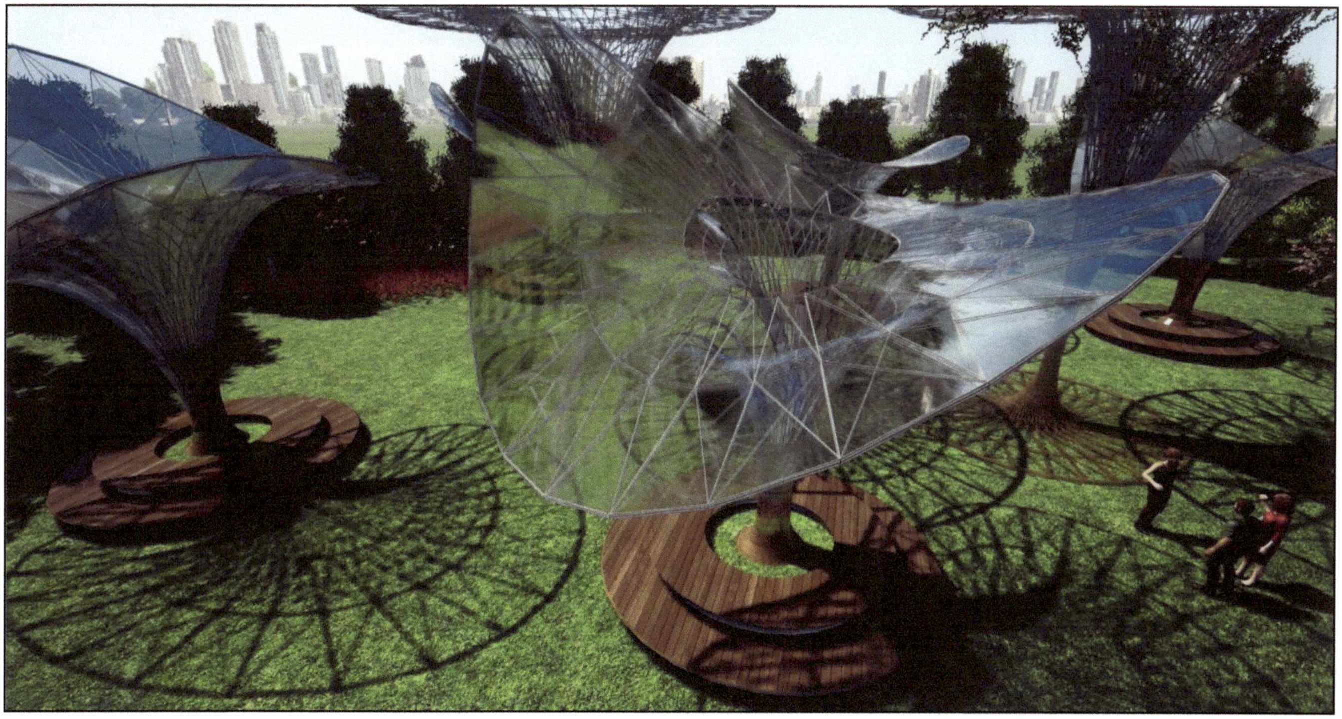

Forum Pavilion
Mahsa Abedi

In the workshop, our initial experiences of the form were mainly limited to cylinder. It was attractive especially when small and big circles were collected to complete the pavilion. The "Circle" form stands for wisdom and it matches with the main idea of the workshop, i.e. to design a space to be together, a space for forum.
Therefore, the main volume was radically organized in different dimensions and height as a symbol of variable thoughts and beliefs. It seems that different people have gathered to talk, interact, and think.

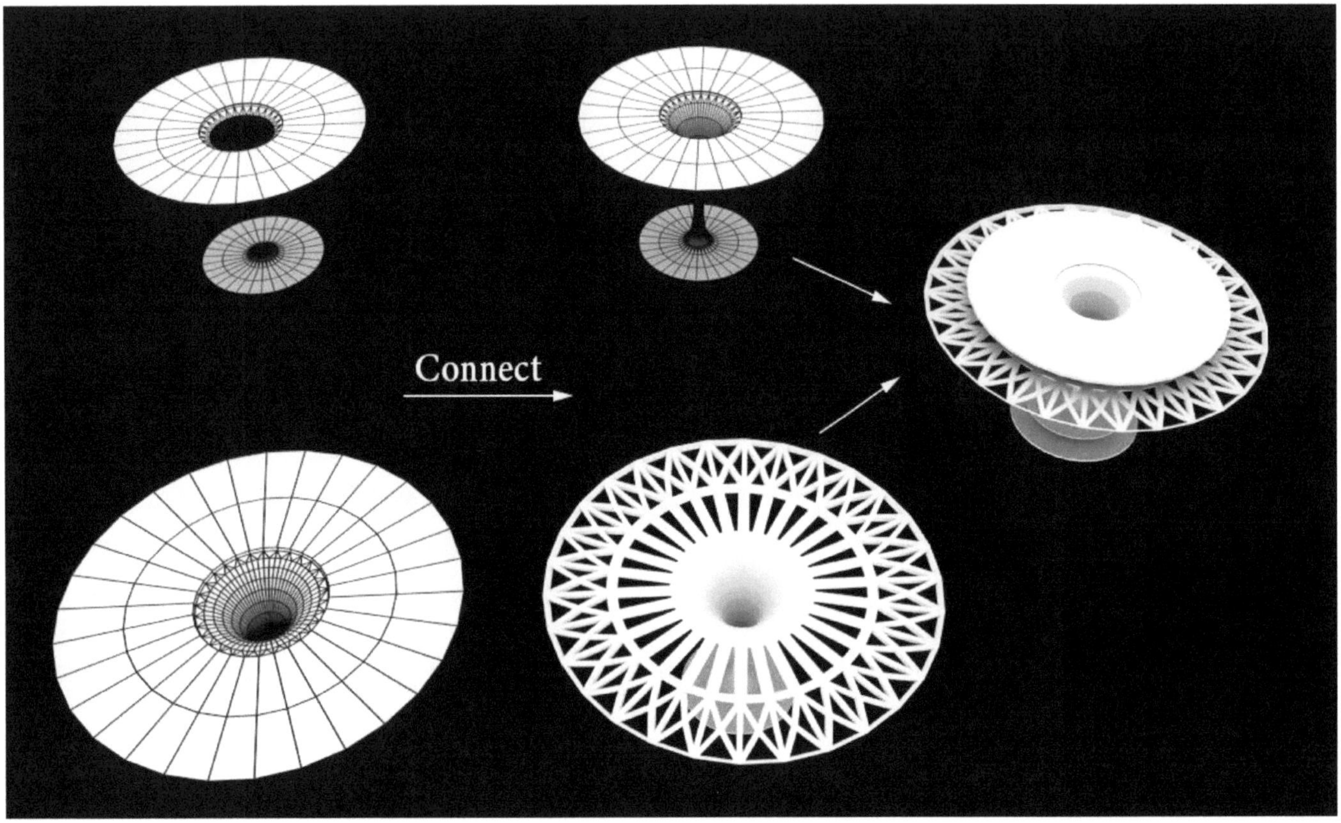

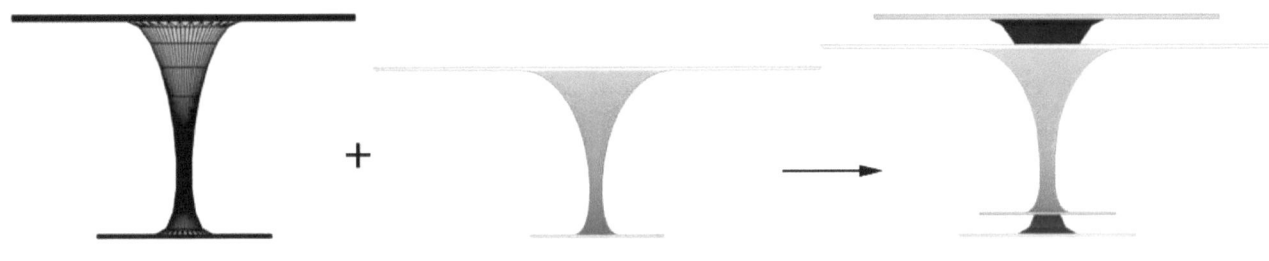

Design Process

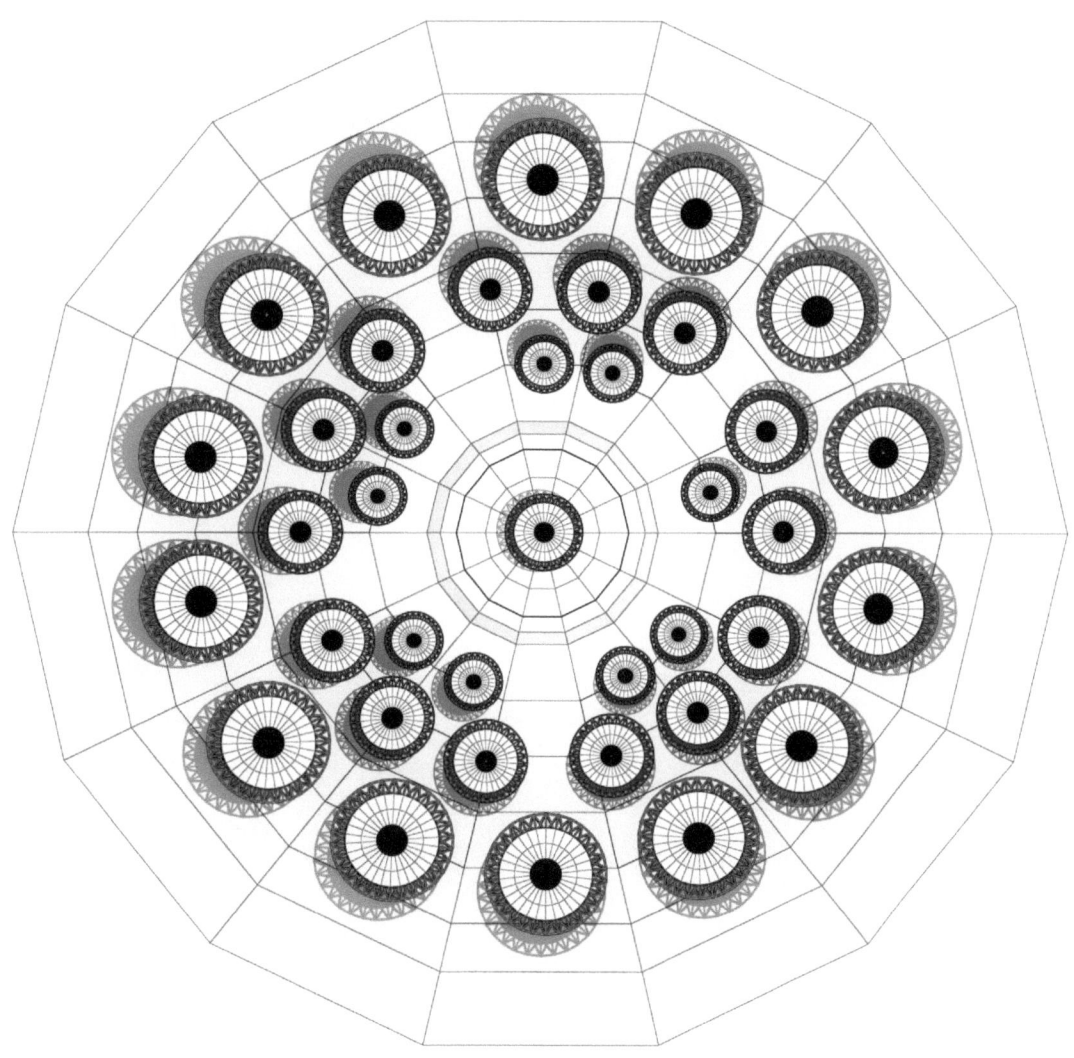

Site plan

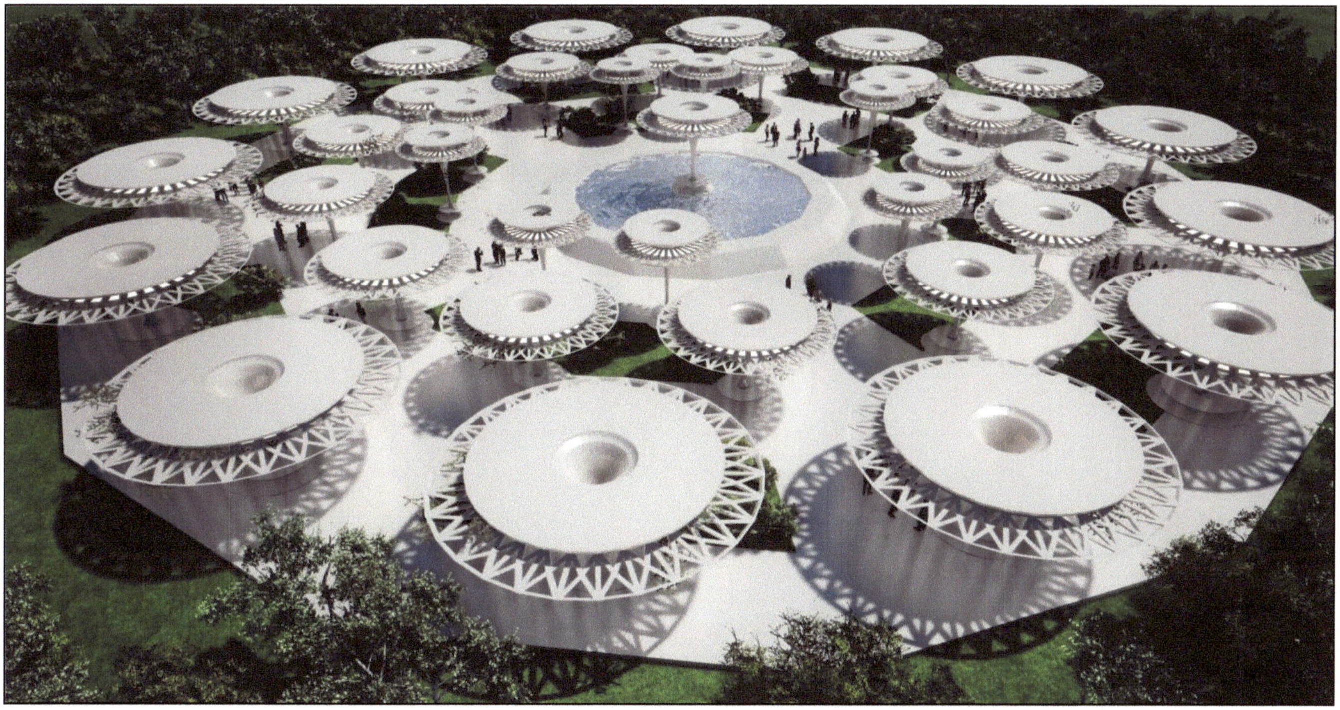

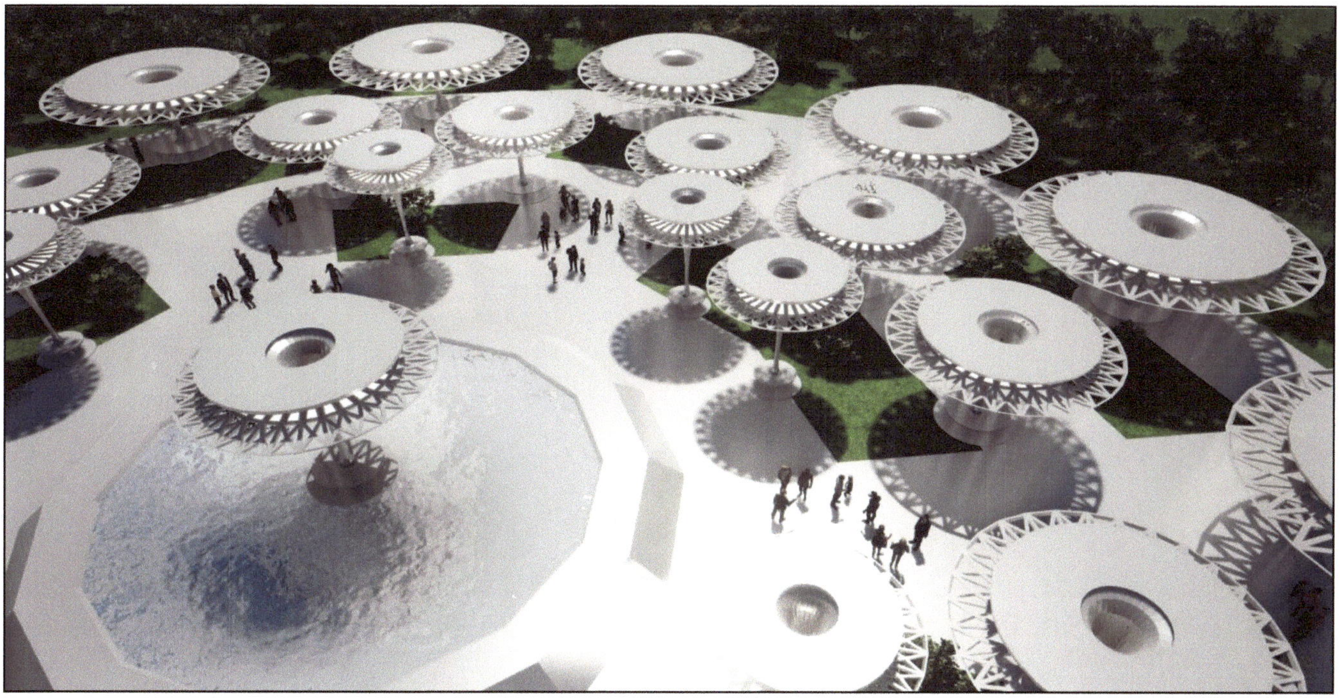

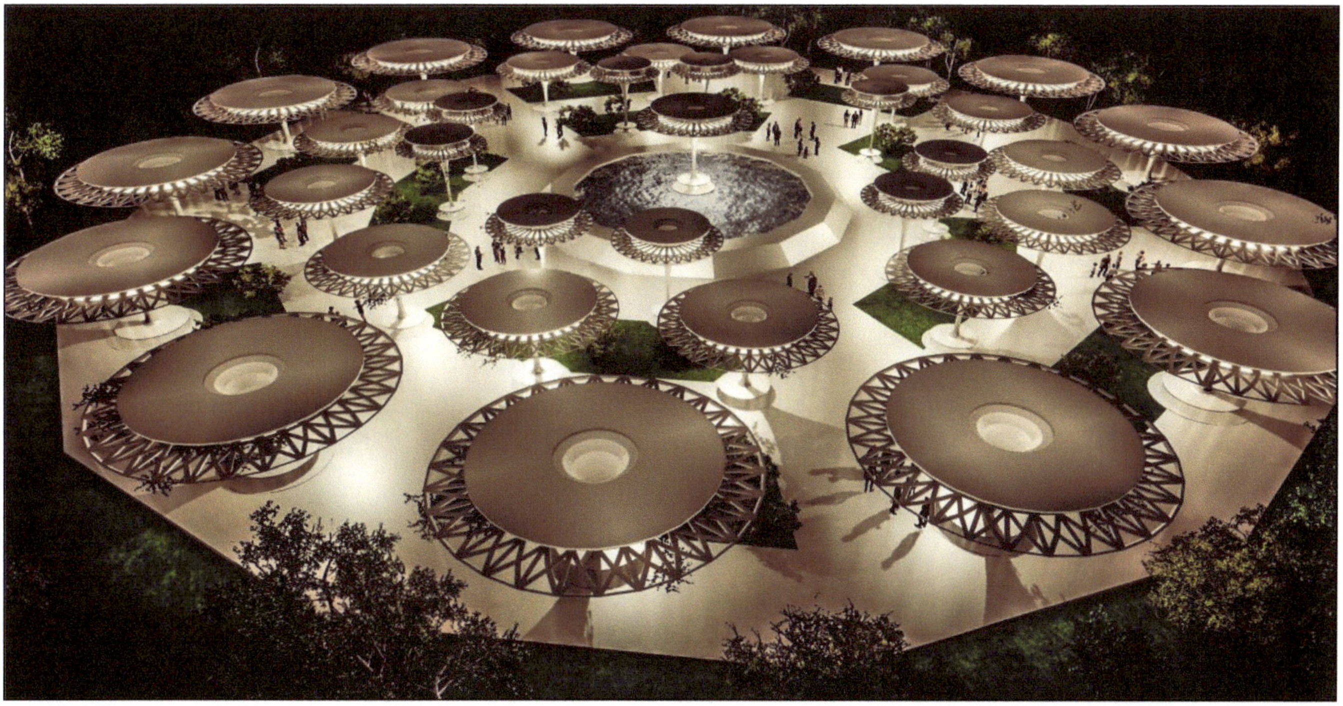

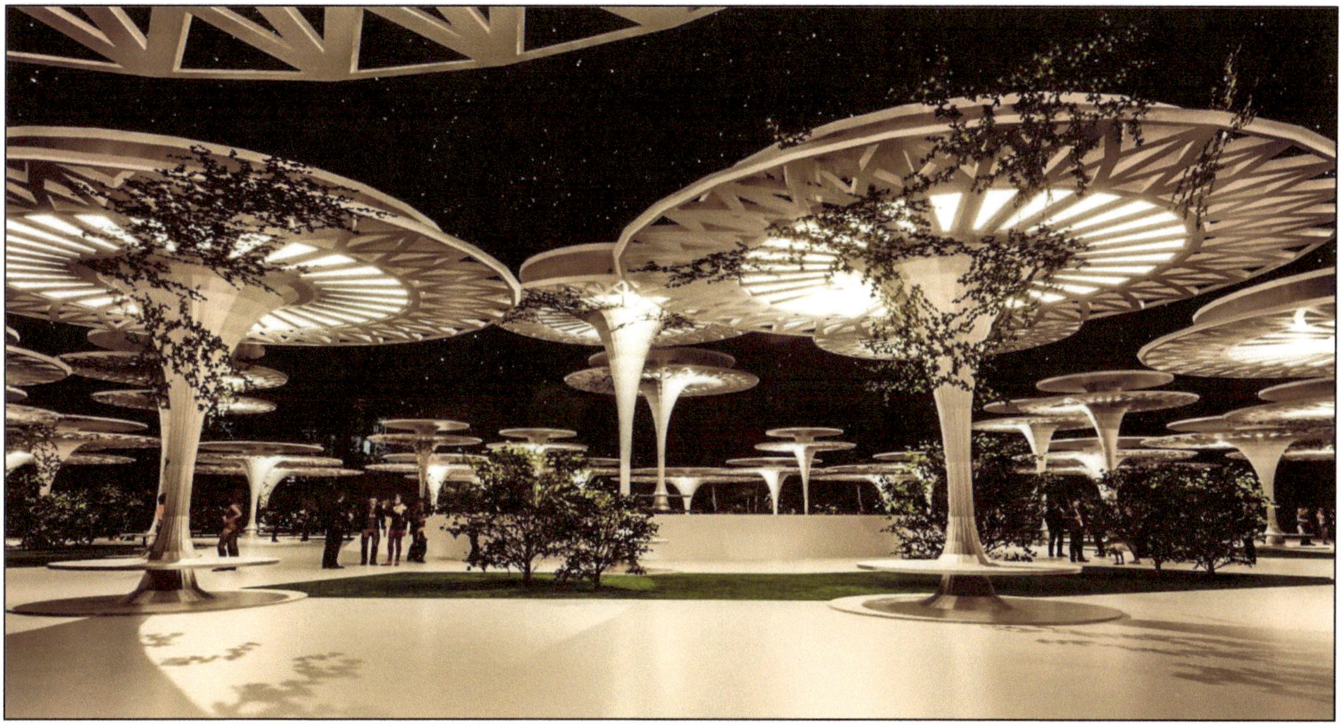

Organic product sales pavilion

Dourna Kiavar

Nowadays, struggling with numerous health problems are correlated to the poor quality of food. Due to health problems that mentioned above, importance of organic food utilization becomes more clear. The idea behind designing of this pavilion is concepting hexagonal bee hives which is originated from nature. So by reforming this base shape try to make an attractive place for costumers.

Site plan

Creation method: rotate the line around the inner axis

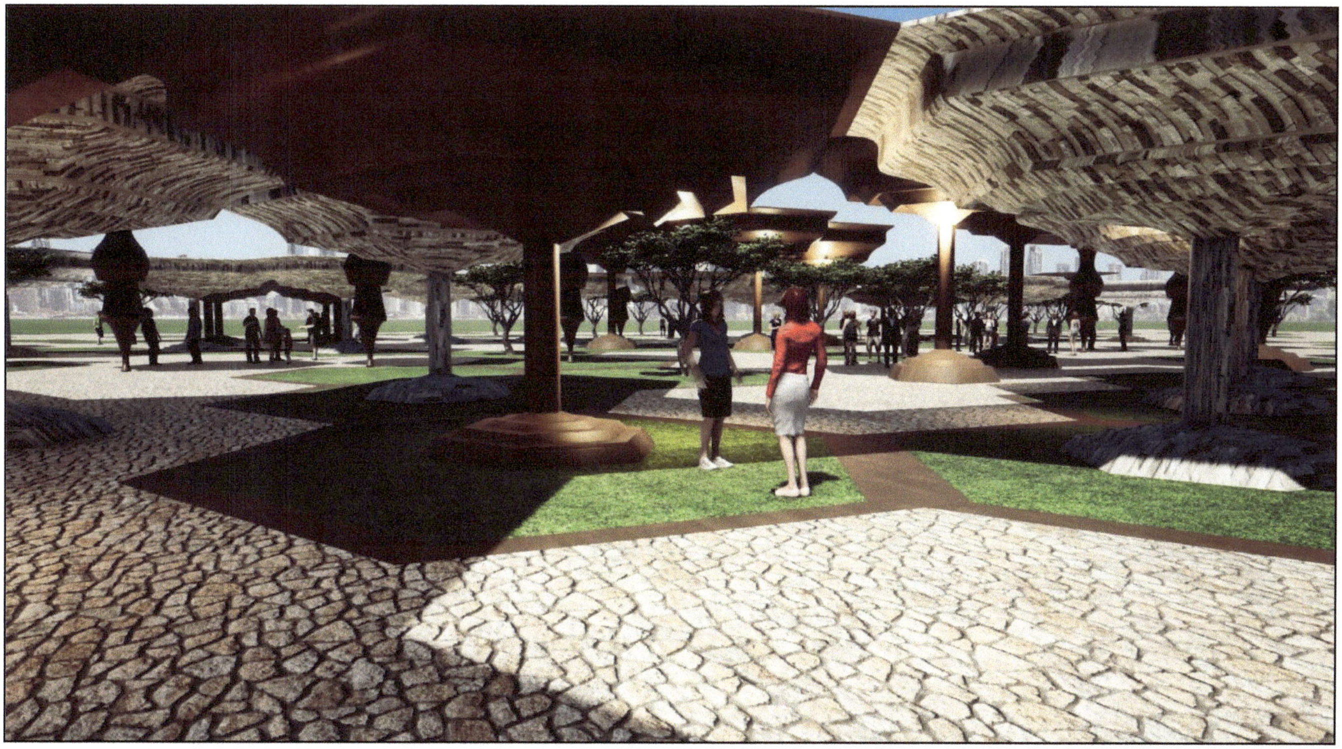

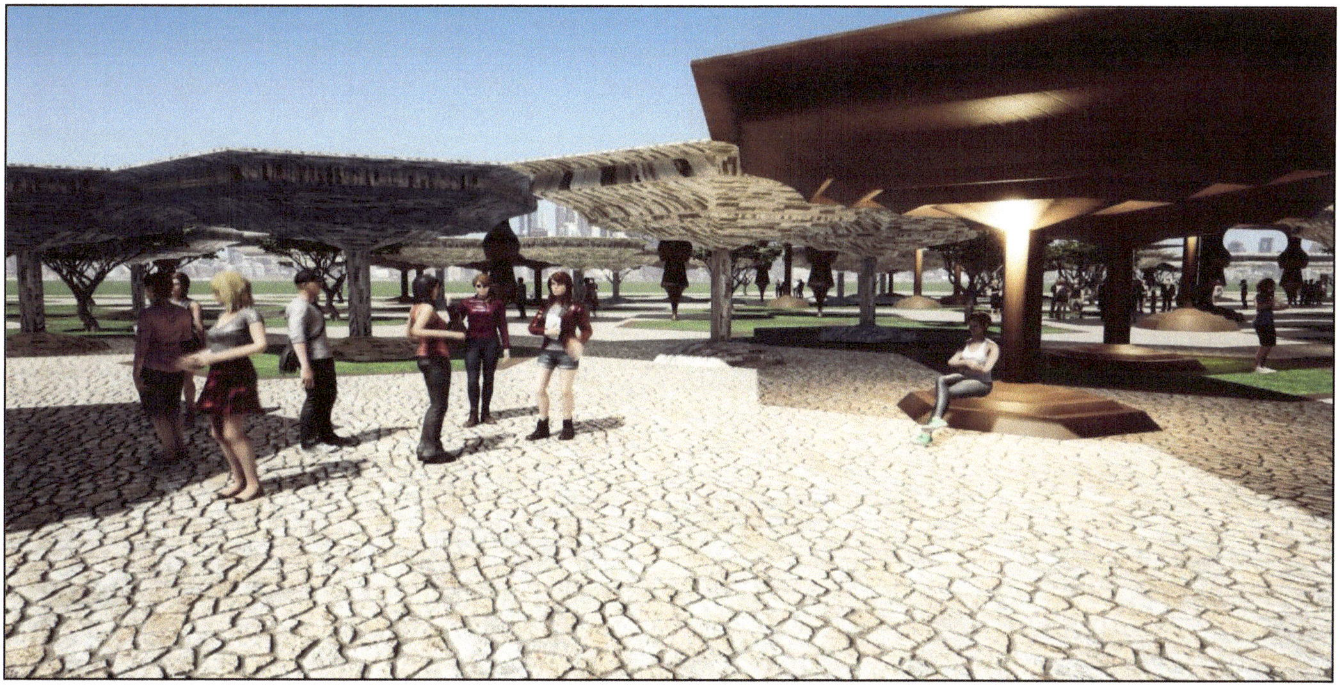

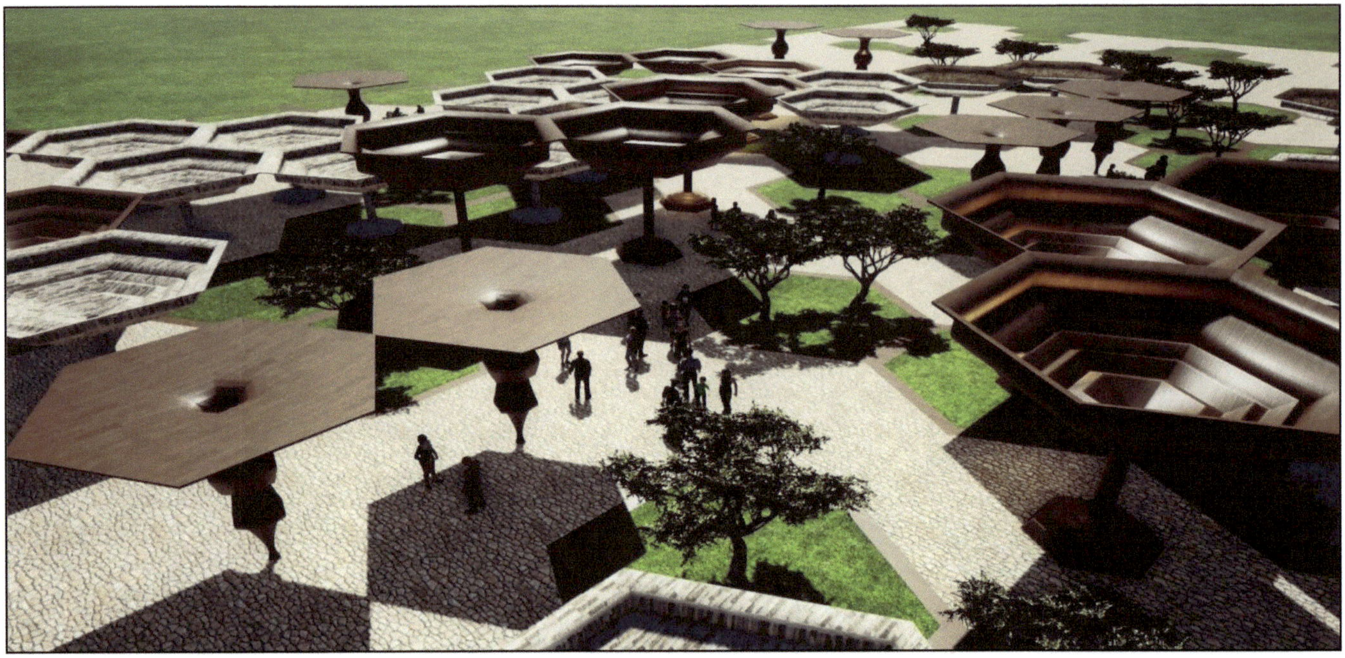

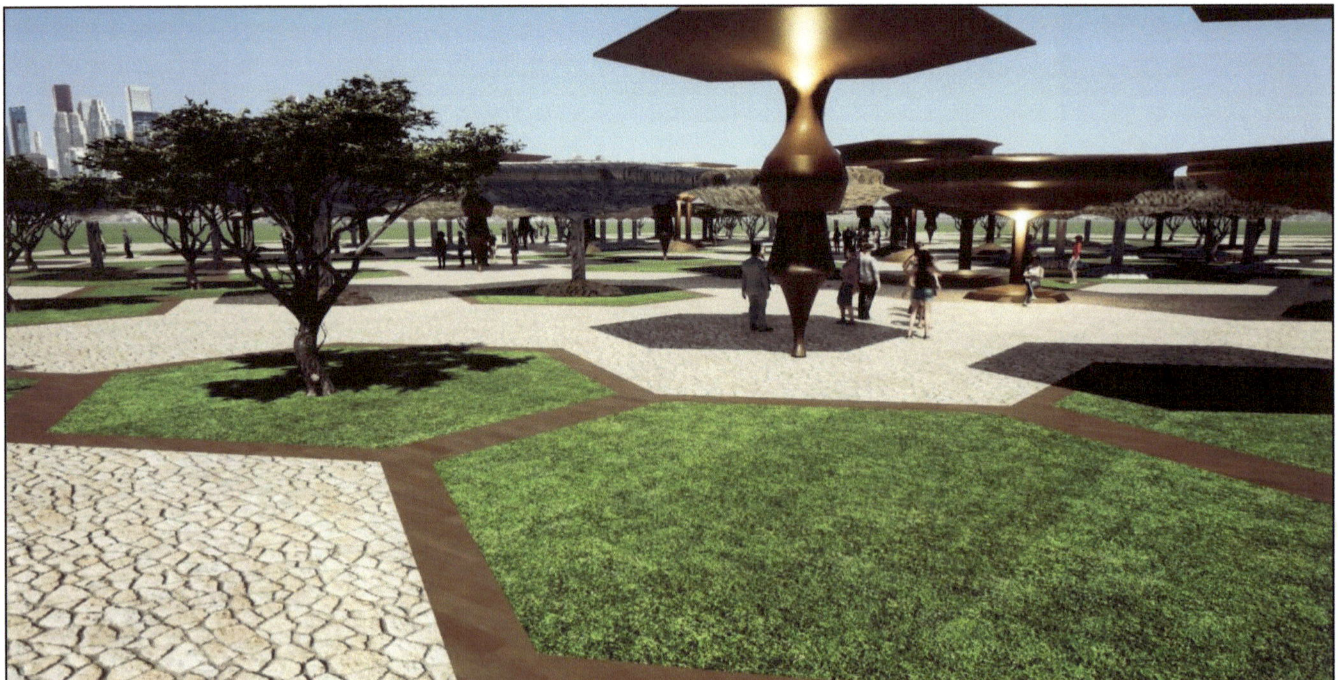

Pendulous pavilion
Kosar Piri

After design of different structures based on "Connect" order, I decided to symmetry them vertically to develop the designed structure. As seen in the design process diagram, the main structure, and its symmetry are place over each other. Suddenly, I encountered with several volumes like flying saucers. The first case that occurred to me was to return to the former structure. However, I continued design at the recommendation of the workshop instructors. I connected the designed structures using oval ceilings to make a double-deck pavilion. Six orange glass elevators were designed in four structures to access the upper story. A double-deck pavilion covered with wood, grass, and trees hanging between the earth and sky or, in better words, this pavilion made the earth and sky closer.

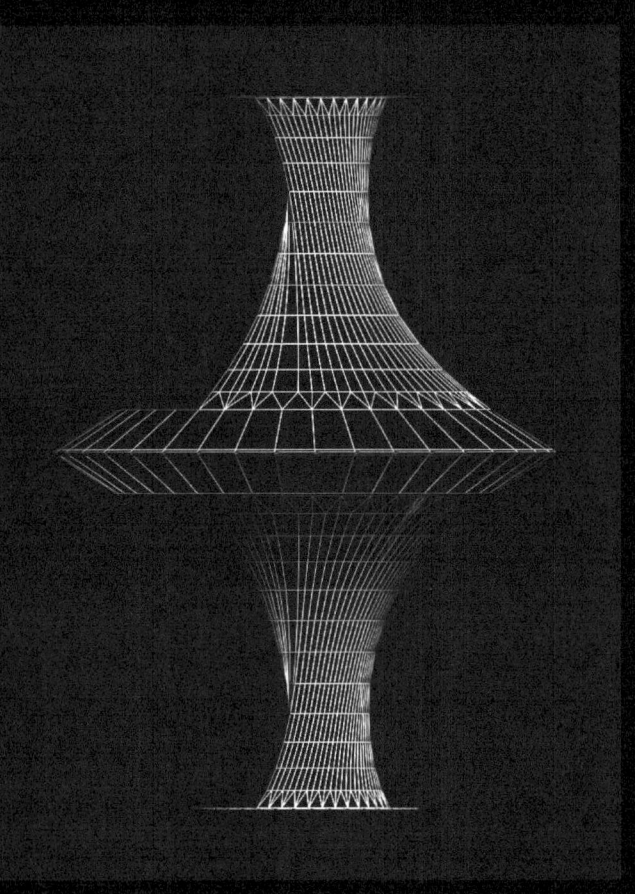

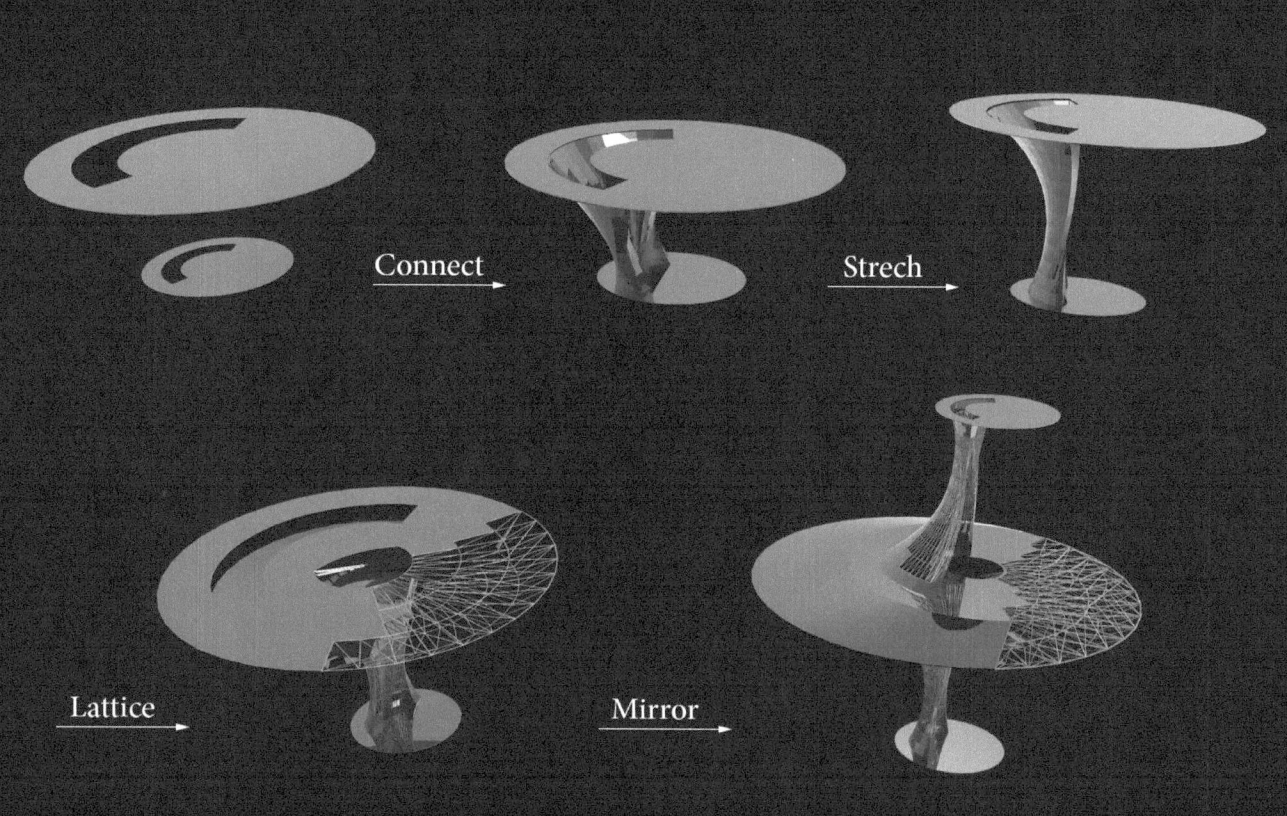

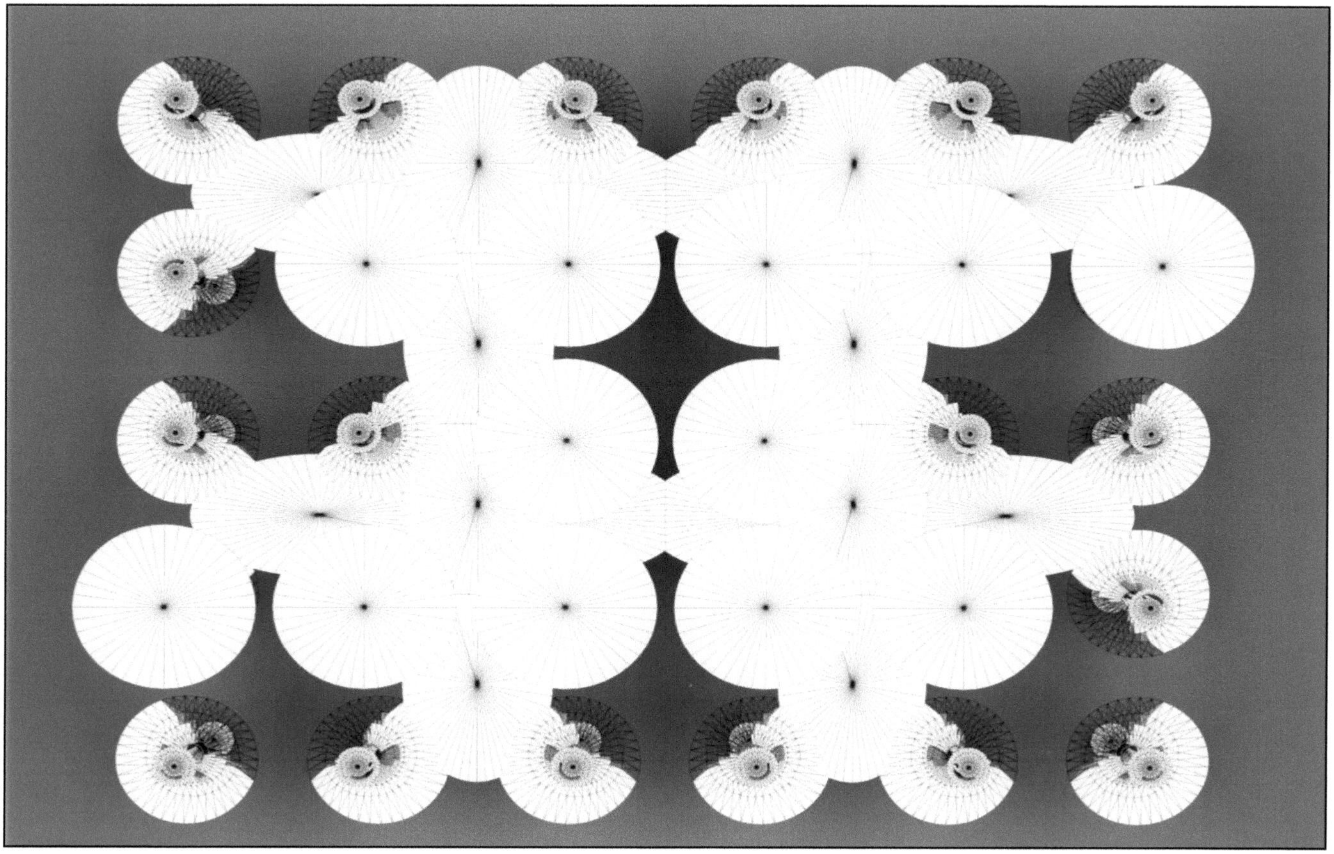

Site plan

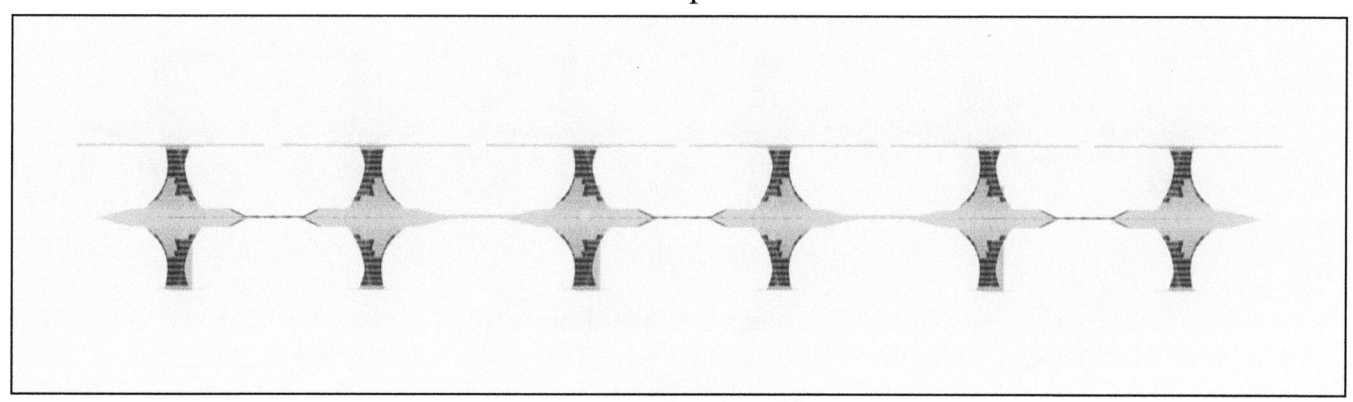

Facade of pavilion

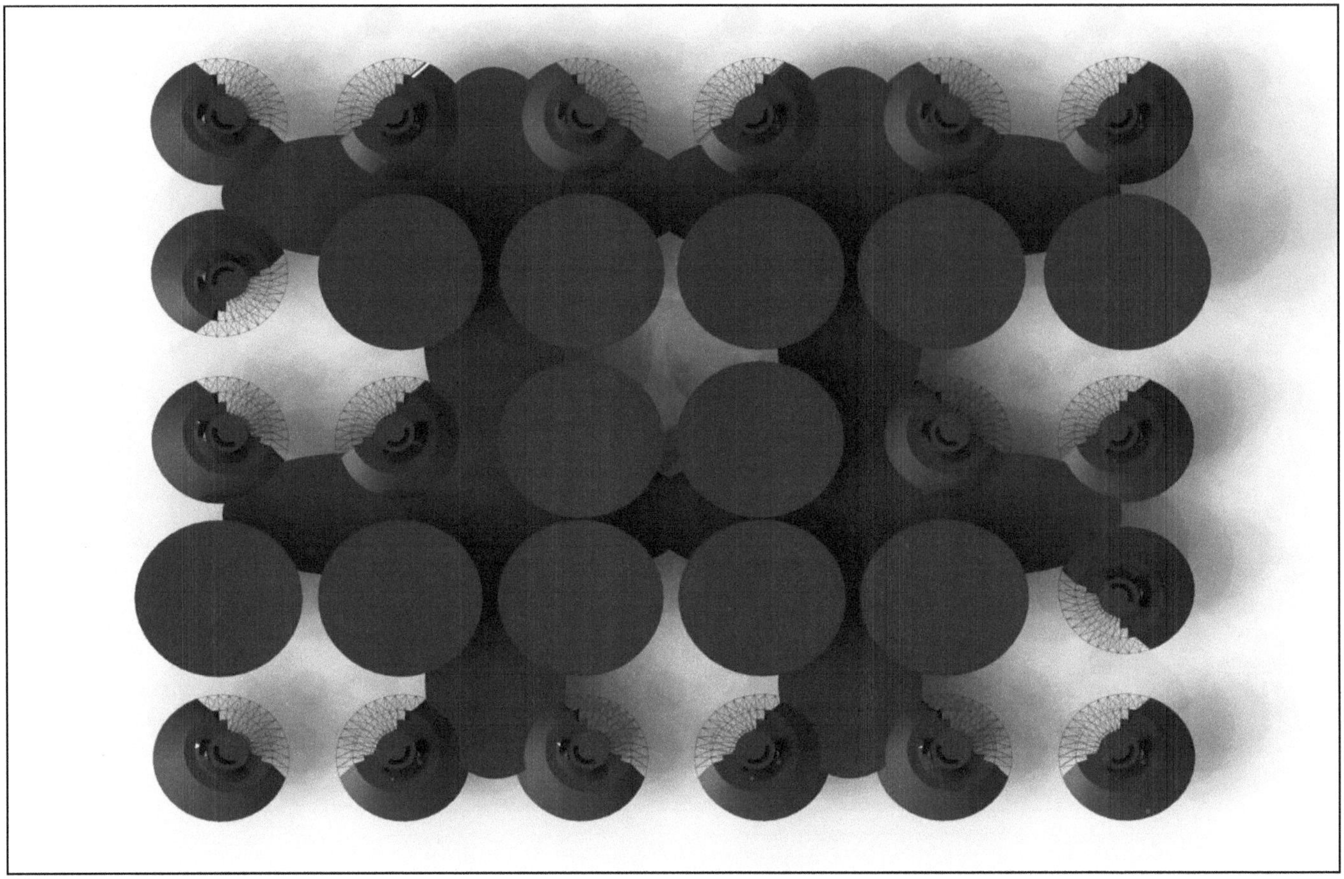

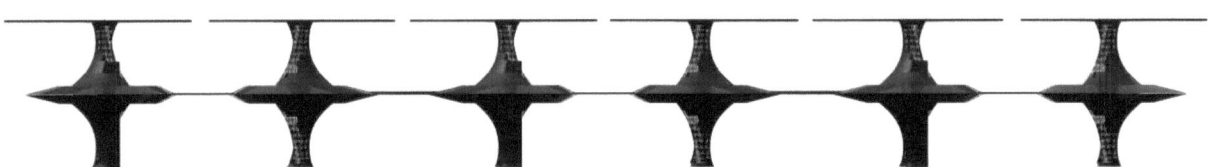

Facade of pavilion

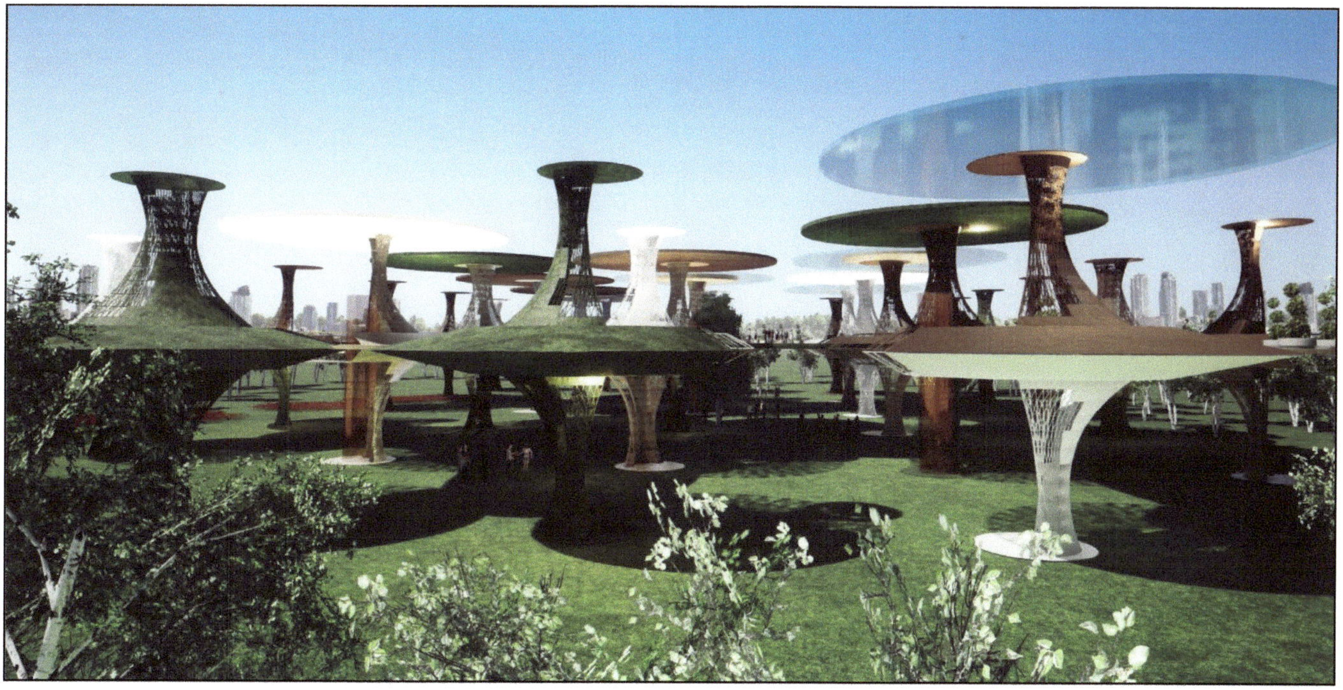

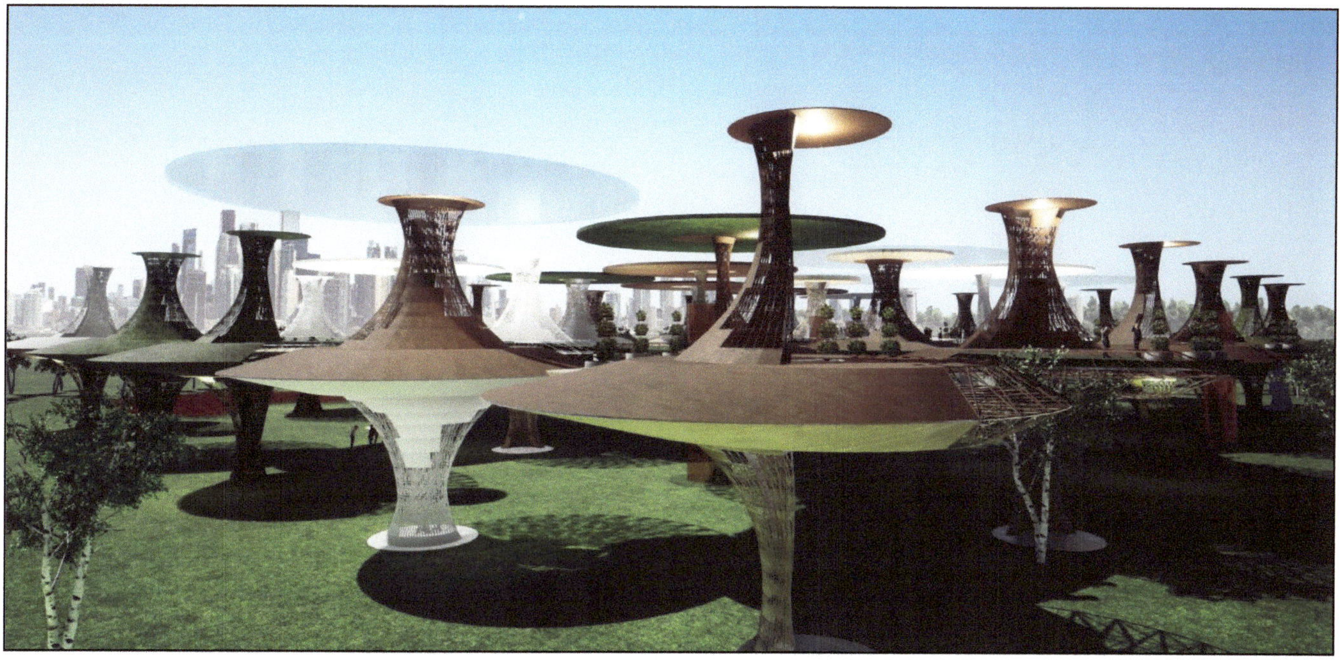

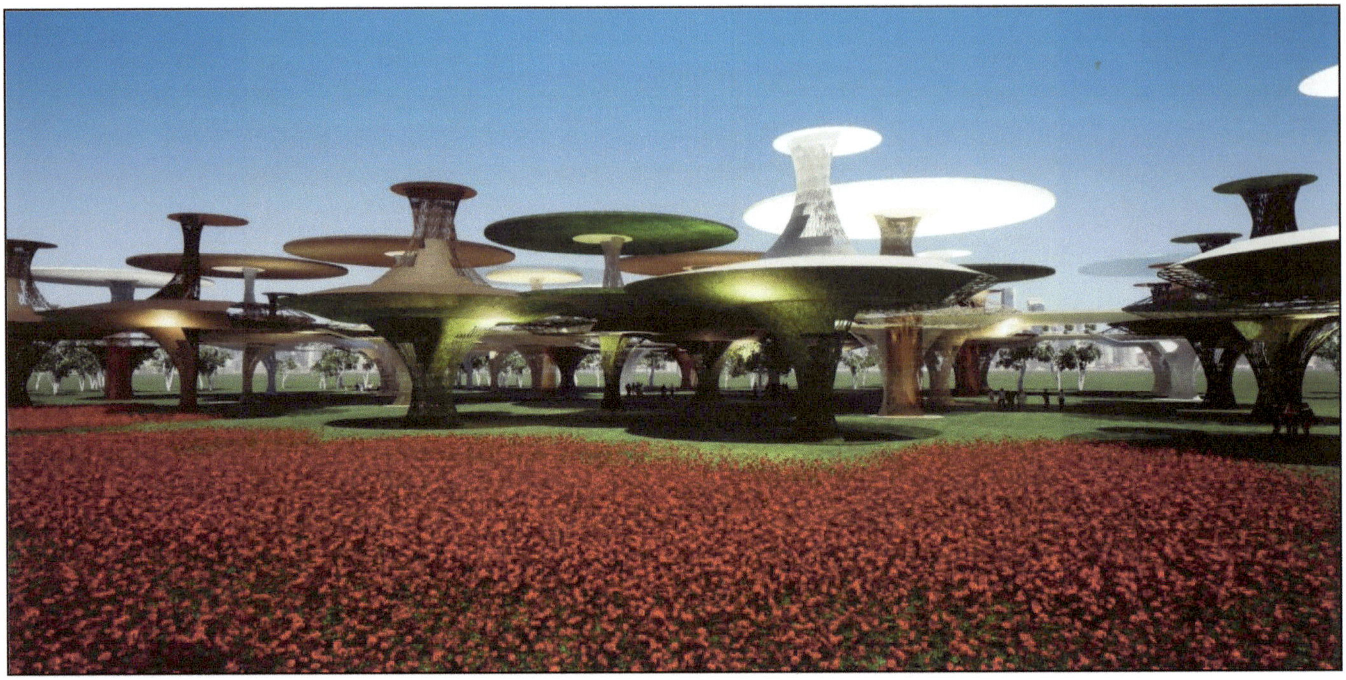

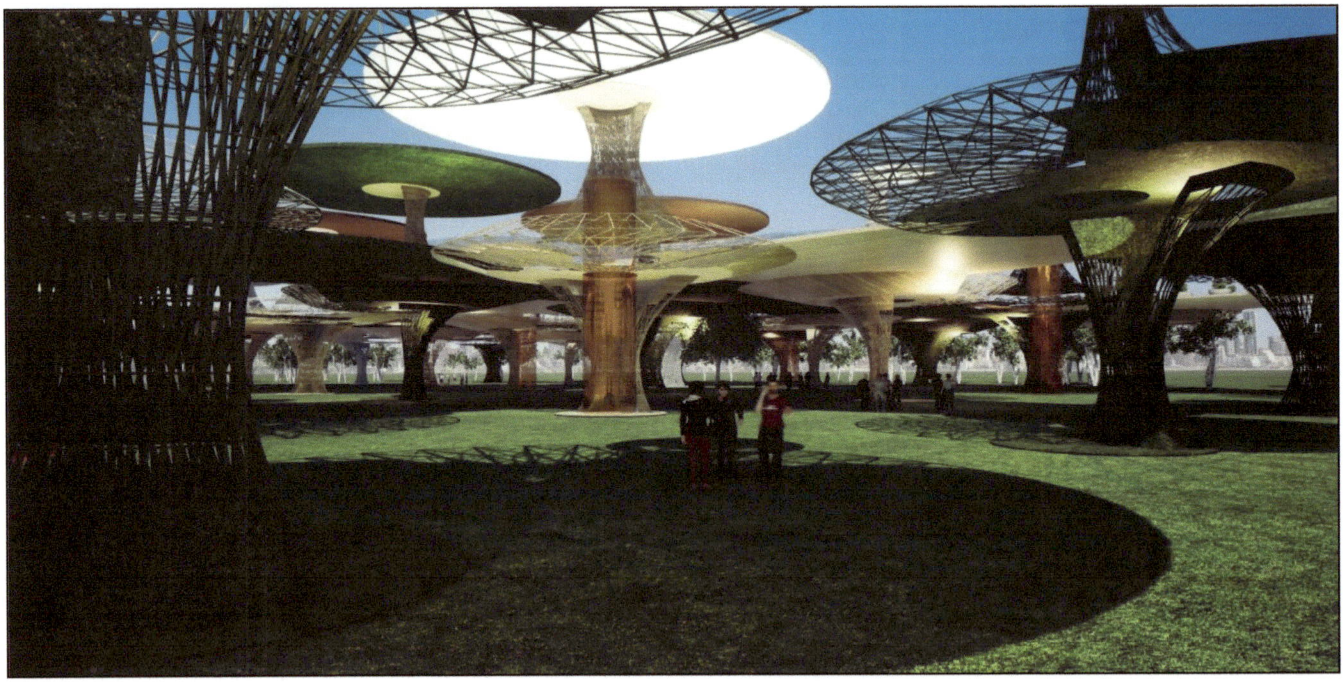

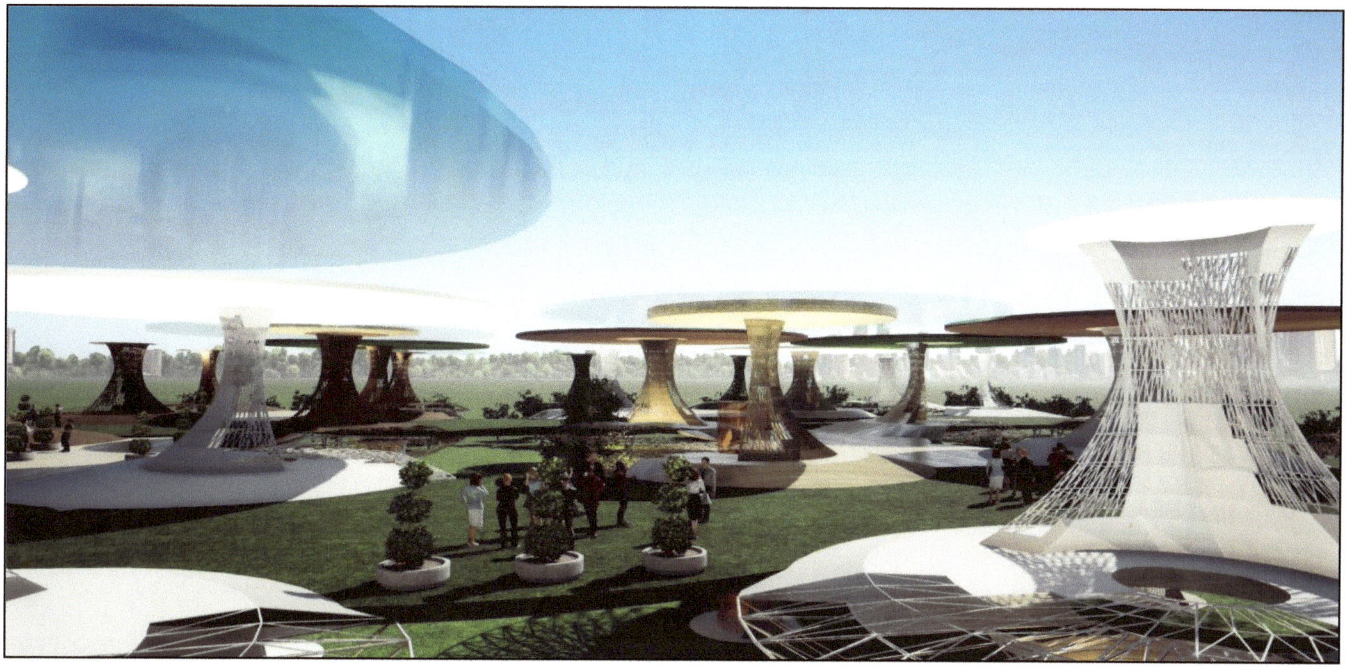

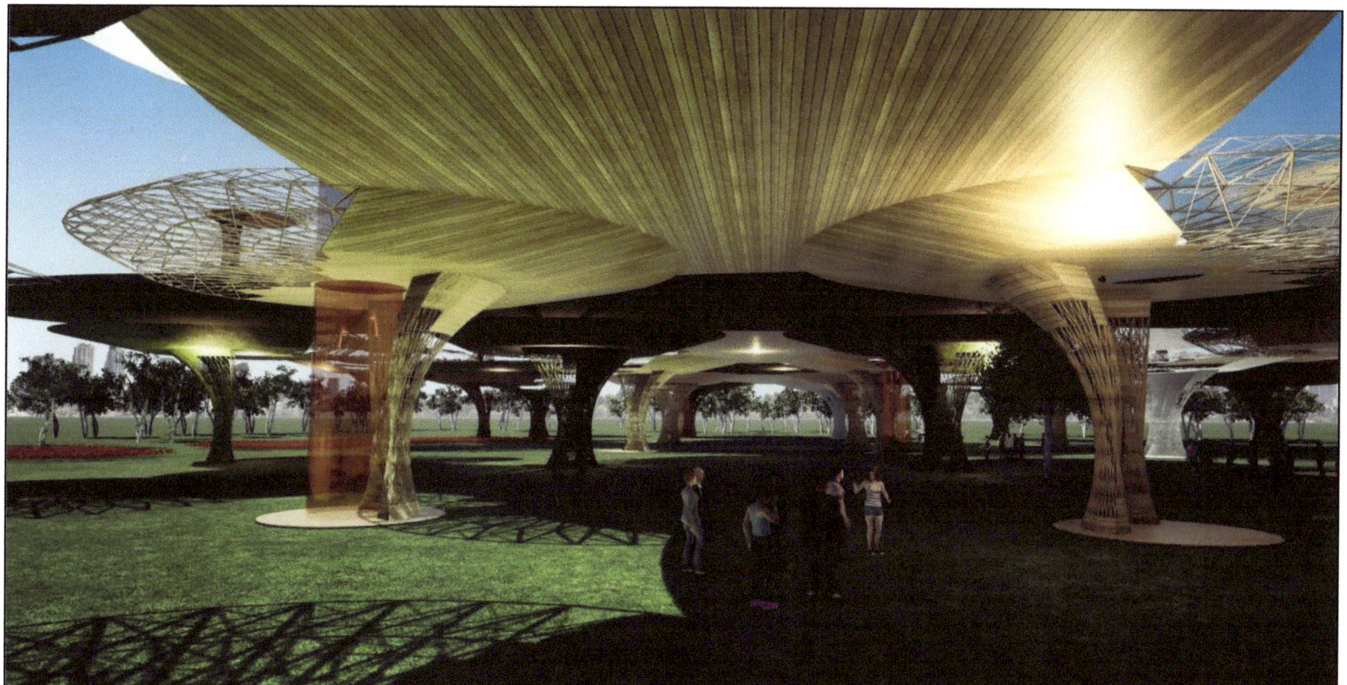

Green Trench

Sanaz Asgari

The green trench with 8 meters of structural radius, is designed by combination of urban elements and green roofs. The purpose of combining waterfall column and local plants on roof of structure is to create a beautiful and relaxing atmosphere. In addition, by staircase landscape designing we created a seating area for visitors. The gap created on the green curved shell is to bring light inside the negative height.

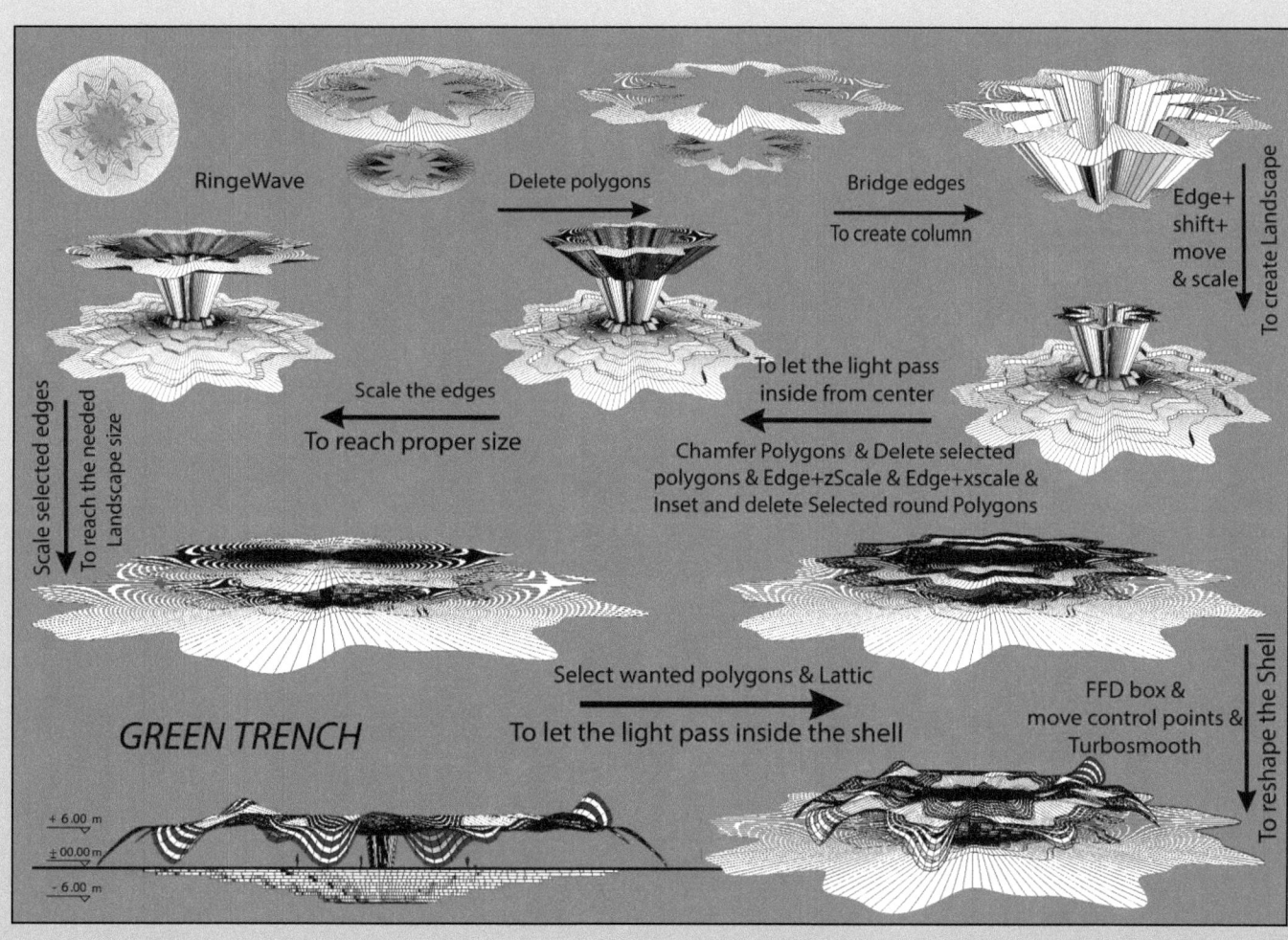

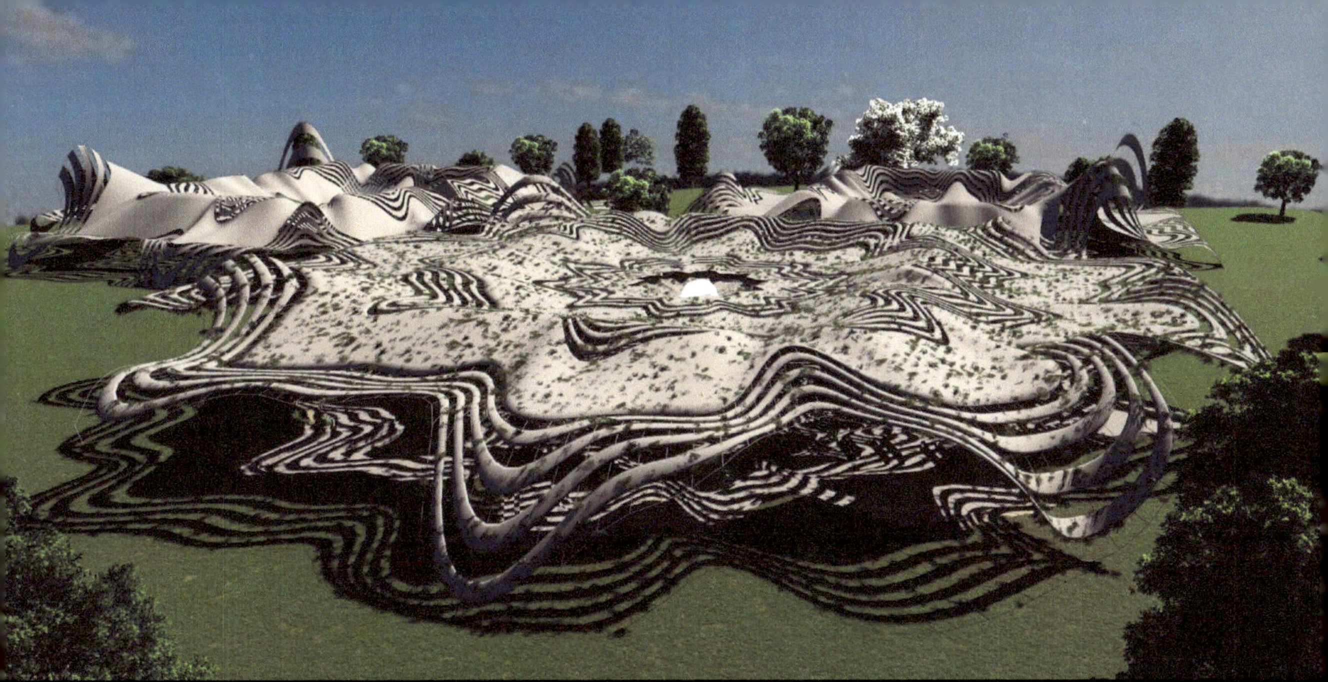

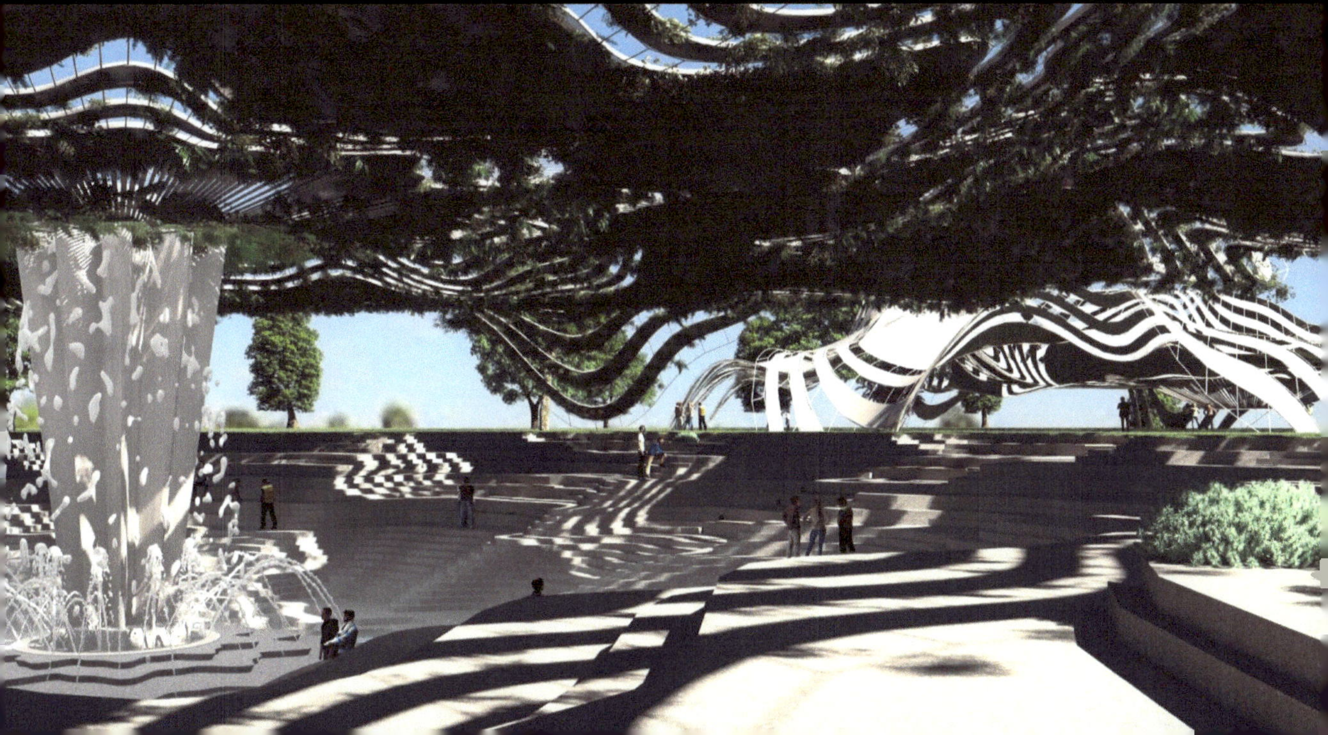

Rainbow skirt
Sanaz Asgari

Urban parks and gardens play a critical role in cities. They provide safe routes for walking and cycling as well as sites for physical activity, social interaction and for recreation. Clothing has always been a factor for looking nice, so why not do this for trees? Clothes that are not only for beauty but also to bring the idea of importance of protecting them. My tree clothes make them beautiful elements in our sites and parks. The clothe is inverted from the foliage of the trees, which provides tent-shape atmosphere for children to play under it.

The shield is designed around the tree trunk connecting to the ground by rods in the center of the volume without attaching to tree's trunk, which can withstand the load of a 2 mm galvanized structure. The color variation used in the material increases the visual vibrancy of the space, plus the harmony between the shape of shield and lighting make it look like colorful butterflies which make rainbow on the ground at nights.

Gometric pattern

Move splines on z axis to make gap between splines →
Cross section the splines + Weld vertecs →
Surface →
Editepoly + Lattic the Selected polygons →
FDD BOX →
Taper + ffd3x3x3 + Turbosmooth →
Slice to remove the top and ffd to wider the top →

TREE Shelter

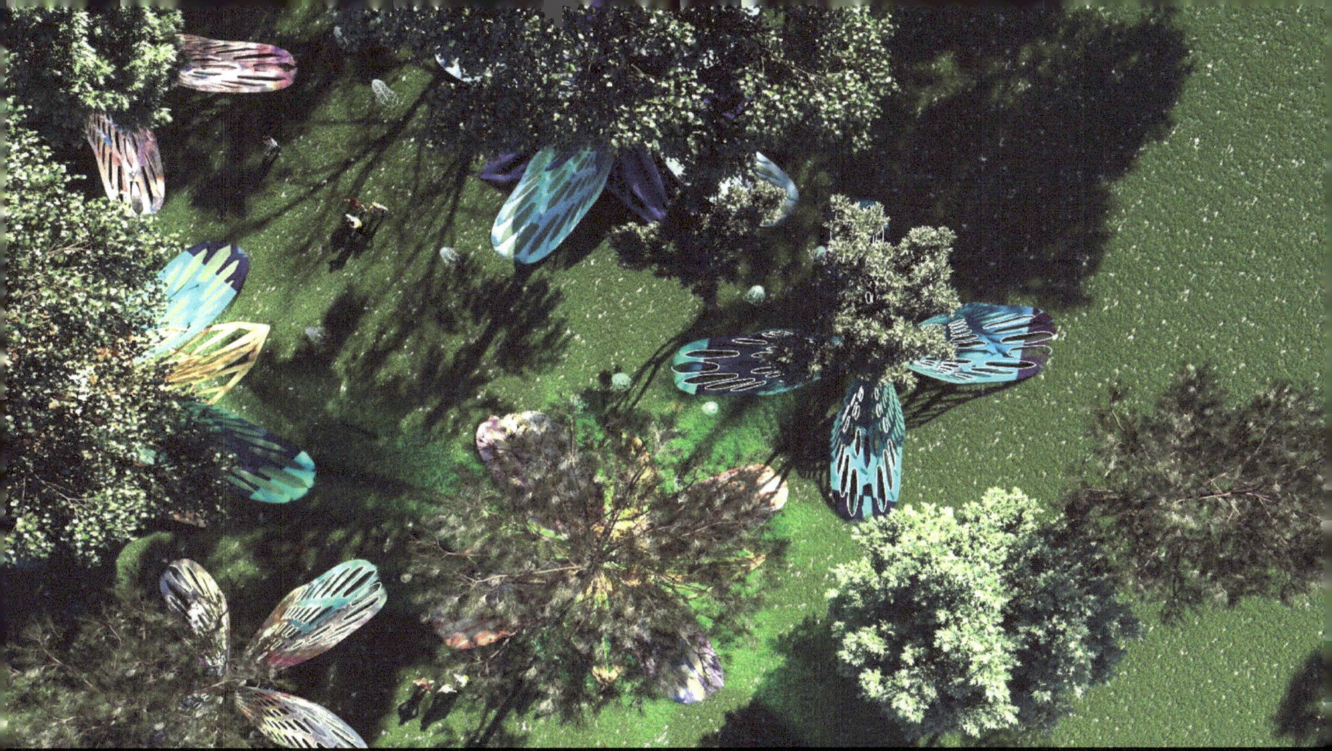

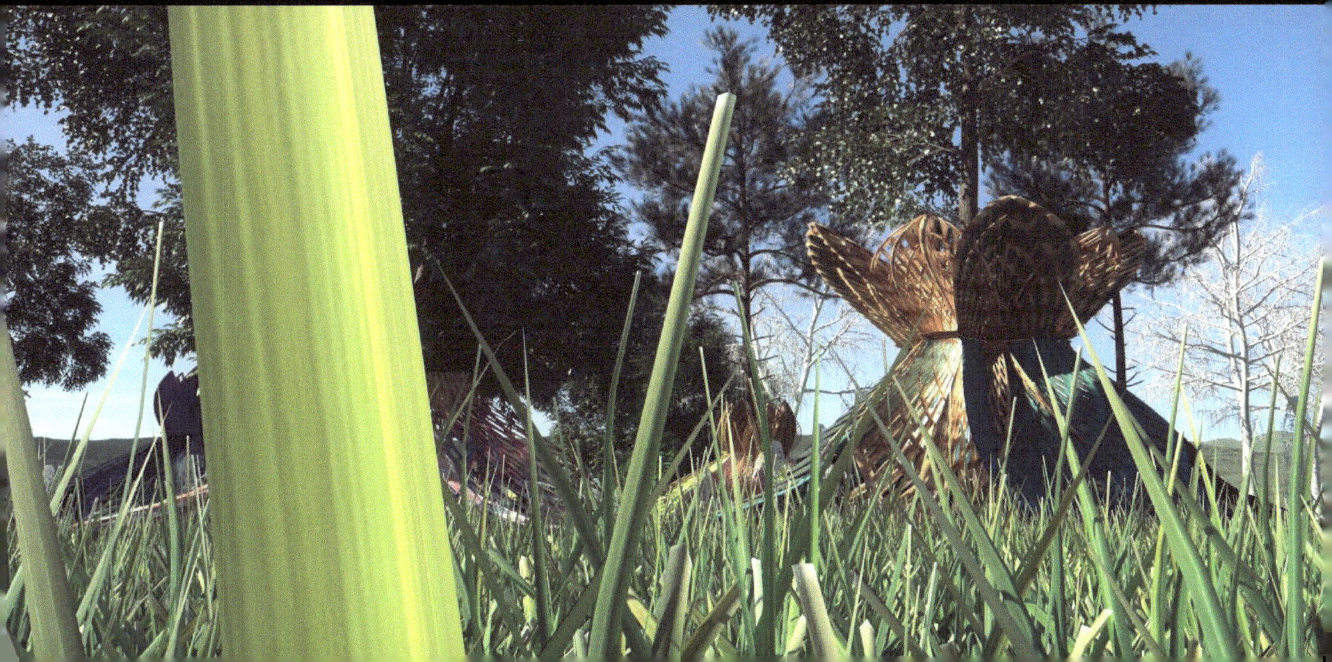

Bio-Gravity Pavilion

Movement-responsive architecture.

Hussein Agoush

The project Bio-Gravity Pavilion explores a mode of movement-responsive architecture, and its primary focus is about direct incorporation of active biological matters into built structures, which can potentially lead to exciting space, forms and functional possibilities.

This design presents how water-containing hydrogels can be adapted to digital fabrication techniques to design a soft responsive skin with integrated skeleton and surface.

Hydrogels, synthetic biomaterials that contain water, provide a soft skeleton that can be potentially used in responsive and kinetic architecture. This material, with different material properties, also can be designed and incorporated into laser-cutting and 3D printing methods typically used in architectural design.

Tough hydrogels with vein pattern are capable of interfacing with biological matters, since they do contain water. Along this design, the structure becomes contracted and actuates in response to electric pulse, since the joints become rigid and deformed in response to electricity and hot water, while they are reversed and become fully extended with the power of gravity and in the absence of electric pulse.

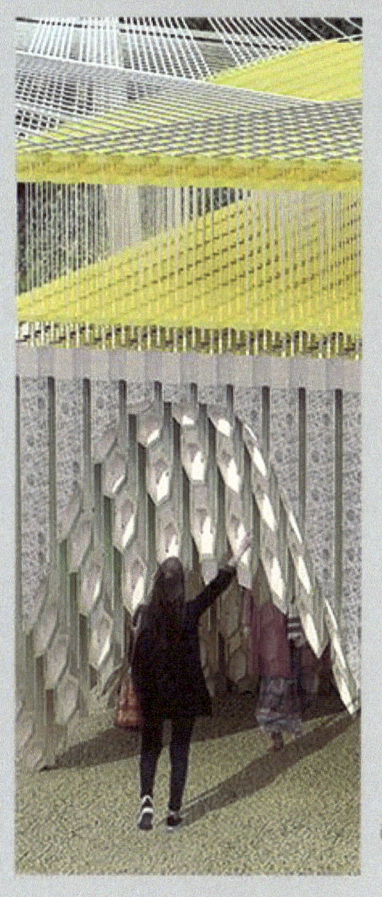
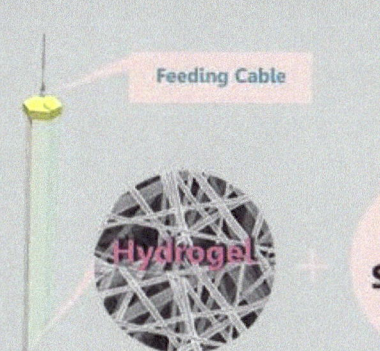
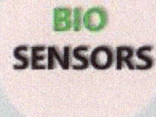

- Incorporating hydrogel materials with bio-sensors that are thermally sensitive, will provide integrated skeletons and skins that can perform multifunctional tasks such as sensing and actuation with minimum active and passive energy.

- The outcomes demonstrate a designed hydrogel skeleton with structural deformation and heat sensitivity capabilities, which can be potentially applied to responsive architectural structures and skins.

  Guided by parametric design, this concept produces a soft responsive structure, which can not only enhance the environmental performance, but also will produce unique and aesthetic architectural forms.

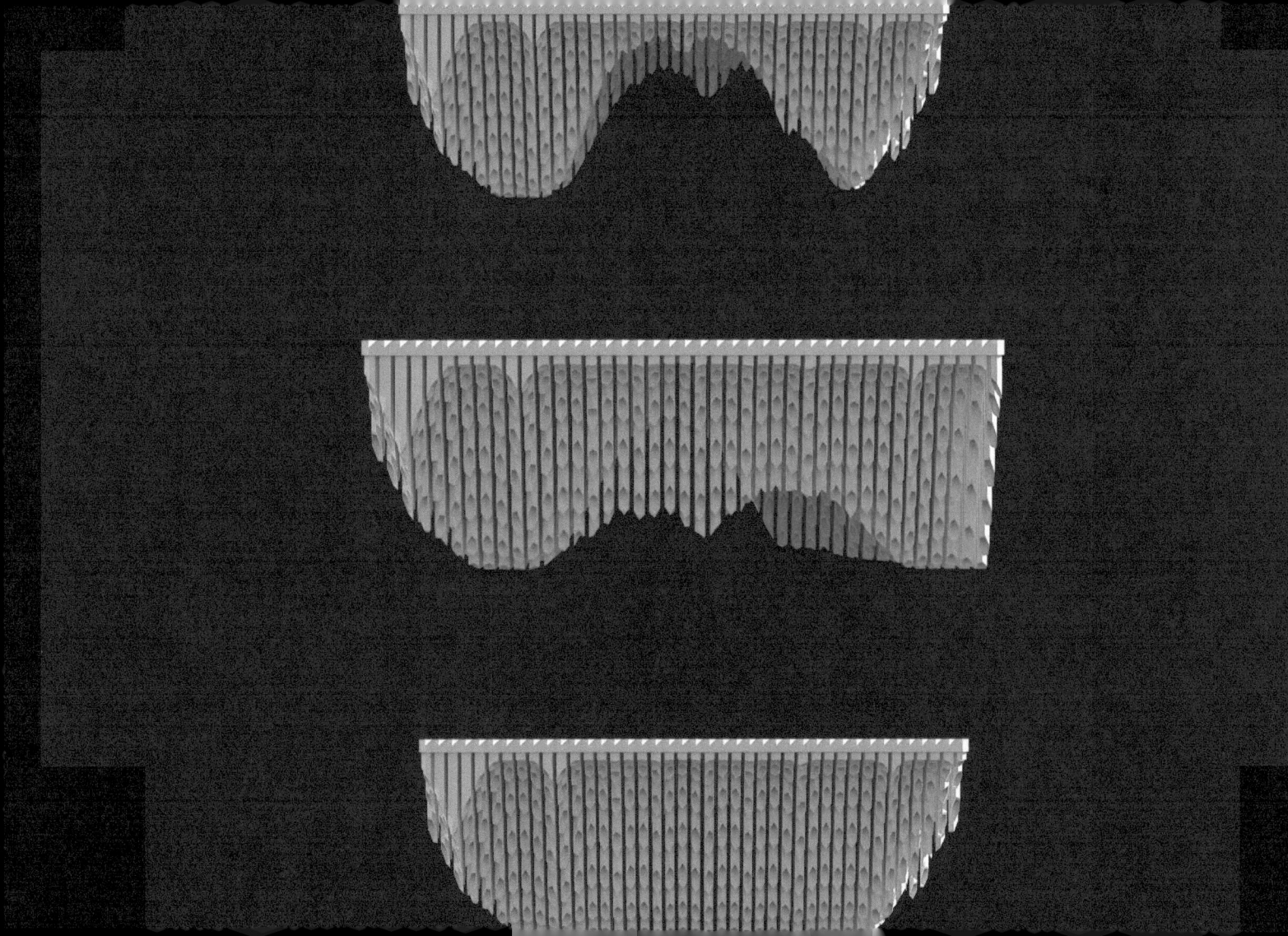

ReUnity Pavilion

Hussein Agoush

Among the spiritually significant symbols, Mobius Strip resembles the infinite unity of the universe. In this pavilion, the unique mathematical shape of the Mobius strip, is used as the main concept and tries to emphasis on the meeting of two human beings. The interconnectedness of the universes within each individual are reflected upon the architecturally merged two Mobius type of forms. The used circulation in this form, which starts from ground level and continues to the rooftop, attempts to create a state of wholeness and connectedness. When individuals enter this pavilion, they will experience an expression of non-duality and will be guided to the central yard where they will meet each other. The interior circulations also follow the same rules and provides a gallery for artists to share their arts.

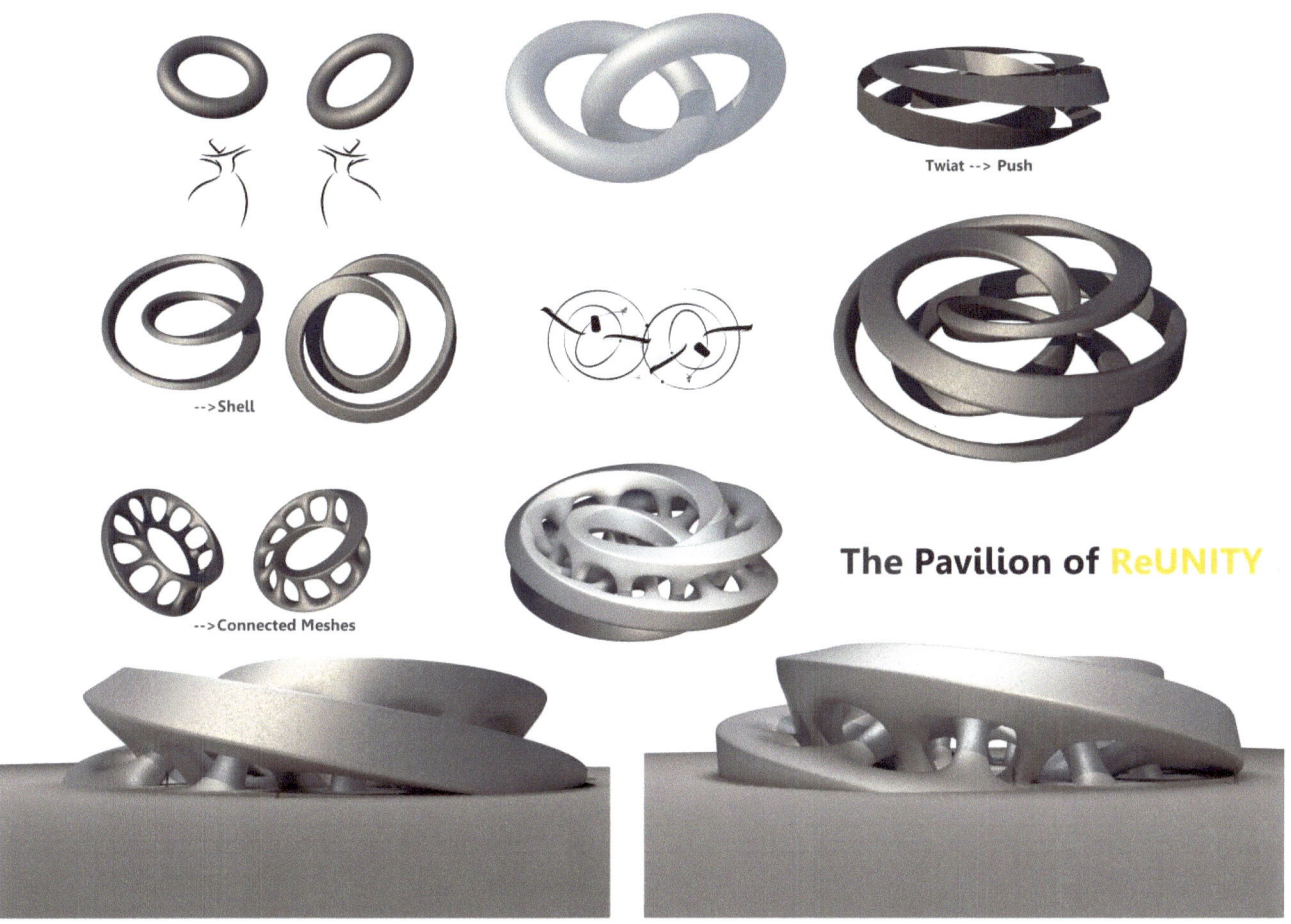

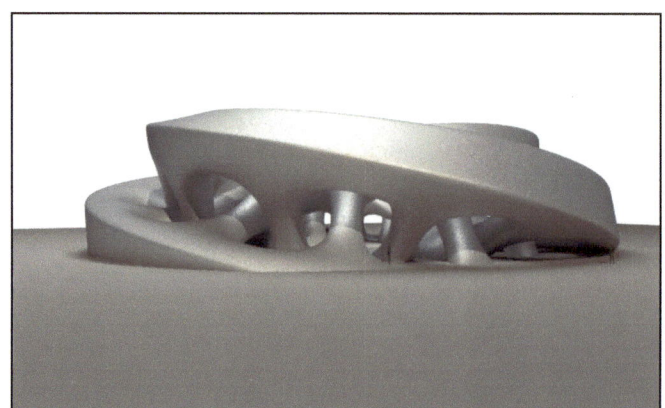

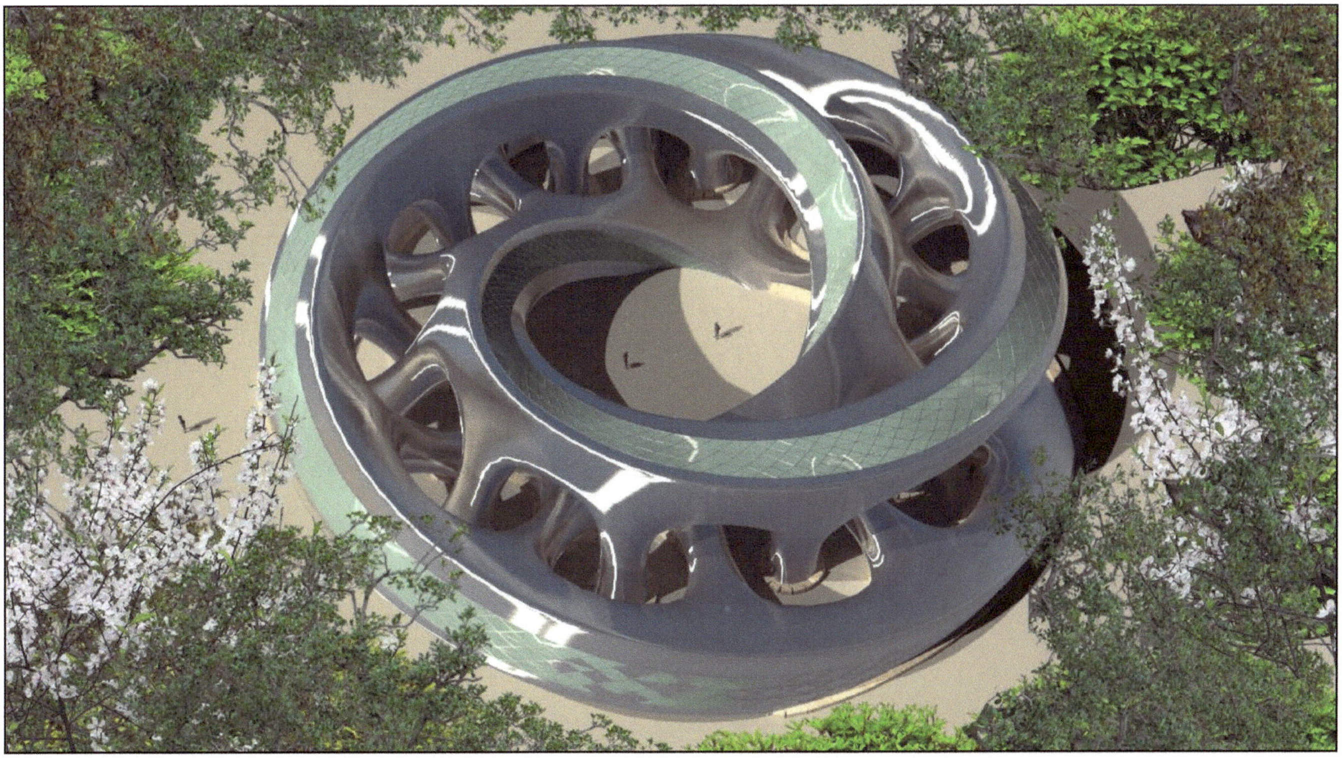

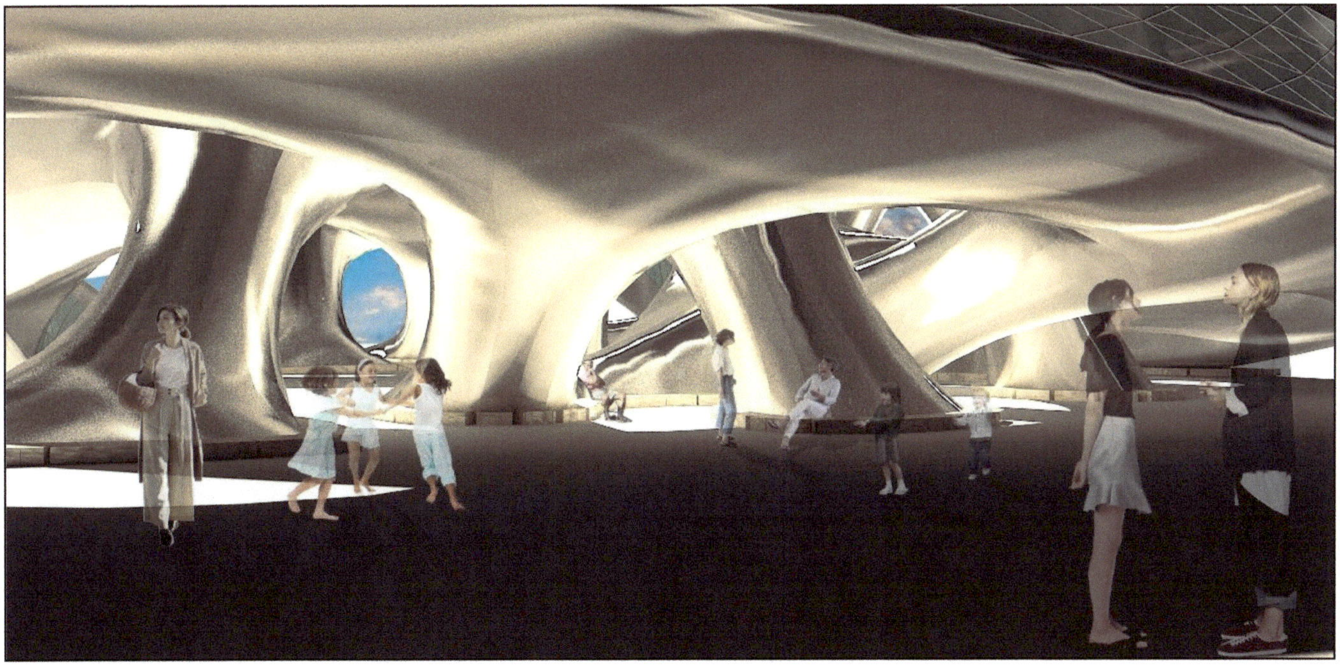

Phoenix Garden

Niloufar Mohammadalizadeh

Phoenix is an Iranian fabulous bird and has several wonderful appearances in fables, sagas, philosophy, mysticism and generally, in Iranian culture and has been repeatedly named in different books. In the Mantegh Alteir Poem of the great poet, i.e. Attar Neyshabouri (the 12th century A.D.), the phoenix is a symbol of truth. Other birds travel to find it and it is the beginning of the story: All birds gathered and said "We should have a king to resign ourselves to its will. We should find it and live under its protection. We should obey it and follow its orders. We heard that there is a king known as "Phoenix" ruling in the west and east. We should go to it and obey it".

Here, the hoopoe is the spiritual leader of the birds. They travel toward the Caucasus, the location of the Phoenix. At the beginning of travel, some birds dispense with continuation of the travel. The hoopoe tells the story of Sheikh Sanan and forces other birds to continue their travel. In this difficult path, the birds have seven stages referring to seven stages of conduct, i.e. seek, love, knowledge, independence, monotheism, amazement, poverty, and death. Passing these stages, some birds are defeated and only thirty birds can reach the phoenix's location. In fact, the phoenix is these thirty birds which have become "phoenix" after passing all these seven stages.

Since the phoenix fable has special position in our culture, this plan tries to use the concept of phoenix, birds and flight and the general plan inspires this story. In this plan, the wings which are symbols of birds are placed sparsely around the garden. When we move toward the center of the garden, the birds unify, obtain general unity, and create the phoenix. The plan presented in the center of the garden indicates such unity of the birds.

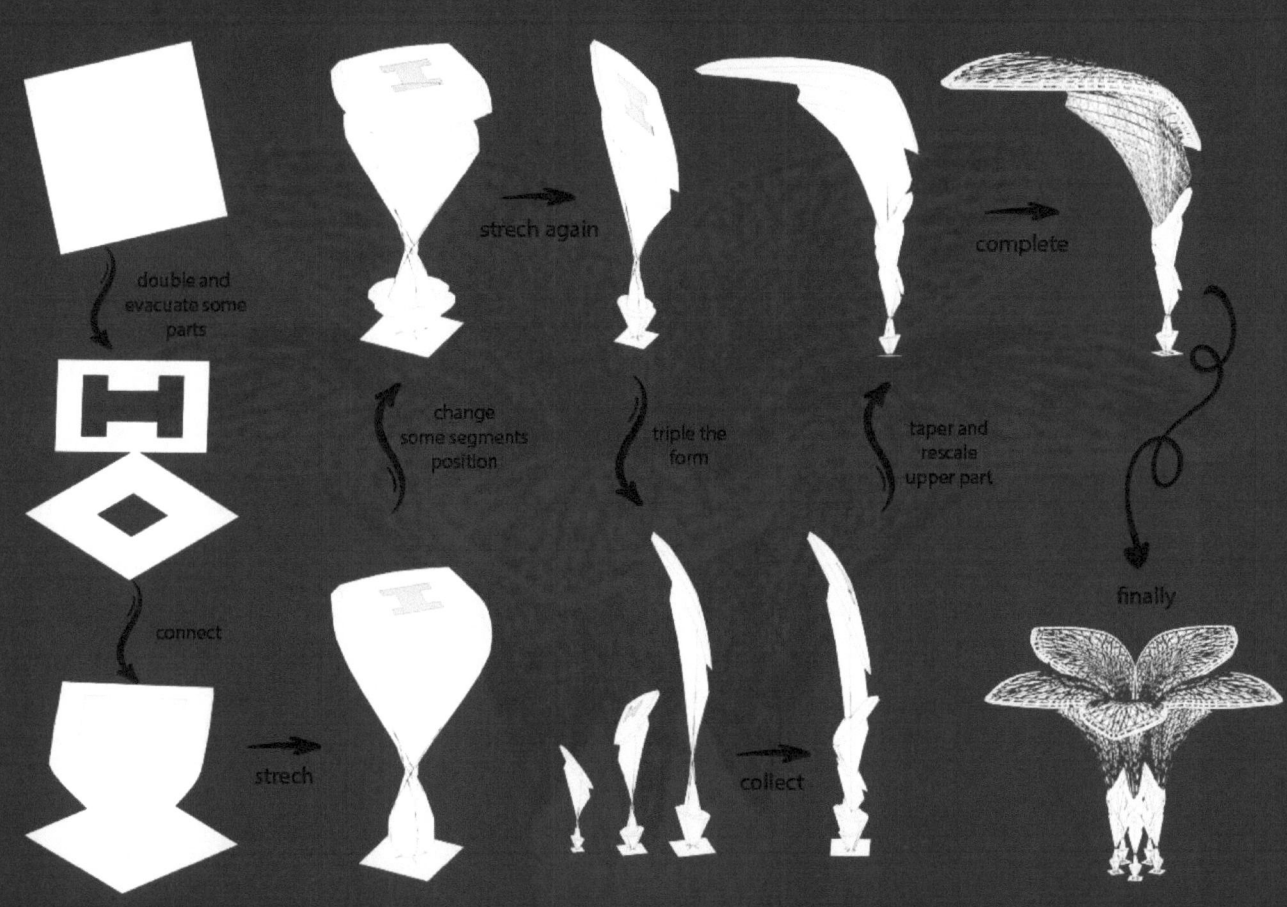

Design process

Site plan

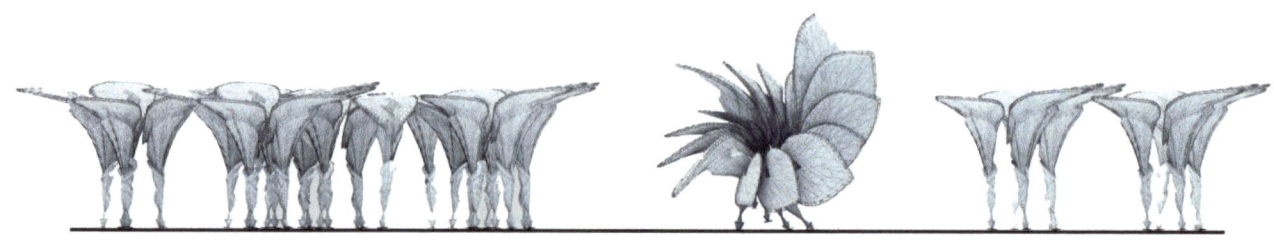

Façade of phoenix garden

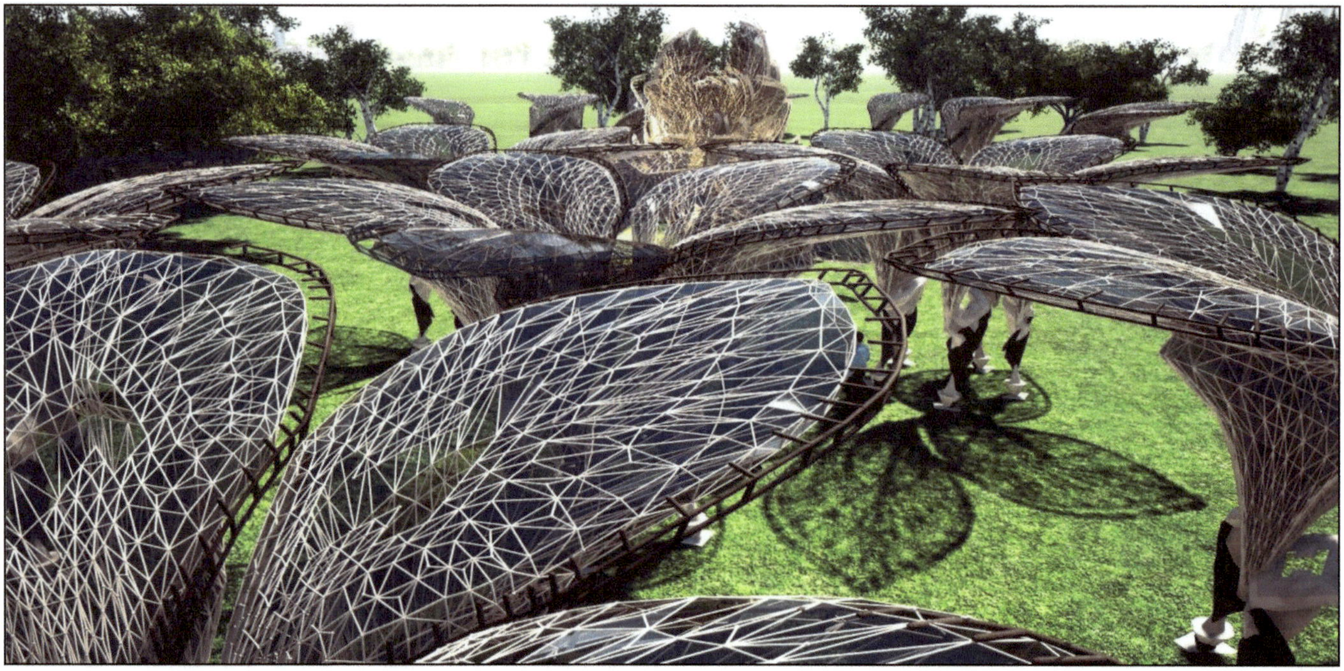

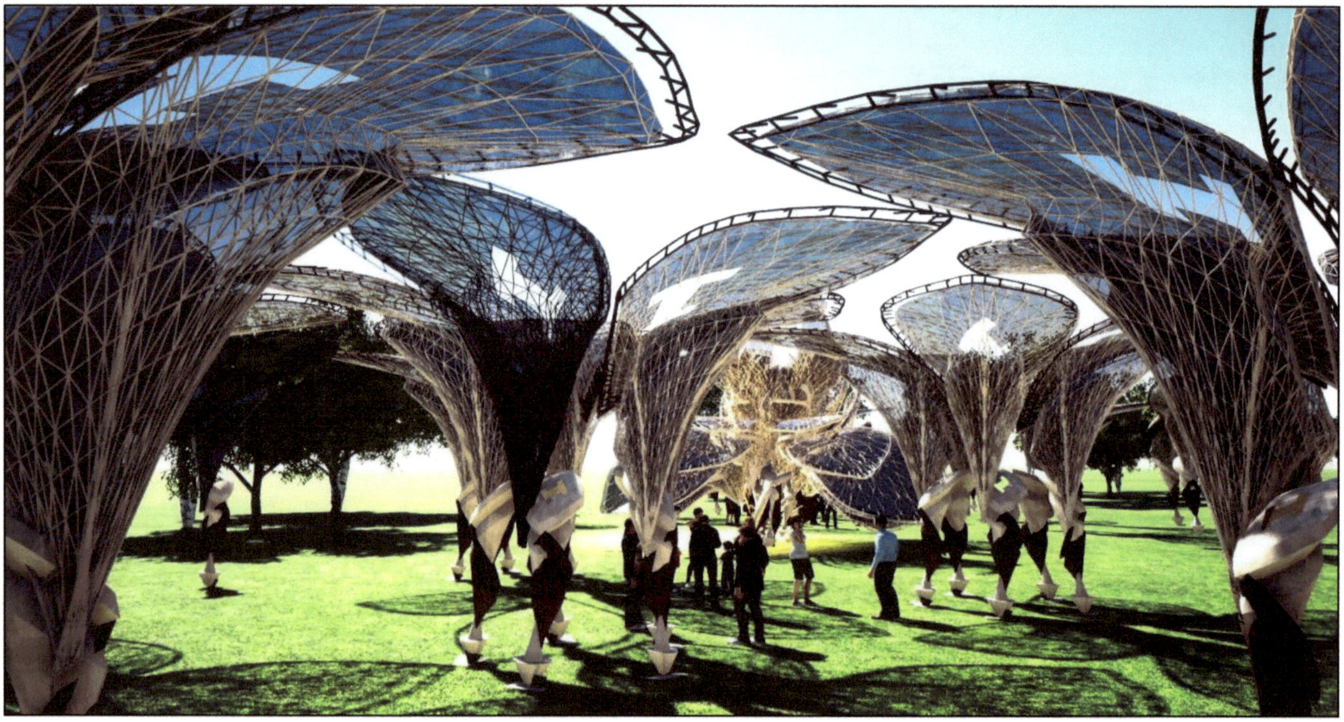

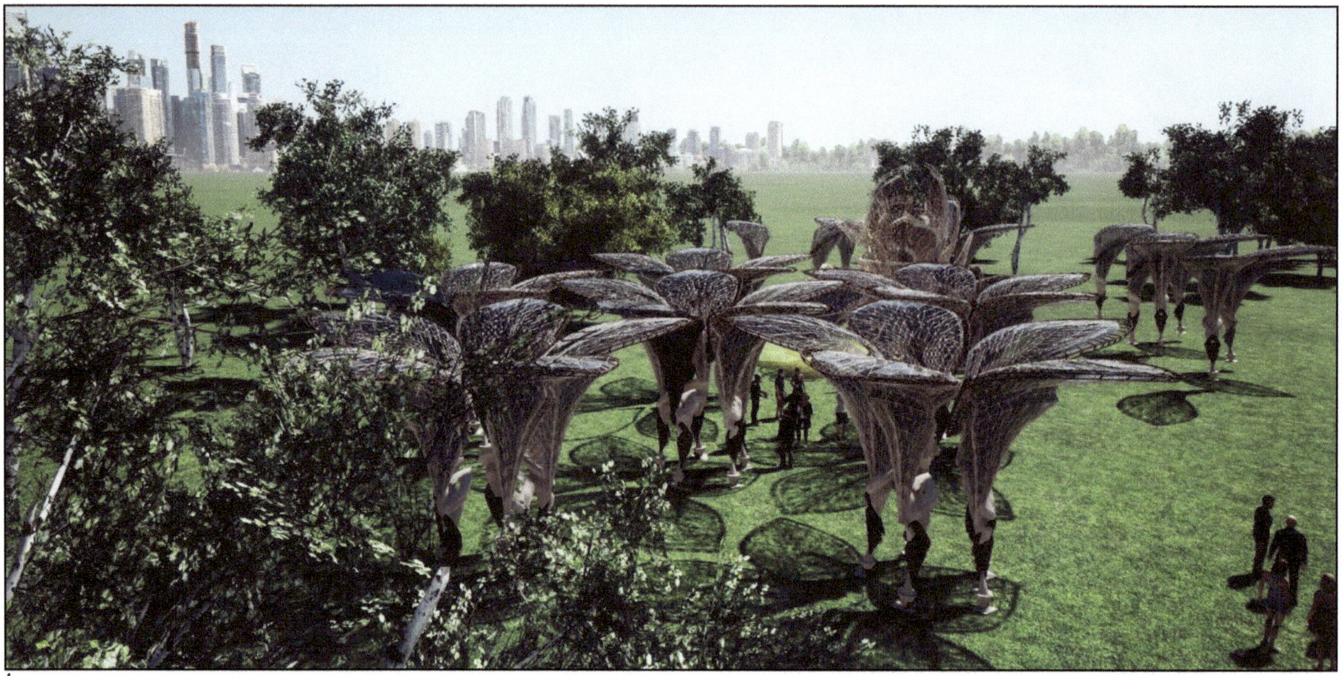

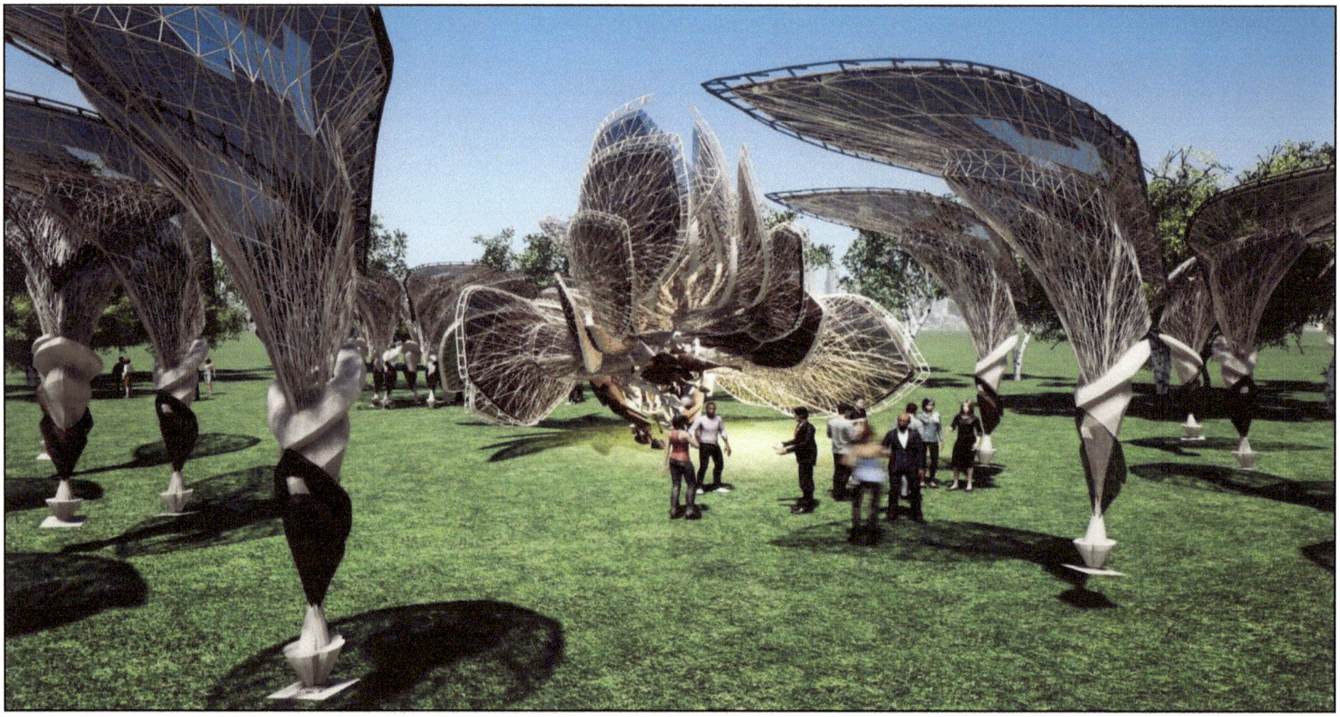

Phoenix Garden
Niloufar Mohammadalizadeh

In line with the former design, we decided to extensively study the phoenix fable of Mantegh Alteir of Attar Neyshabouri considering variety and number of the designed forms and design of the site plan of the complex. This project aims at providing a tourism space to introduce one of the old fables of Iranian culture and literature in addition to creating a place for spending free time and recreation of different people.

The project design is based on three structures:
- The main structure which is softly extended as the bird's wing with the mild slope in the center of the site plan where the visitors may climb it and have a general sight to the complex and its adjacency.
- The second one plays the role of a sunshade and is so wide that prevents from direct sunlight and guarantees tranquility of the visitors even in warm weather.
- The third structure is designed for the complex being inspired of the phoenix fable as the light and gives a special elegance to the phoenix garden at night. This plan shall be used for a land located at the municipality of district 9, Shahrak Khavaran, Southeast Tabriz. Form of the site plan and its inside circulation is designed in a way to inspire the bird form and phoenix fable.

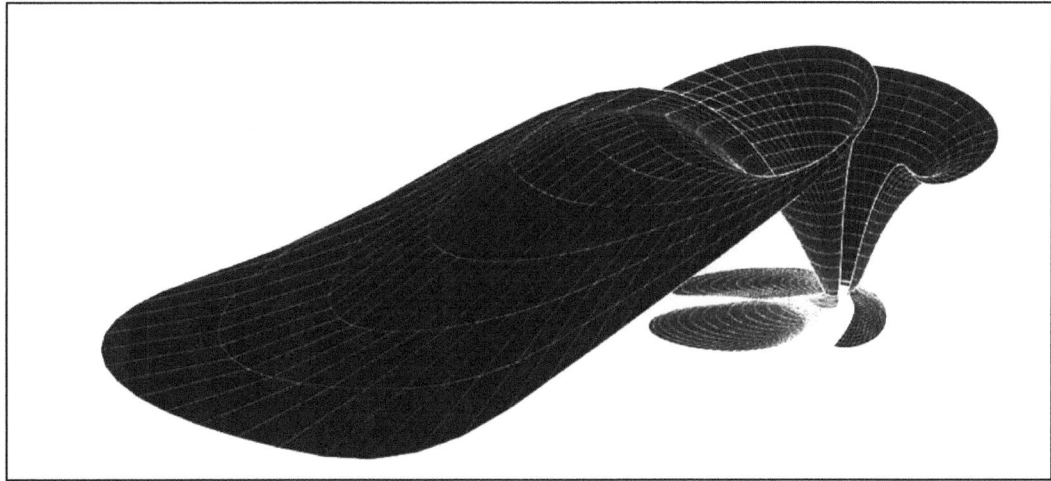

The main structure

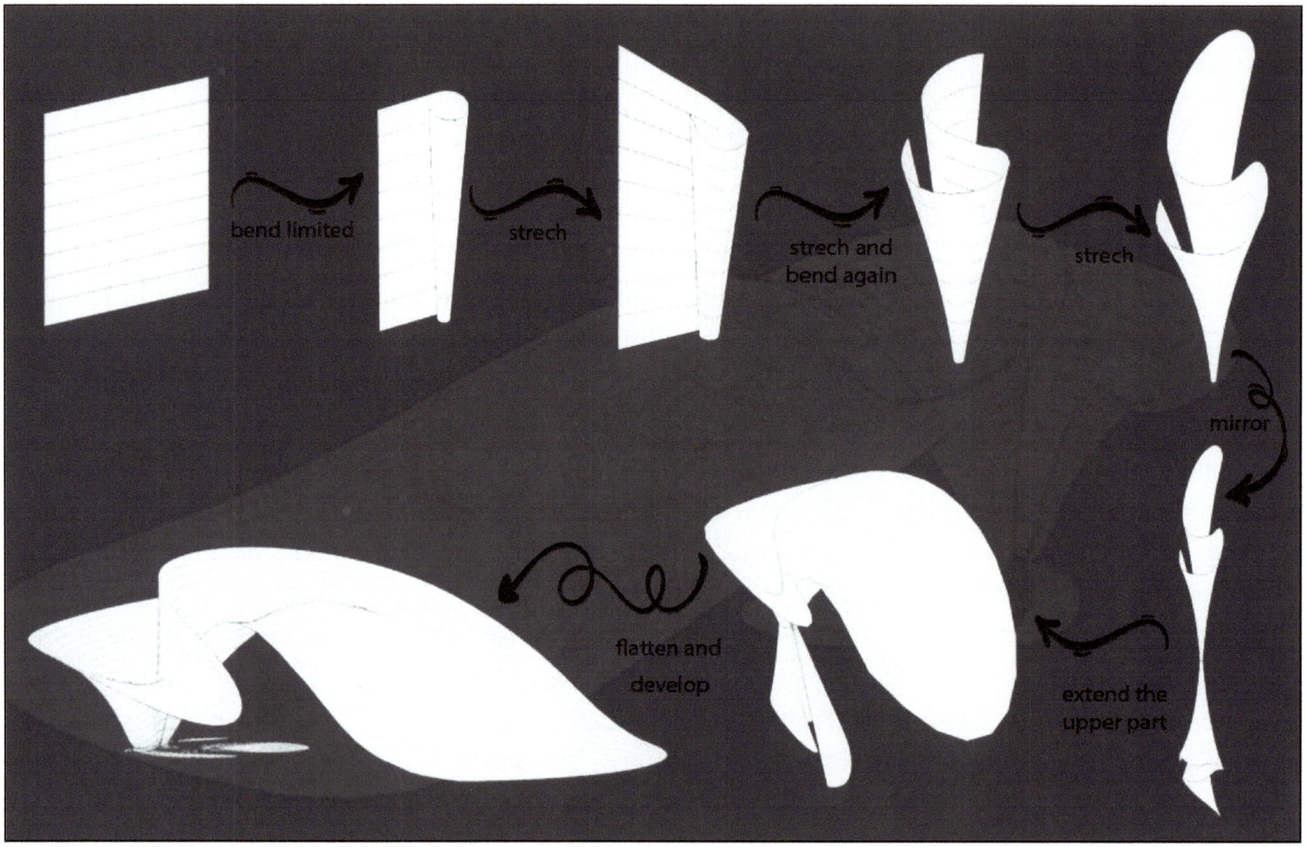

Design process of main structure

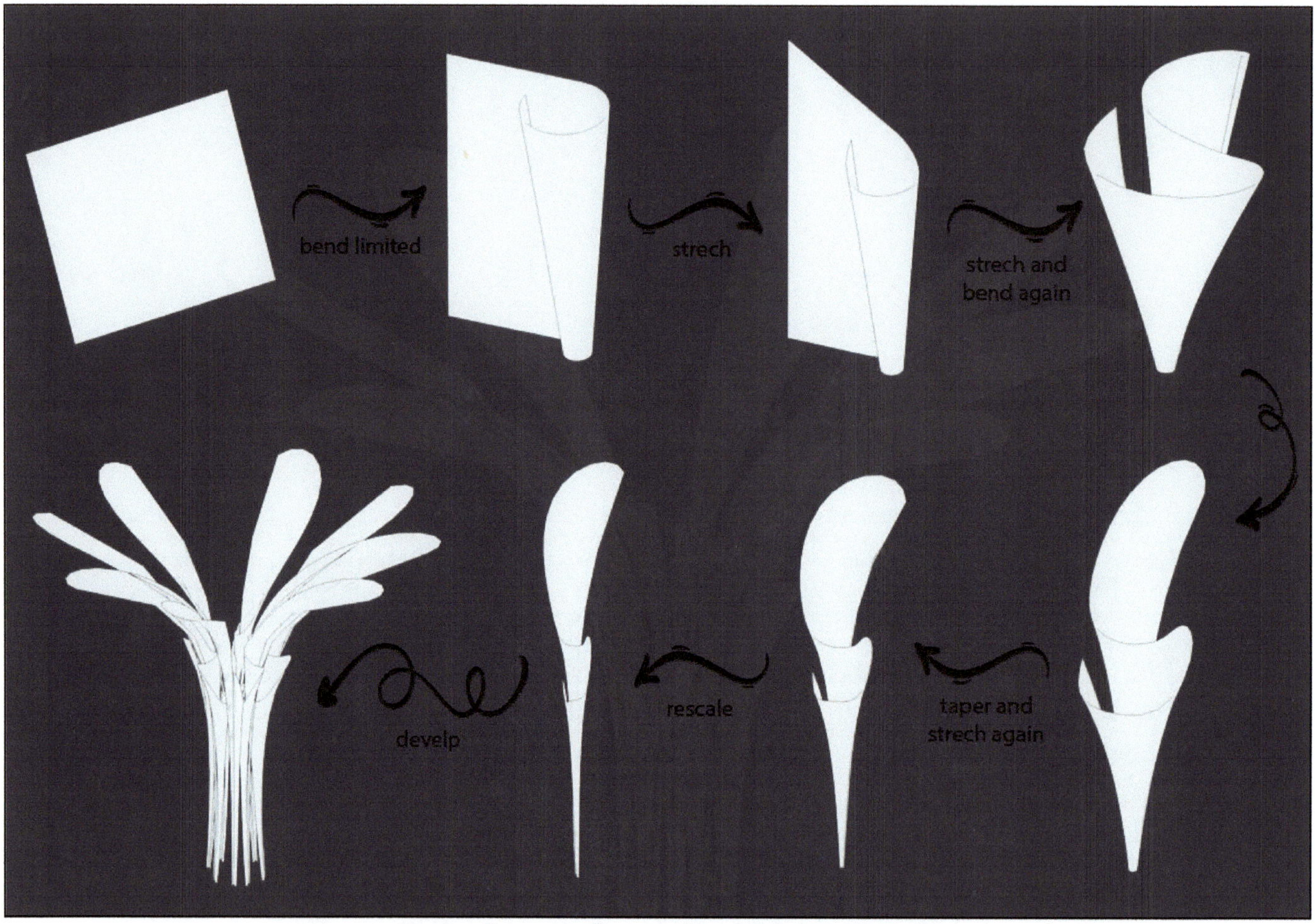

Design Process of second and third structure

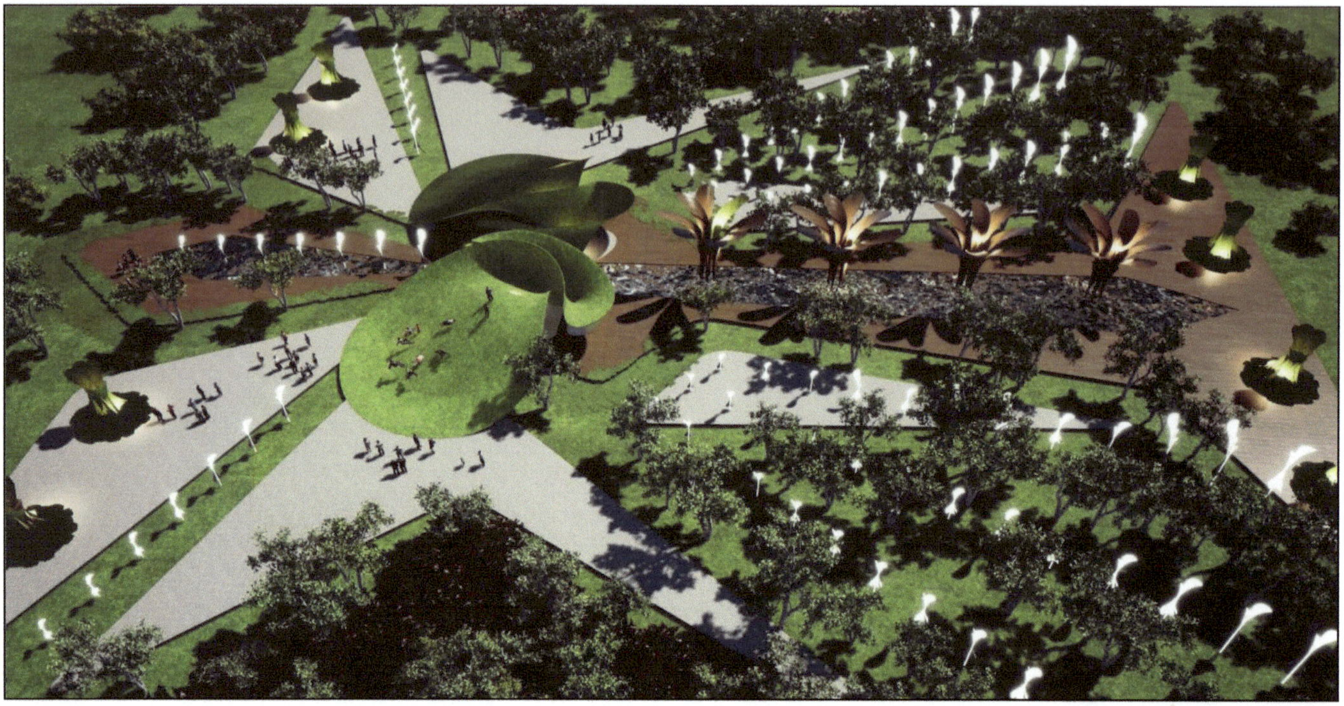

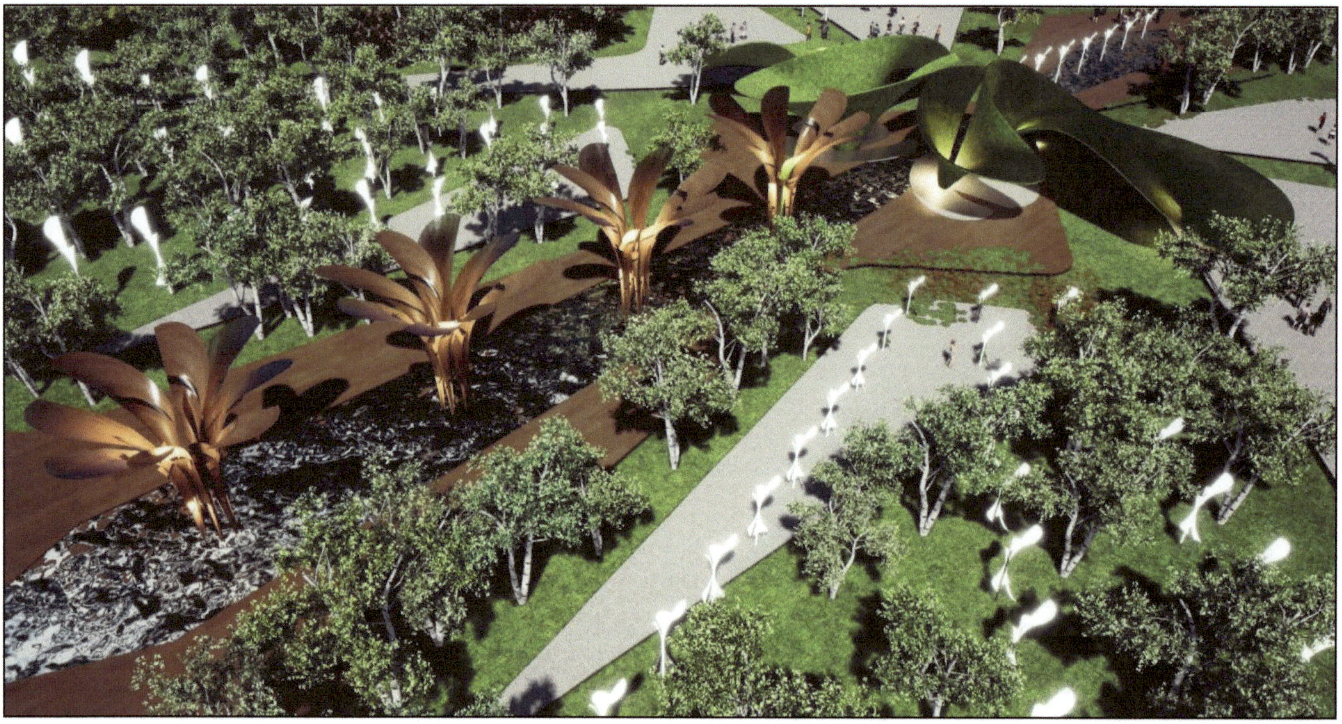

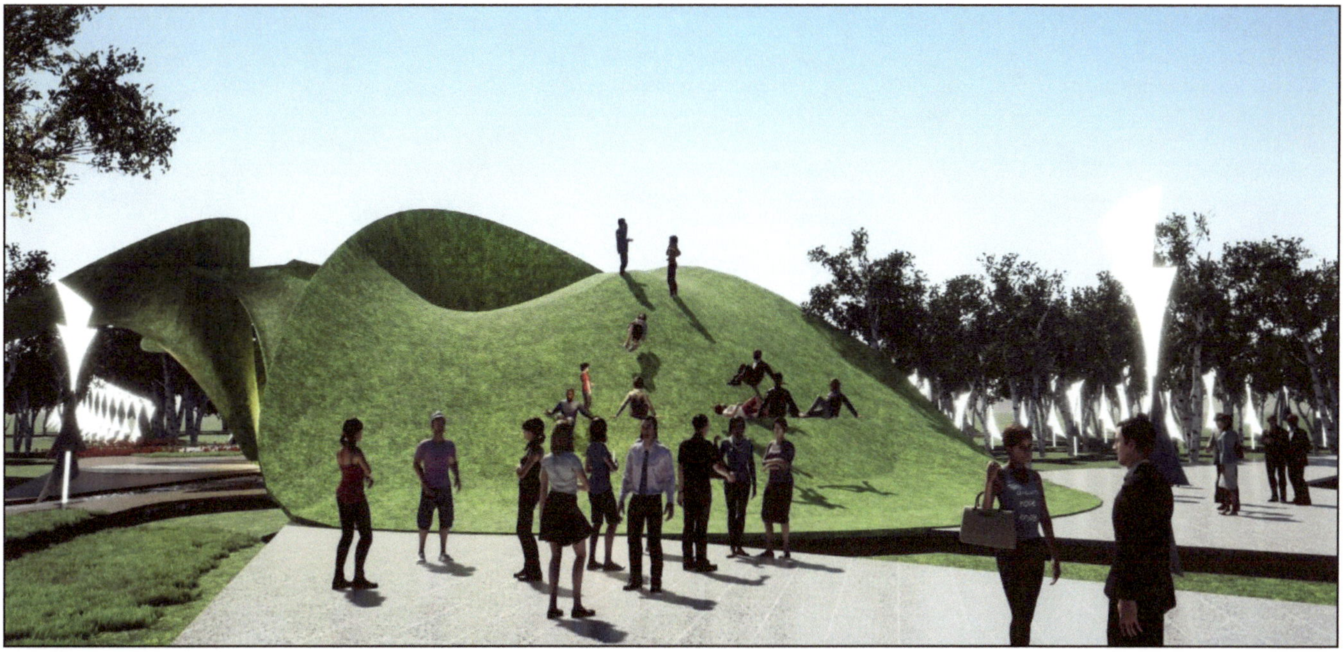

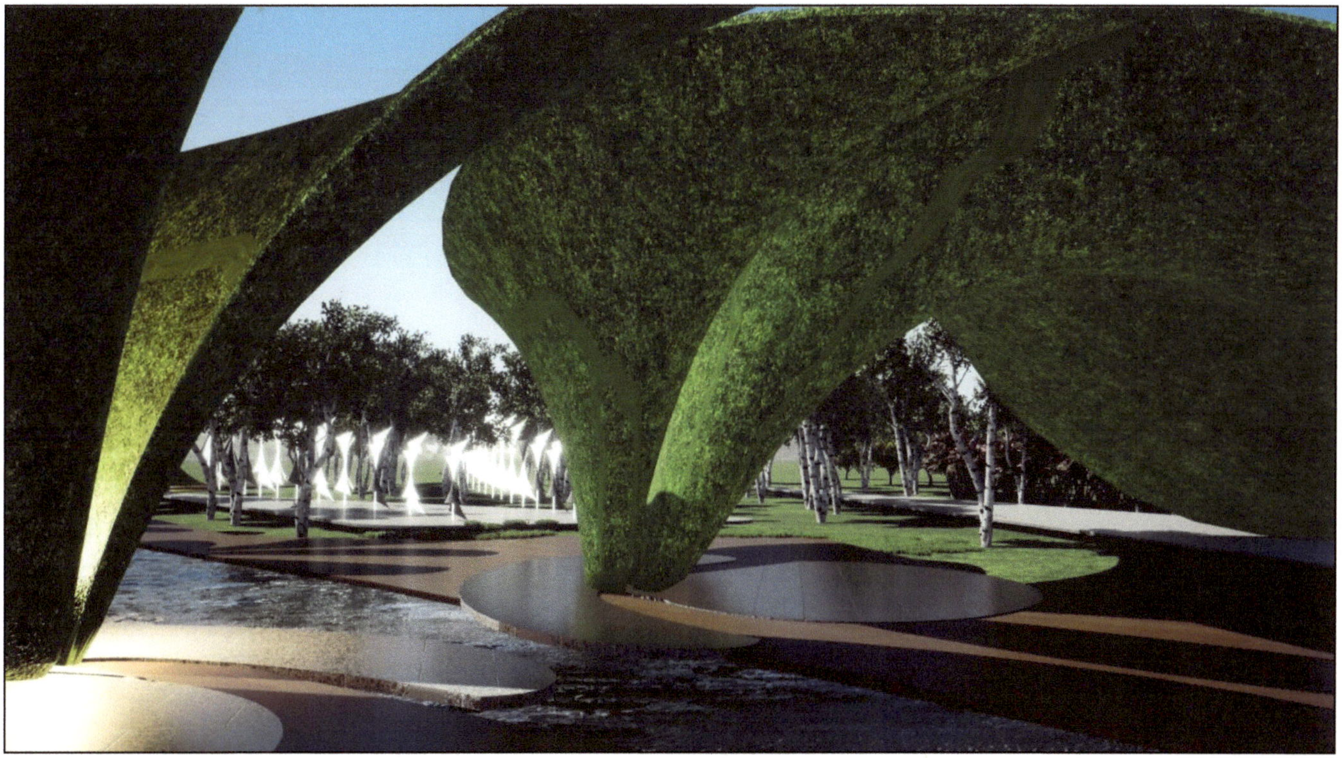

Music Pavilion

Neda Sadeghinahr

Music is an art branch that can influence people all over the world even with different languages. It is a bridge over linguistic, cultural, social and even historical gaps. Music can connect people with different beliefs and races. It can also create a relaxing atmosphere or evoke enthusiasm and even creativity. Such a possibility has many social, cultural and economic benefits and plays an important role in improving the quality of public space and social behaviors.

This music pavilion is a public space for live music performances. The musicians can gather in the center of the pavilion, and the spectators can sit on the stairs. The form of stairs, which are a quarter of a circle, is inspired by the shape of a piano. Also roofs design's concept is the wings of a bird ready to fly. By combining these two concepts try to inspire the effects of music on human's soils. This pavilion aims to bring happiness and togetherness for the post-quarantine Period.

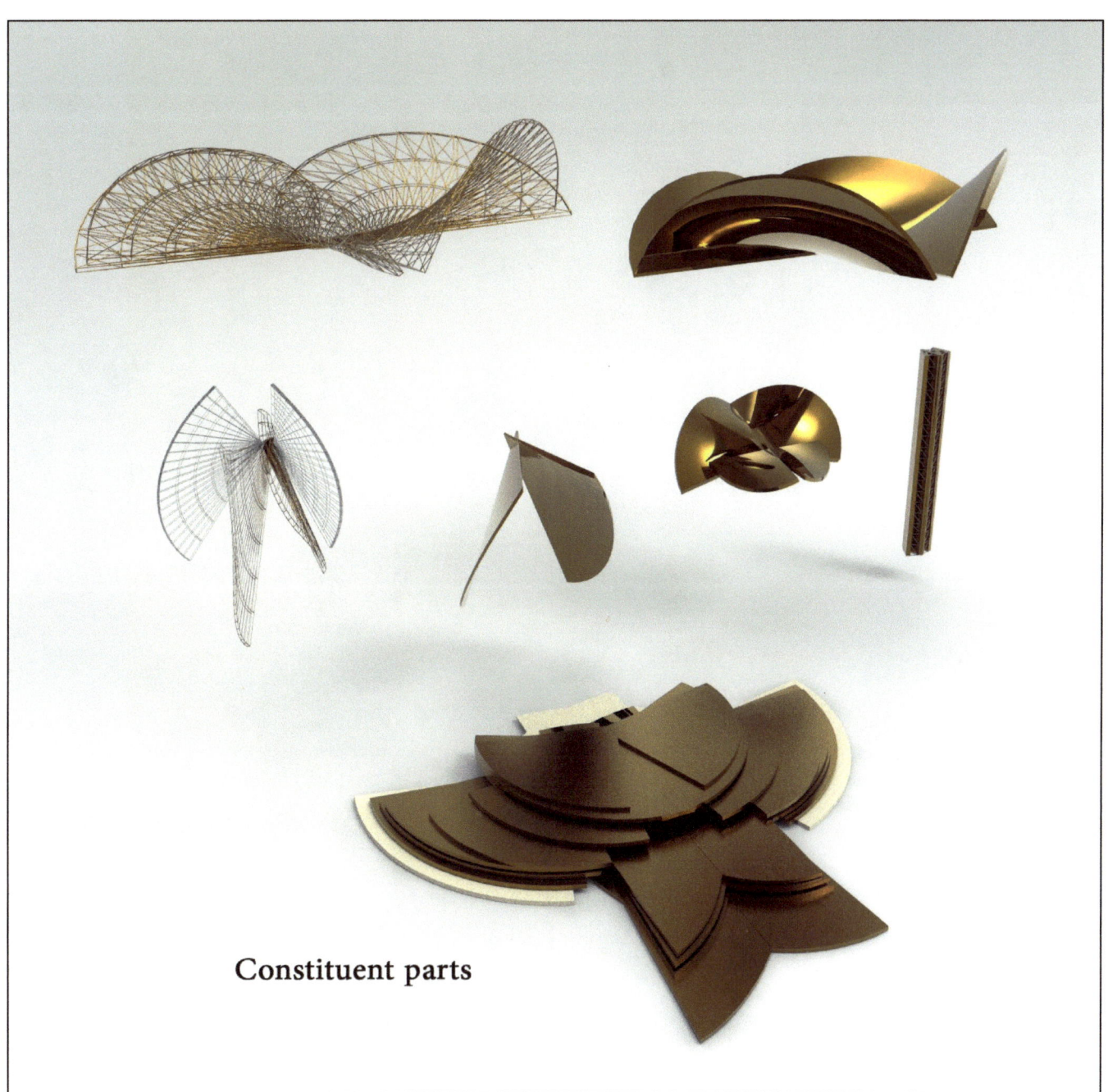

Constituent parts

Project description

Neda Sadeghinahr

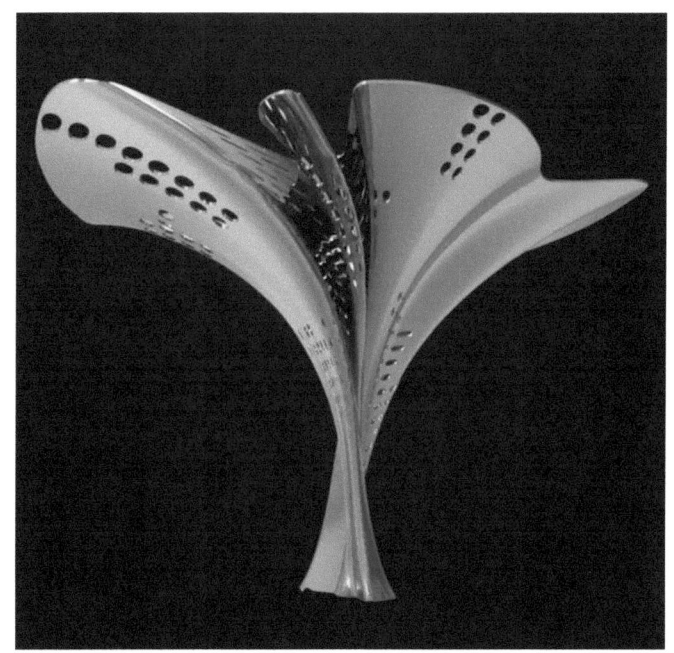

The digital world provided infinite amenities to the designers through its ever-increasing capacity. Design of curved and organic volumes has become easily possible. Usually, curved lines are seen less in architecture while the nature is full of curved lines and surfaces. I mainly aimed at designing a pavilion which is different from the conventional forms, made through combination of platonic volumes and is organic.

Human experiences a feeling different from the spaces encountered daily, a feeling inspiring dynamism, vivacity and fluidity.

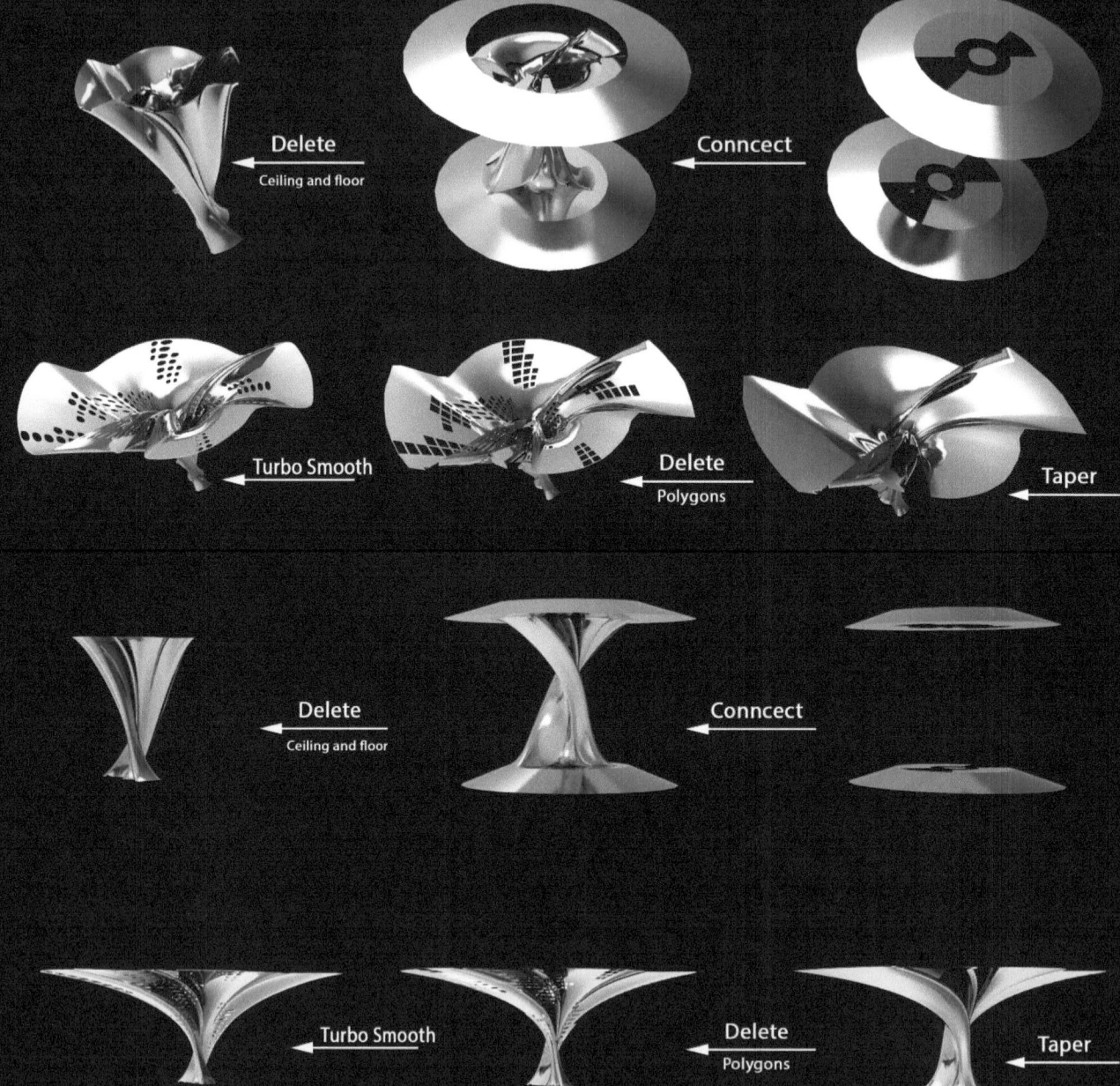

Perspectives of structures

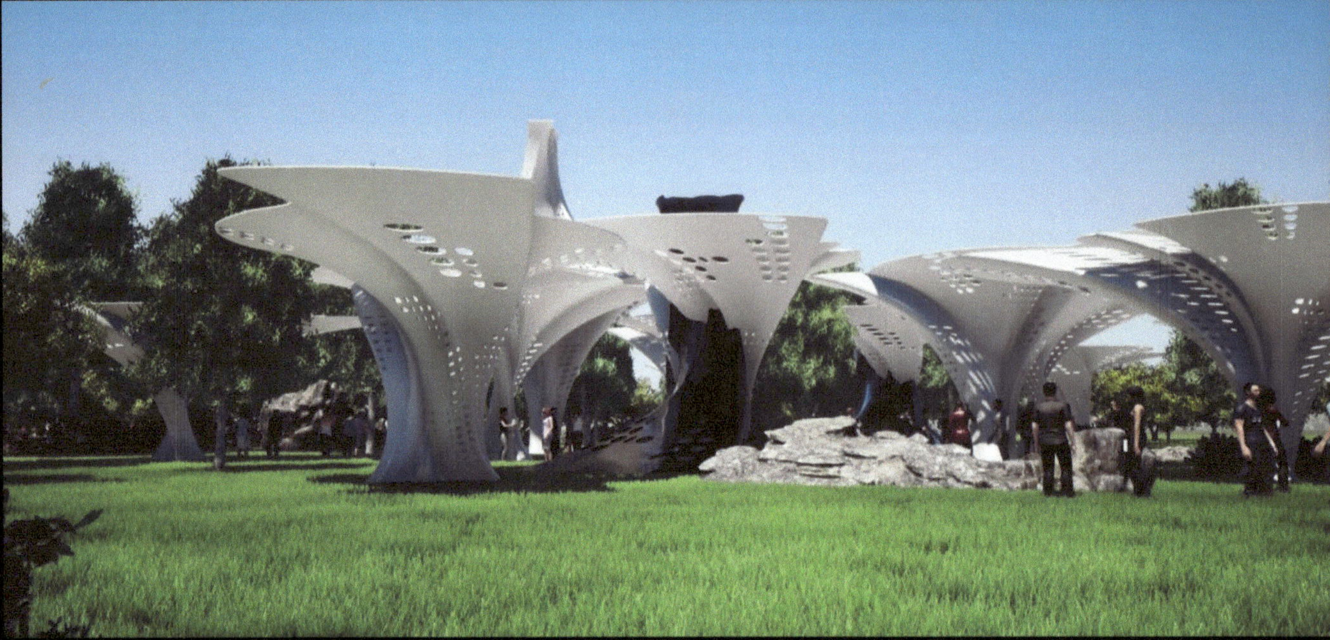

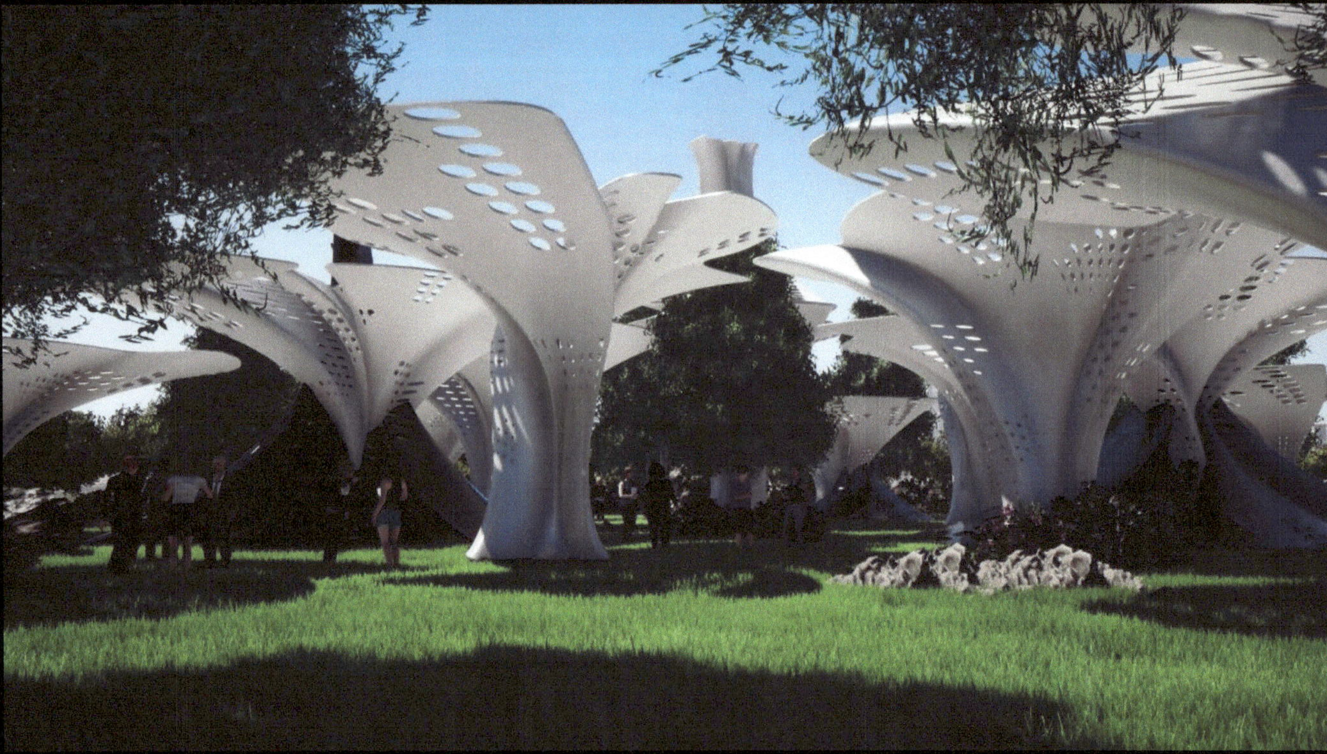

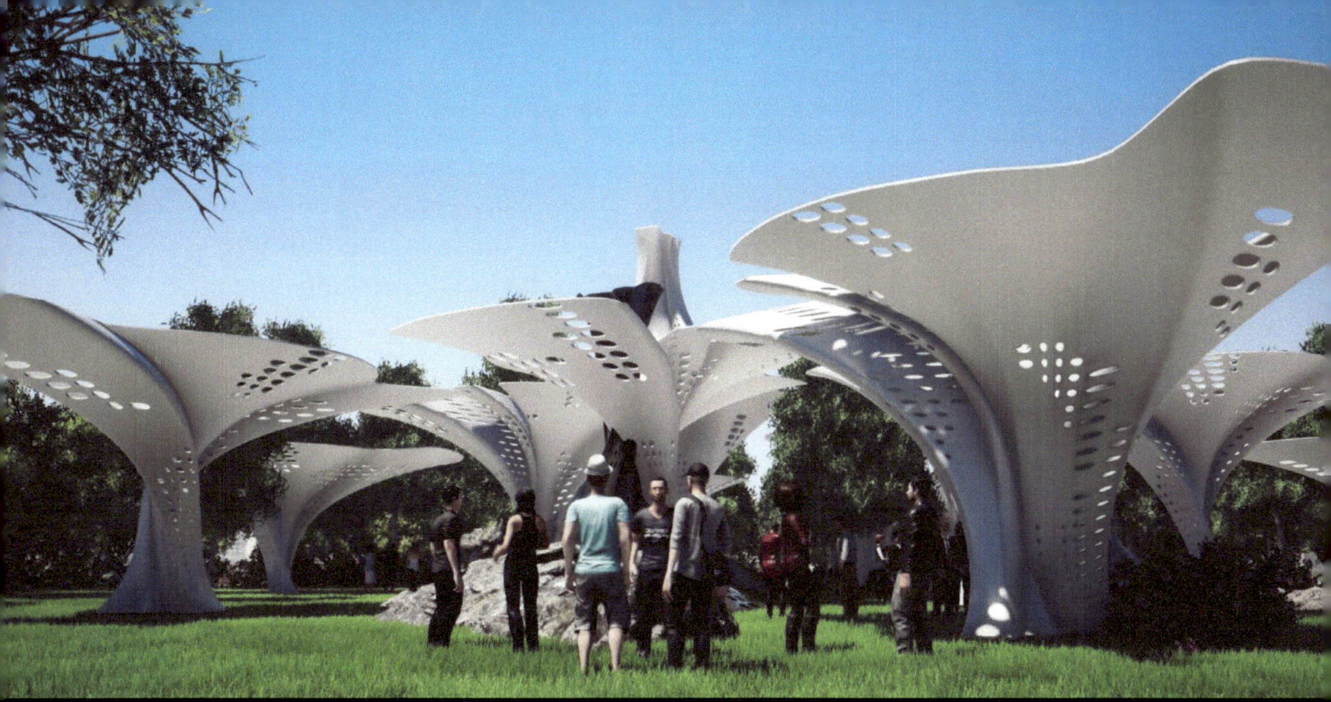
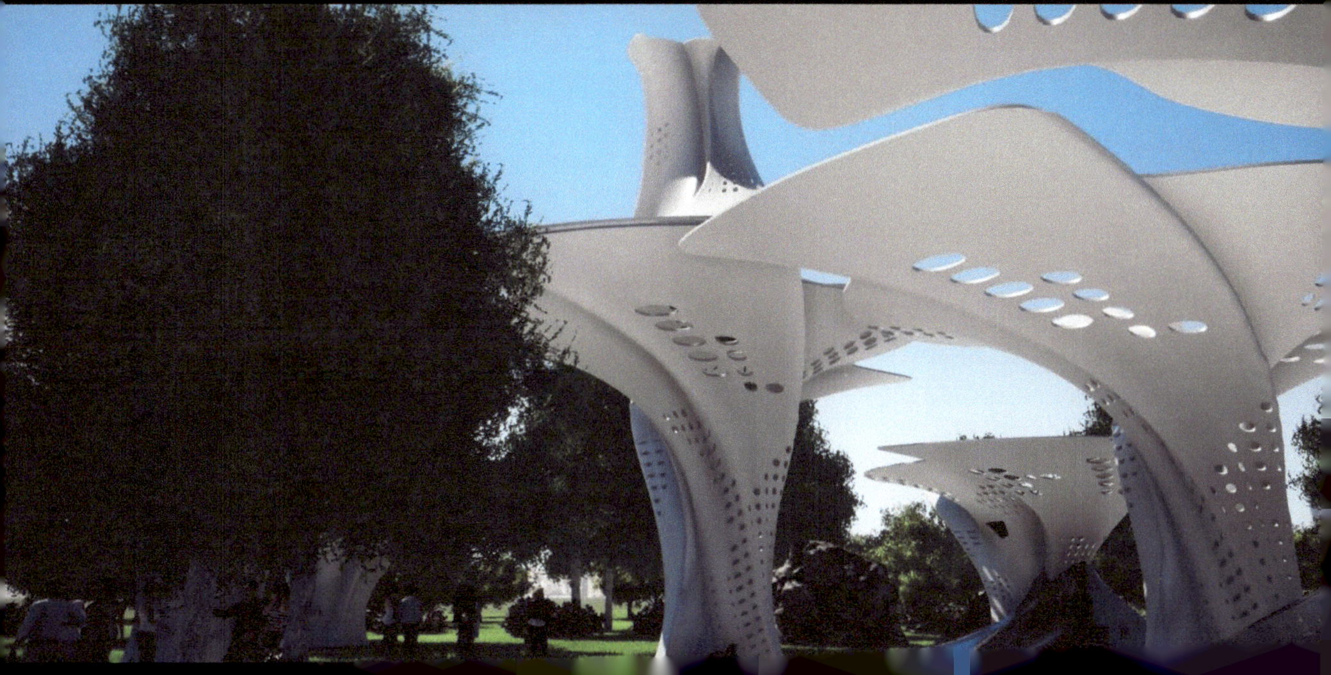

Dovecote
Sevda Javadi

Dovecotes are regarded as the old buildings of Iranian architecture. These buildings and their exceptional interior architecture show innovation and genius of Iranian architecture to the world. The towers which are built inside of cities to be nested by the doves are generally cylindrical and built of mud, mud brick, plaster and lime. Their diameter varies between 10 to 22 meter and their height is 18 meters or more. Each of these towers may nest about 14000 doves. The entrance of such towers is built narrow to prevent from the entrance of big doves such as falcons and eagles.

The immensity of these buildings is wonderful considering their expansion and variety. They are excellent samples of form elegance and performance. The interior space has a checkered design covering all walls equally and the doves may nest there. The size of the nests is approximately 20*20*28cm.

As narrated, Esfahan had about 3000 dovecotes and now, there are only 300 dovecotes in suburb which should be repaired. Fertilizers and modern chemicals have made these grand towers useless.

Pictures: Meybod dovecote tower - www.eligasht.com

The dovecotes in Iranian urban custom and in any climate were general opportunities to supply part of agriculture fertilizers and improve the quality of general life. Additionally, such towers played an important role as urban symbols. This is a reason for biological interaction with nonhuman species in Iranian old cities. In fact, the dovecotes are a symbol of sustainable and eco-friendly architecture and

urban development.

At present, cities are defined based on their greenery and relation with plant species and interaction of humans and animals are regarded as inseparable part of urban sustainable policies. modern dovecotes may improve the quality of urban spaces and revival the quarters. In such case, we encounter with more behavioral participation among members of a quarter and/or a residential complex and more sense of responsibility and belonging to the place. Also, rotary flight of the birds over the site shall result in enhancement of relations quality through stimulation of emotions of the residences and creation of peripheral happiness.

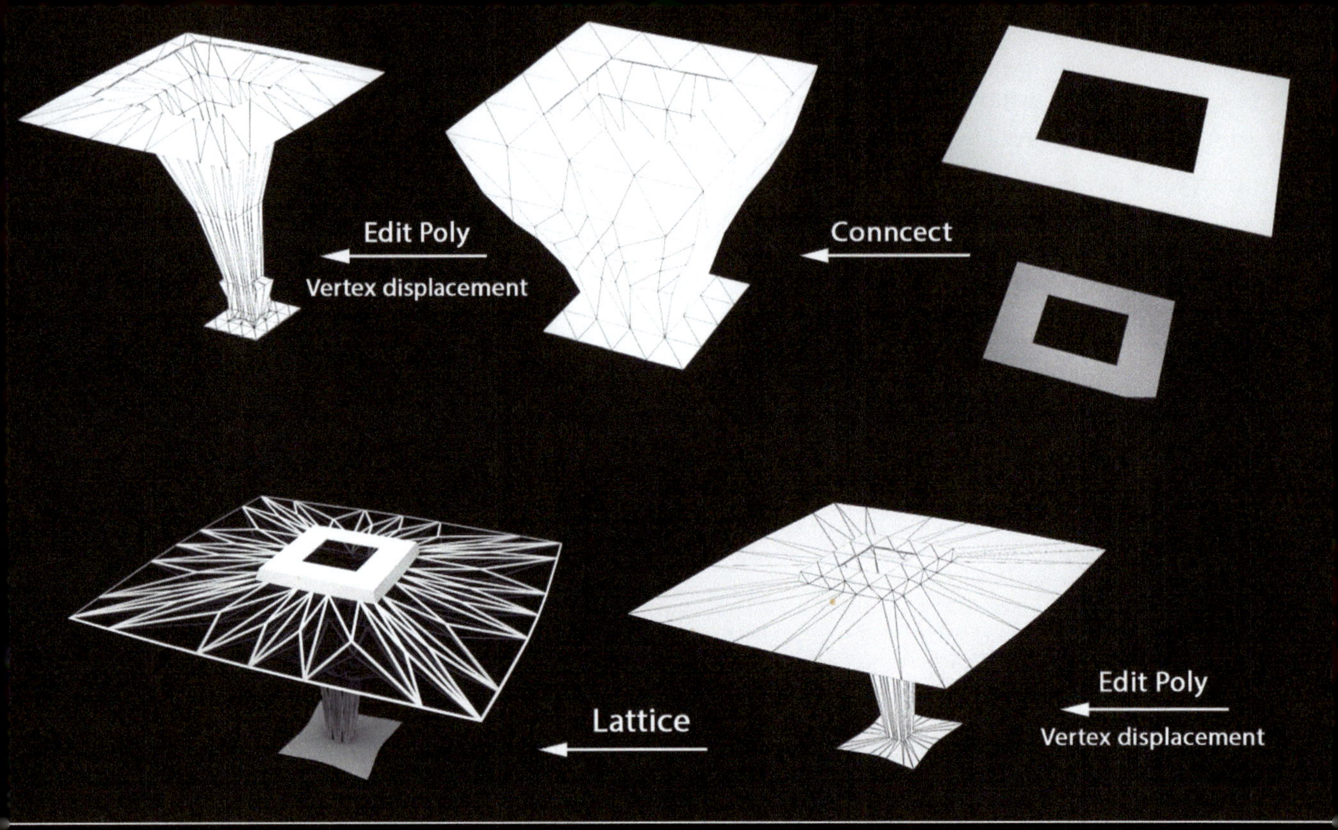

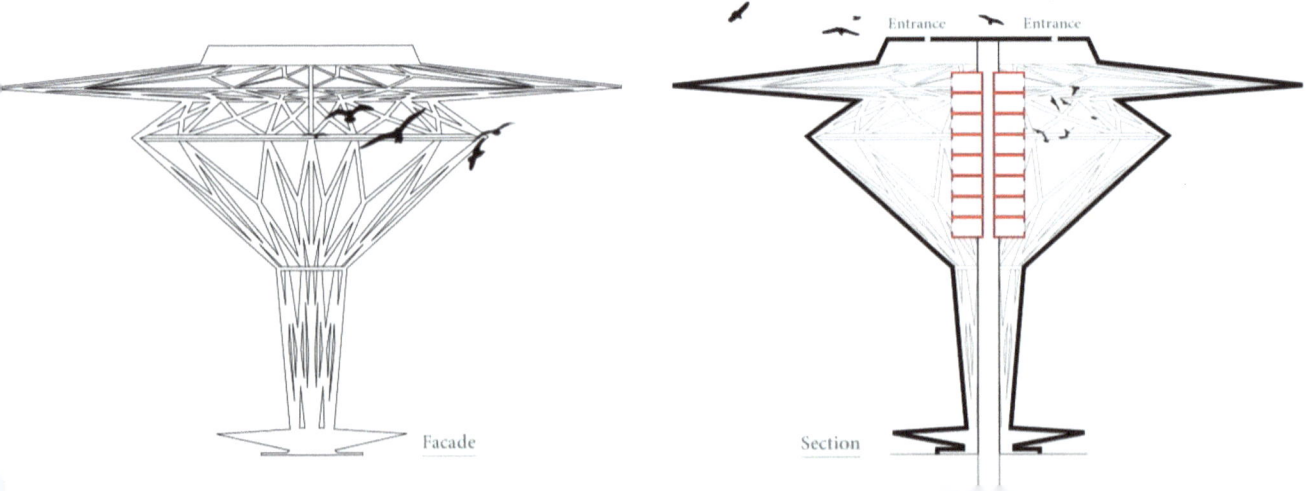

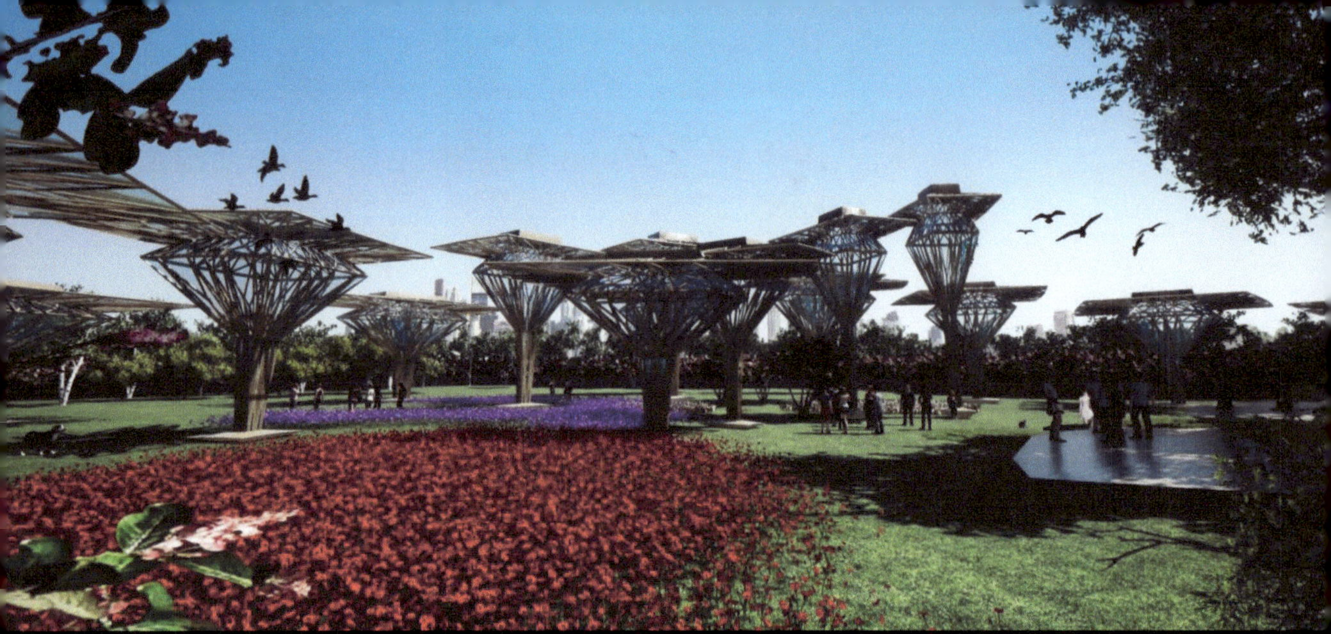
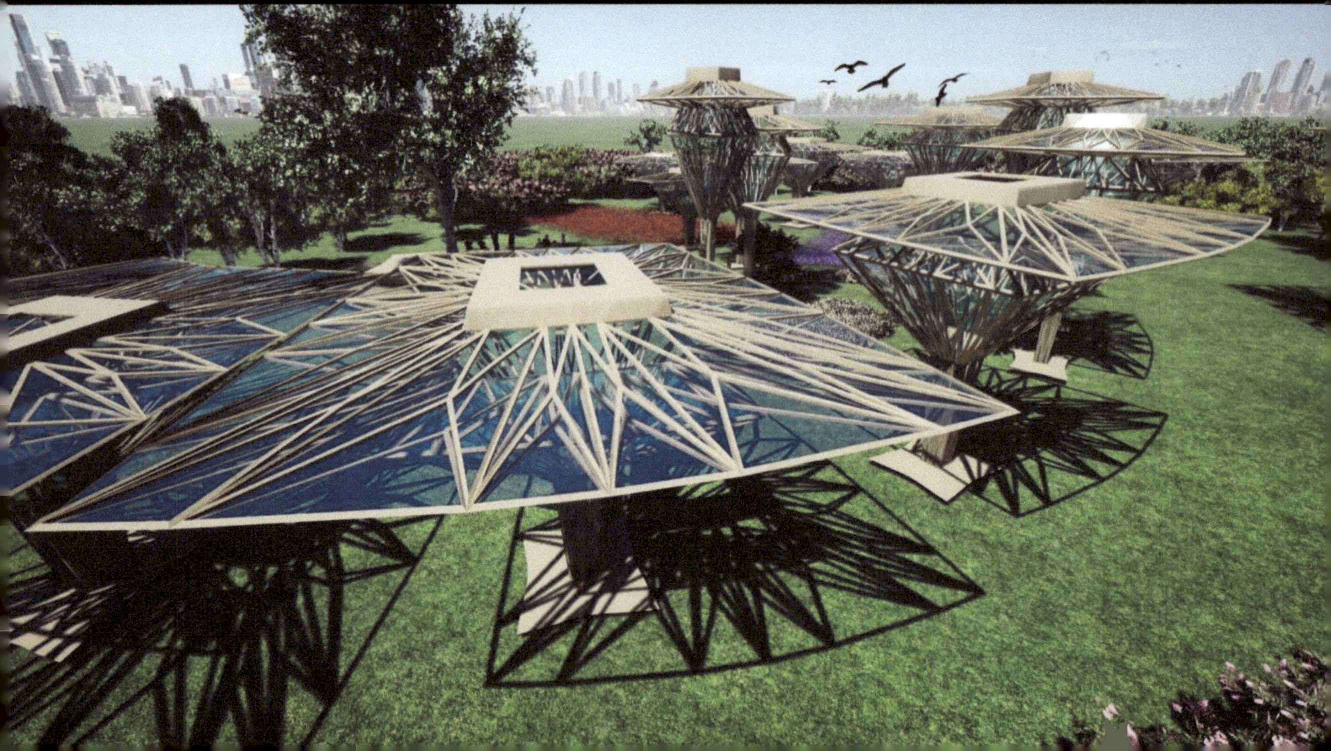

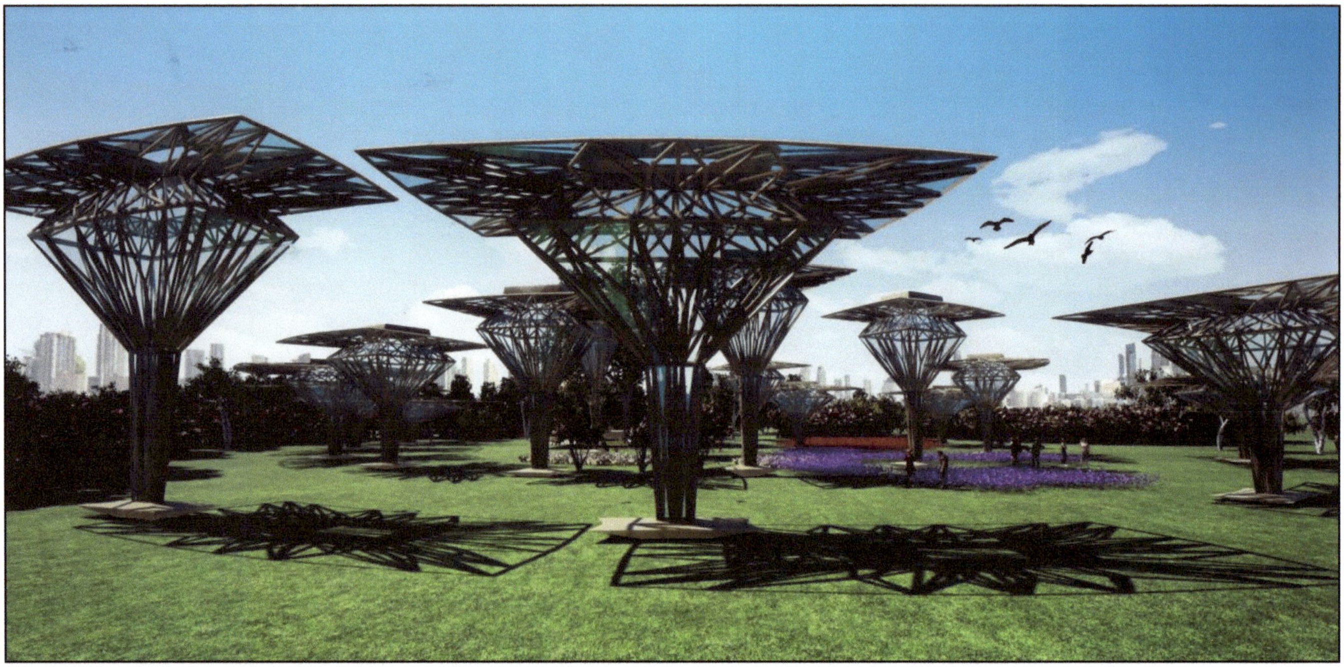

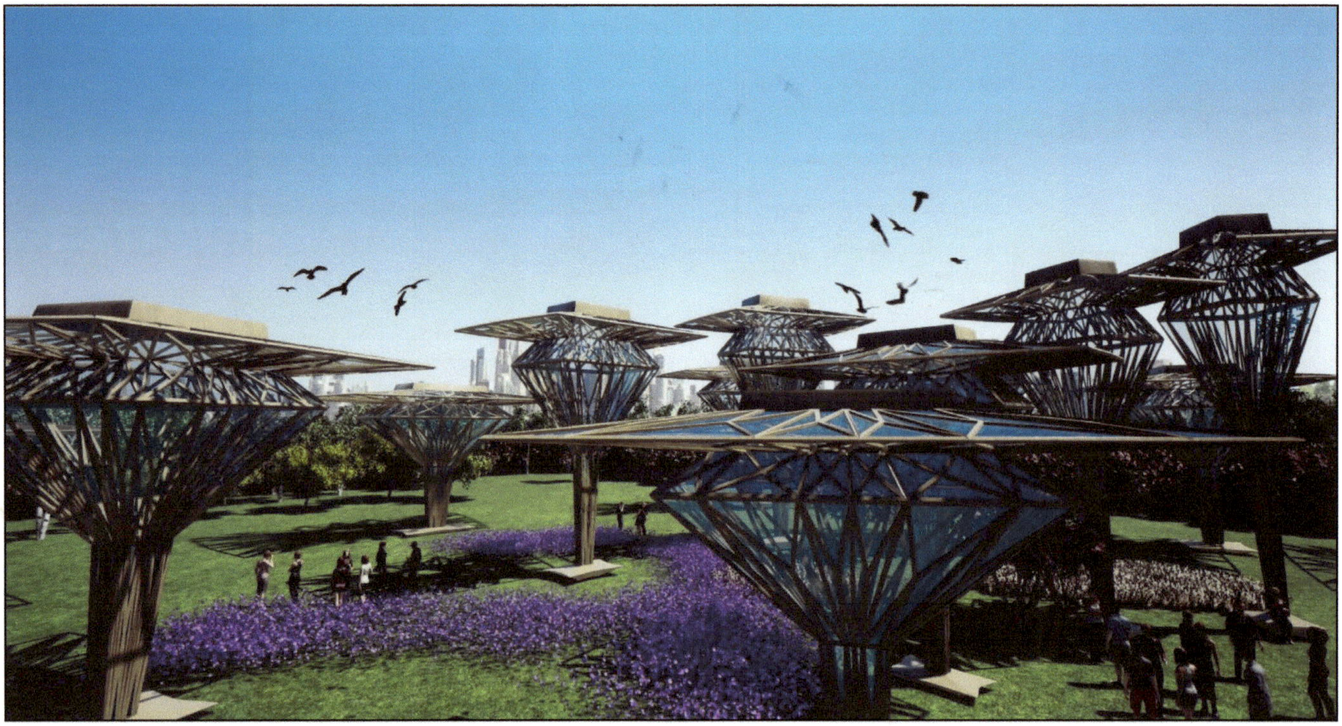

Pattern Pavilion
Mina Alizadeh

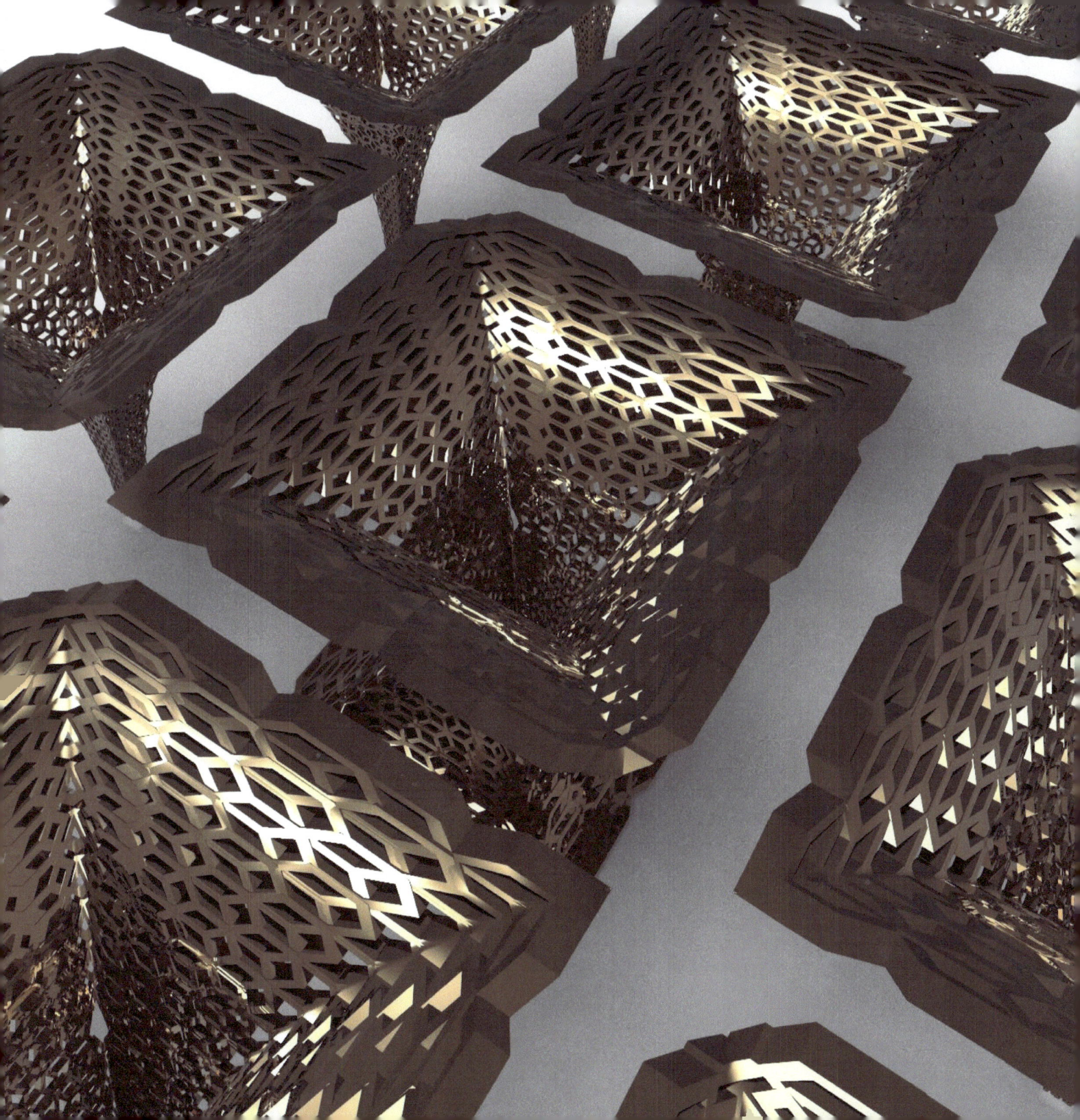

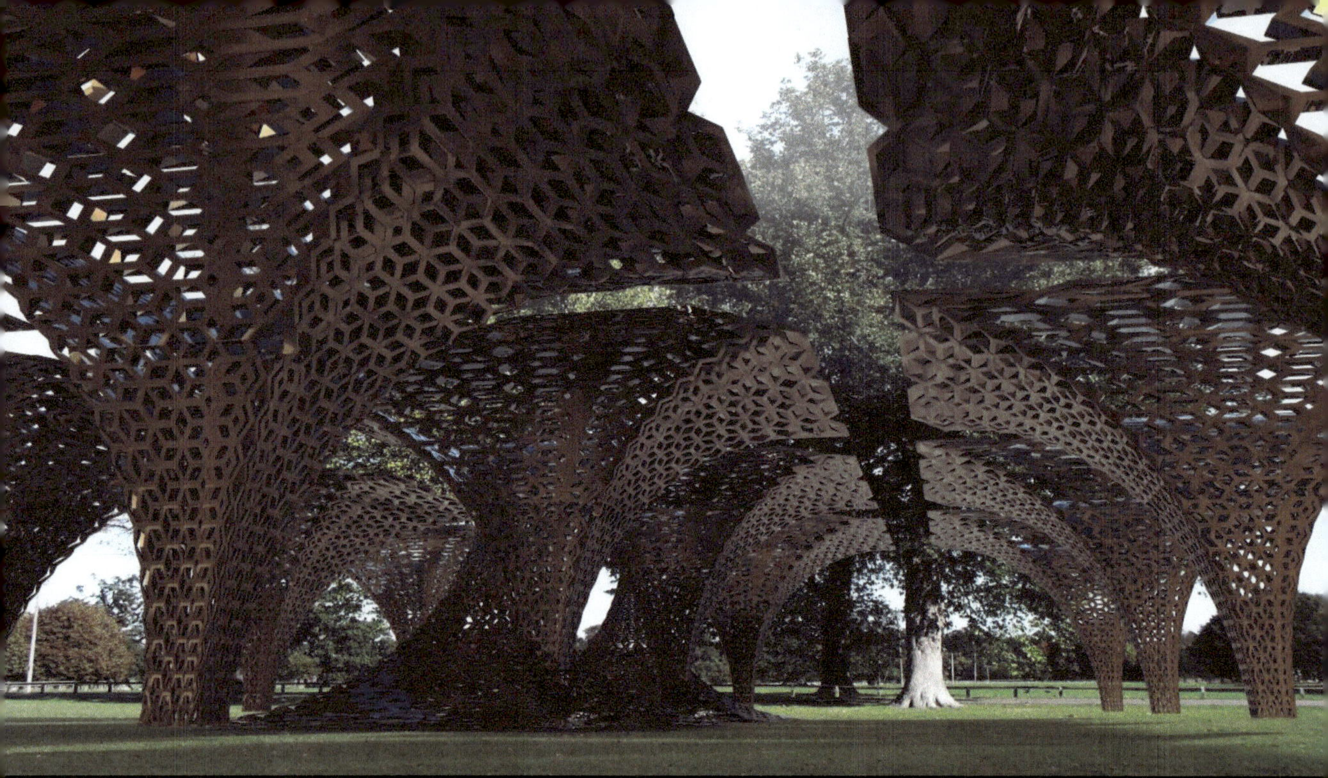

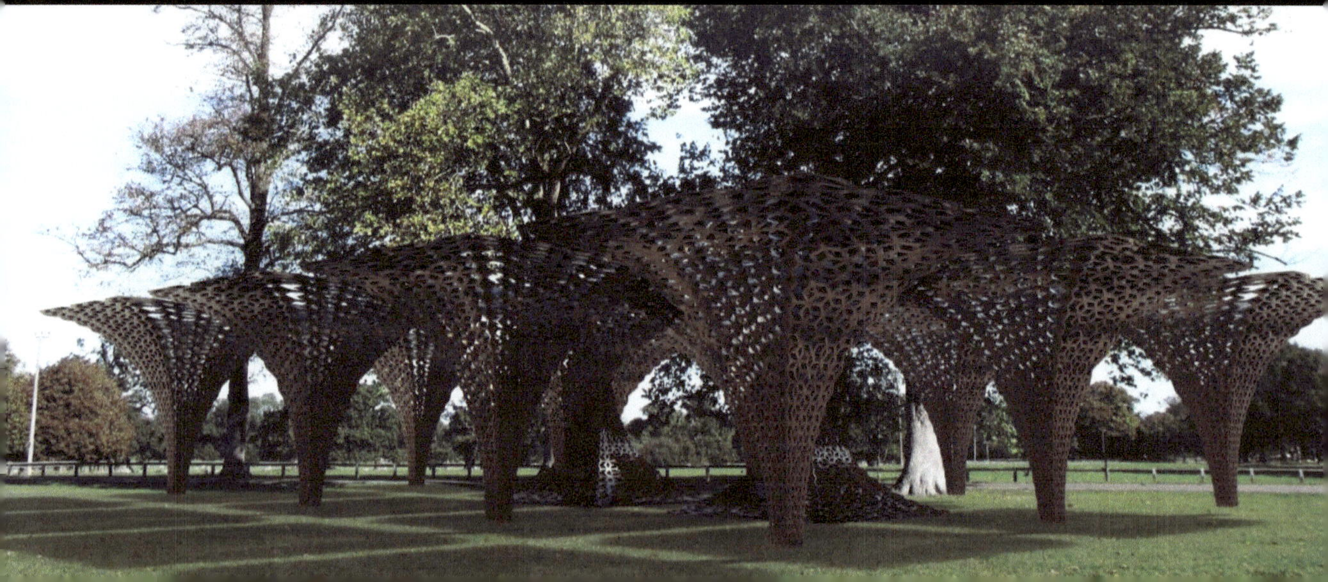

Lotus Pavilion

Shabnam Javankar

Lotus is the symbol of fertility, prosperity, land fertility, protection from beings, global peace, beauty, health, love, mortification, worship, popularity, nobility, spiritual growth, perfection, human birth and growth cycle, purity, life power, knowledge and wisdom. Lotus is the symbol of light and is a result of creative powers of fire, sun and moon and is known as the product of sun and waters. Lotus is the symbol of the world and several layers of its petals indicate to different eras of the world and hierarchies of existence. Eight petals of the lotus show eight directions (right, left, front, behind, up, down, outside, inside). In Iranian myths, this flower is the symbol of Nahid Goddess. The lotus is also known as Anahita Flower which is used as decoration of the buildings of Hakhamaneshian Era as a symbol of purity. Public space is a space where citizens of any class, age, race, and job may enter and attend there without any limitation. In this regard, the lotus pavilion is the place for gathering of citizens in El Gol Park, located at Tabriz southeast.

Section

Constituent Parts

Considering importance of this flower in Iranian culture, this pavilion is designed in form of lotus standing as a symbol in the El Goli Park of Tabriz to hold cultural, religious and sport gatherings.
Relatively high height of this pavilion makes it appropriate to hold religious ceremonies such as Ashura, public sports and spring exhibitions. Considering climate of Tabriz where it rains more, a continuous ceiling is created through repeating the patterns. Colorful glasses in the roof make it possible to use the gentle sunlight of summer.

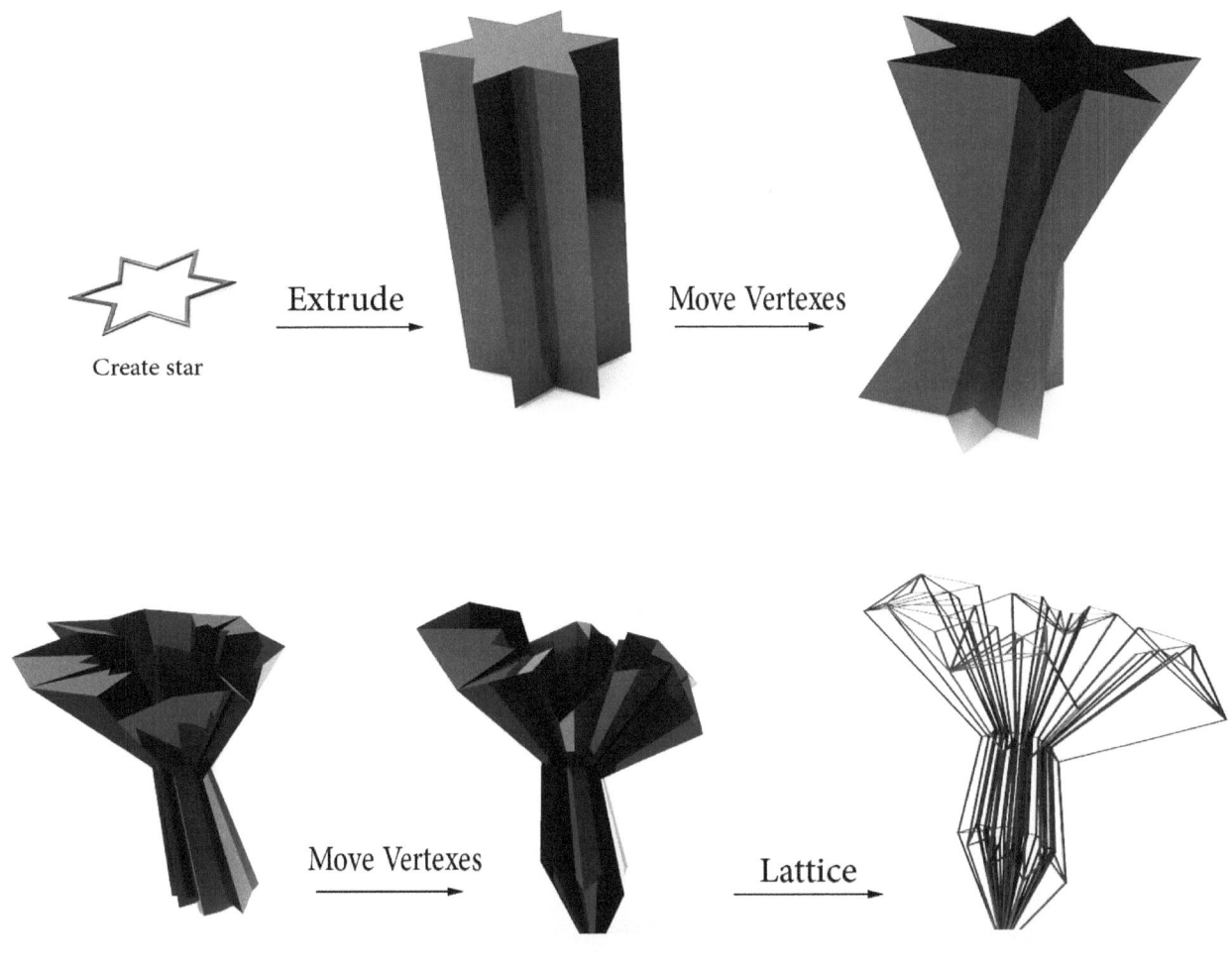

Design Process

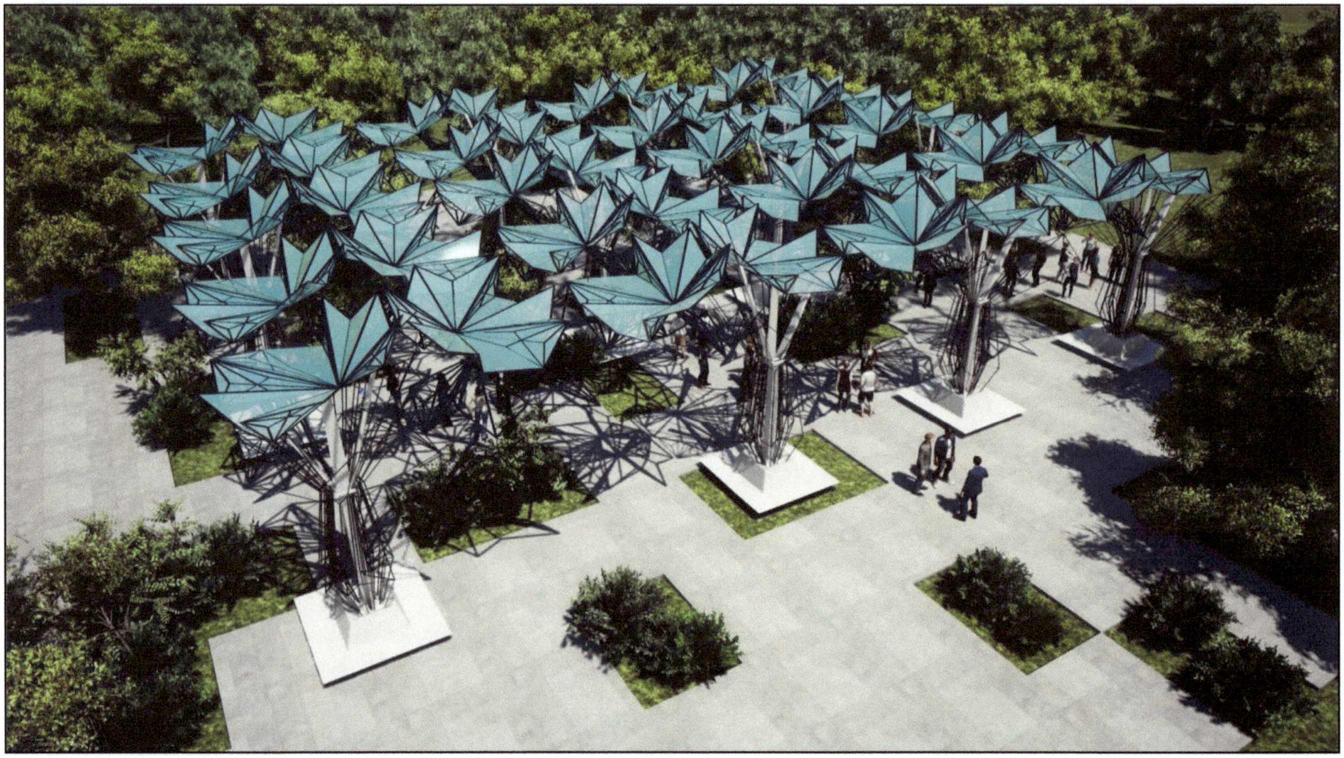

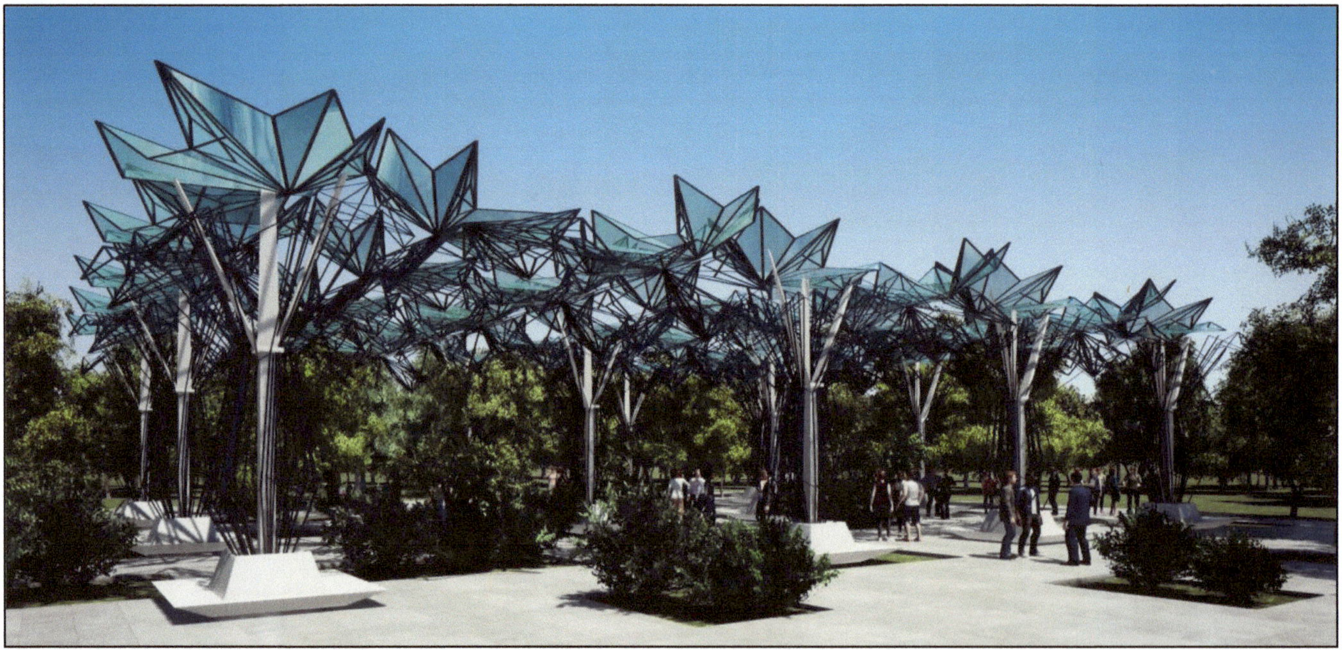

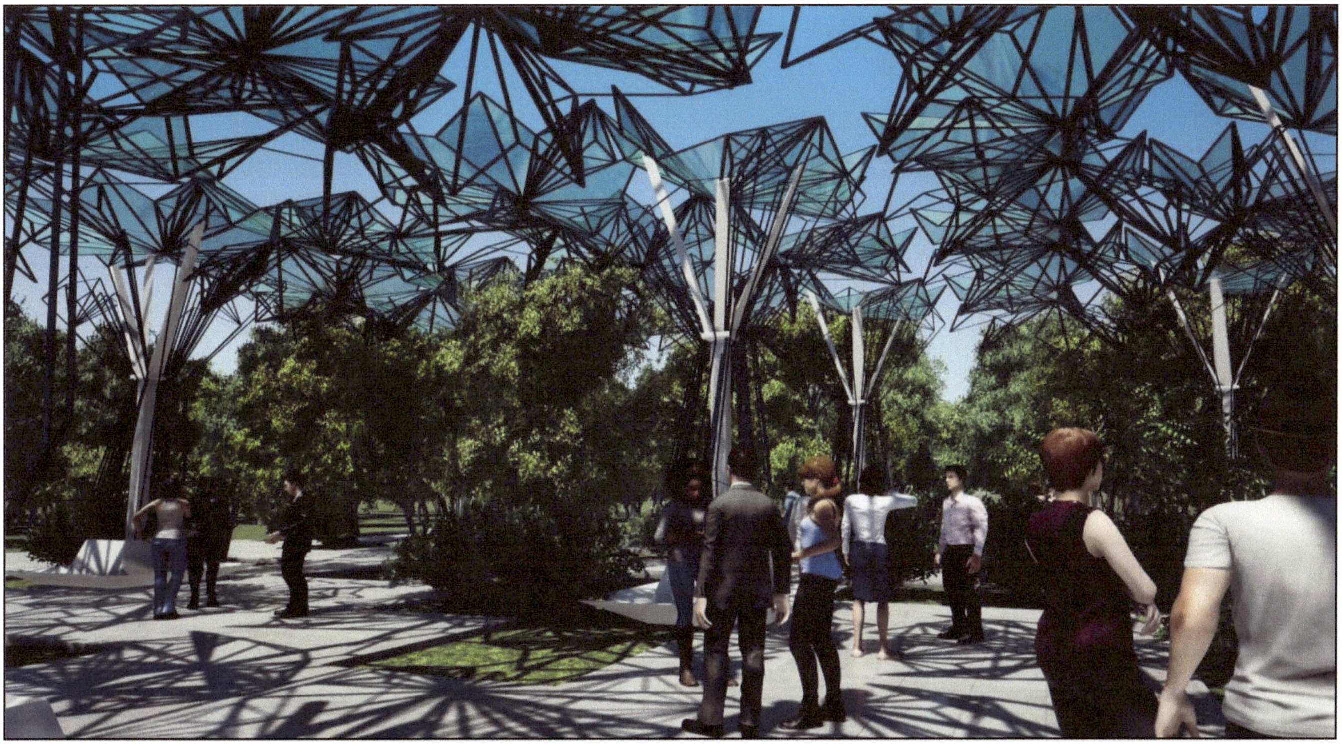

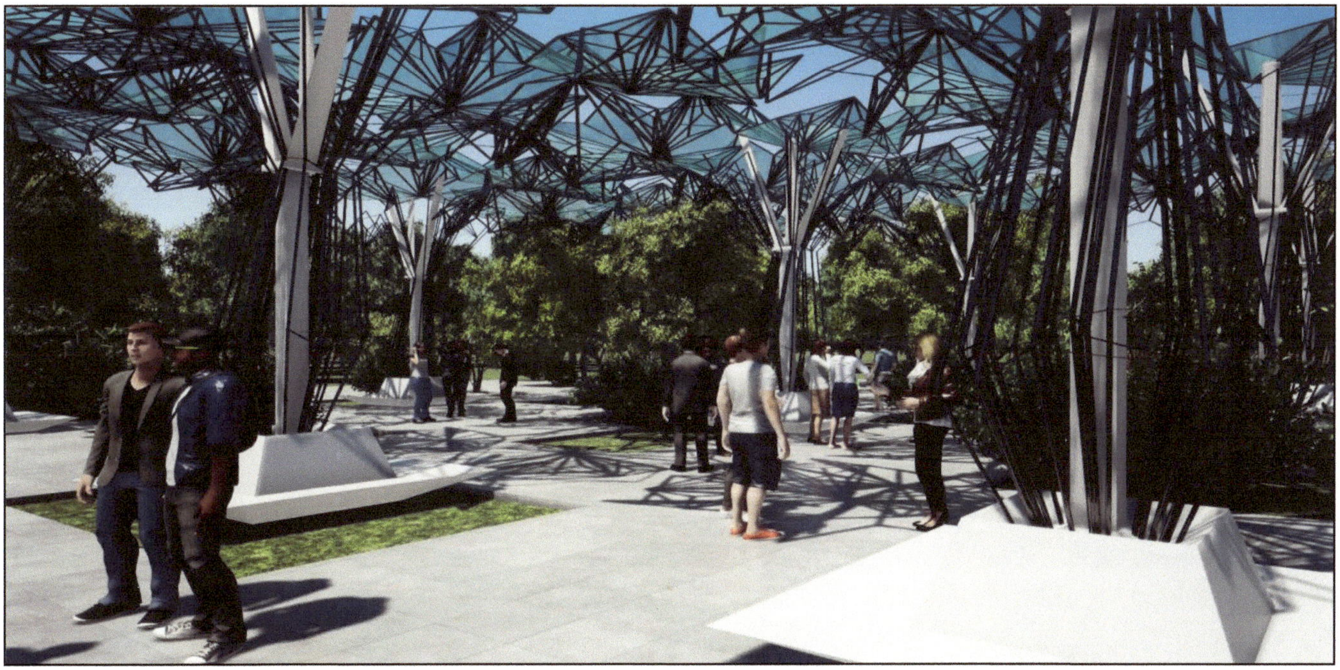

Wicker Pavilion
Shabnam Javankar

Traditional mats were used to decorate windows and balconies of the old houses to prevent from entrance of intense light and heat of the sun and insects. Modernization of urban lives put the mat-making and mat-selling shops aside in cities and a few of such mat-selling shops may be seen in the big cities.

Application of traditional mats:
- Curtain
- Cover of the balcony rails
- Cover of air-conditioners against sunlight
-

This project resembles a mat standing up the earth and transformed by the wind. It has opened its wings and wants to fly. Relying on its height, fluid form and meshed structure, it shows itself to the city and people who take no notice of their traditions and past, ignore light and shade, and live in homes and offices with low ceilings and small windows. It wants to remind important issues of the life in a limited space.

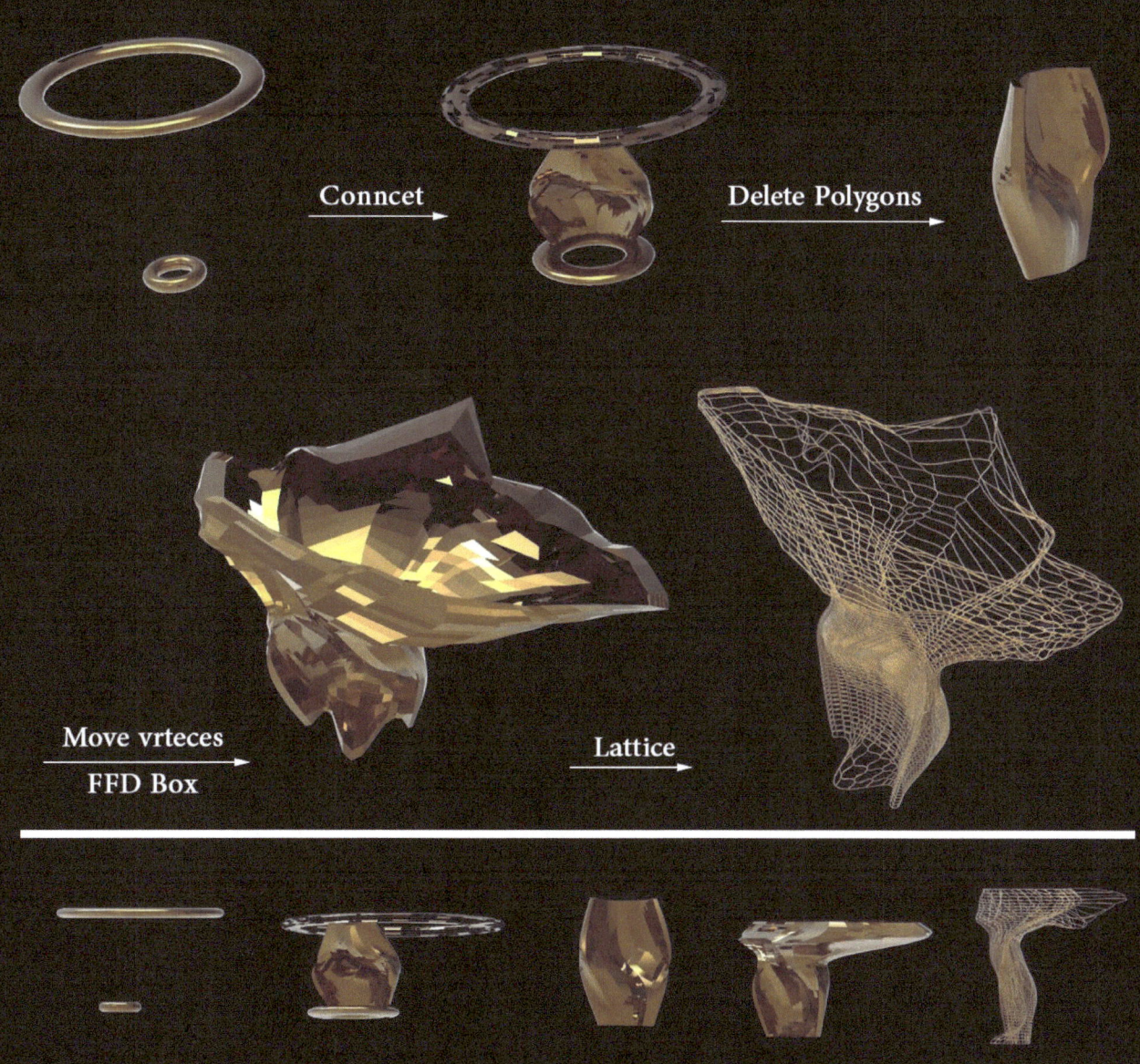

206

Project description
Nasim Tabrizi

Birds are sign of peace, freedom and reconcile with the ecosystem and nature. Due to its form, structure, wings and beauty of its feather, birds associate with the concept of flight and ascension in the viewer's mind, passing from the material world to freedom and infinite world. Birds are of common species of beings recorded in different forms and symbols in the history, culture and art of every society, whether the picture of the birds is used in form of painting or sculpture or an abstract image of the birds is created. This attitude has special position in the architectural design. Inspired from the mentioned cases, this plan tries to show flight and tranquility in form of a pavilion indicating to the birds gathered together.

To be inspired of upward and downward curved form of the birds, a close form and special union is created among the forms which are free from any violence and sharp movements. Also, repetition of volume and hierarchies invite the viewer to its inside.

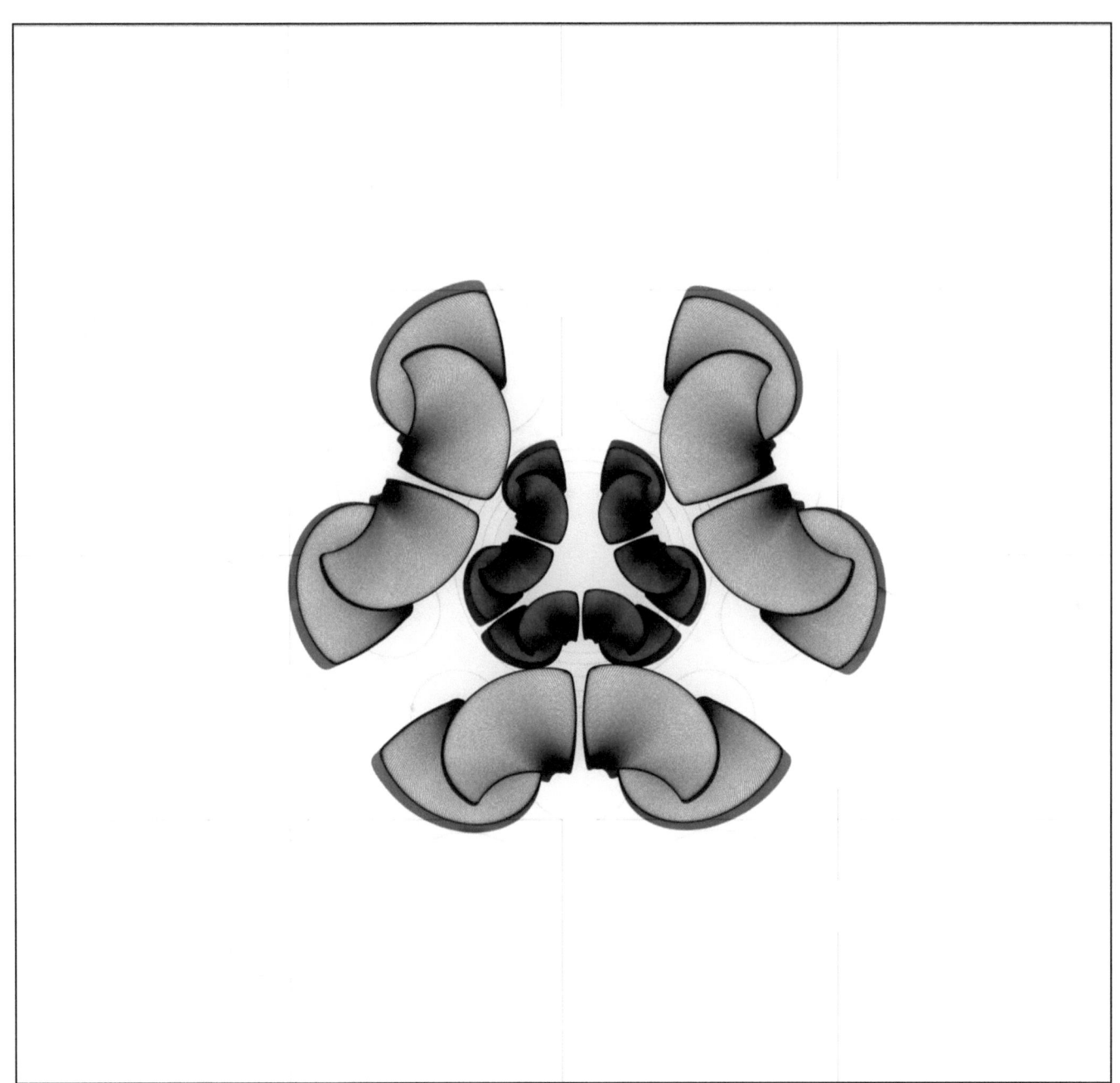

Site plan

210

Temporary Forest Residence in Arasbaran
Zahra Lotfi

Tourism development is one the most essential infrastructures of development of each country. Considering its climate diversity, Iran has special amenities to tourist attraction. Arasbaran forests are regarded as one of the favorite tourism zones in Northwest Iran because of its natural and wonderful perspectives and tourism may be emphasized in this zone through providing appropriate conditions and amenities such as residential facilities and installations matching with the environment. Babak Fort which is historically important for the Azarbaijan people attracts many tourists and mountain climbers.

A space between the hills of Arasbaran forests in one of the main paths shall be used to design this temporary forest residence. This residence was designed through combination of interior and exterior space and use of natural environment materials. The dominant idea is a naturalist and organic perception. It simulates a space between the branches of trees such that it keeps the person between the interior and exterior space and creates the scene of presence in nature and mental calm for the person.

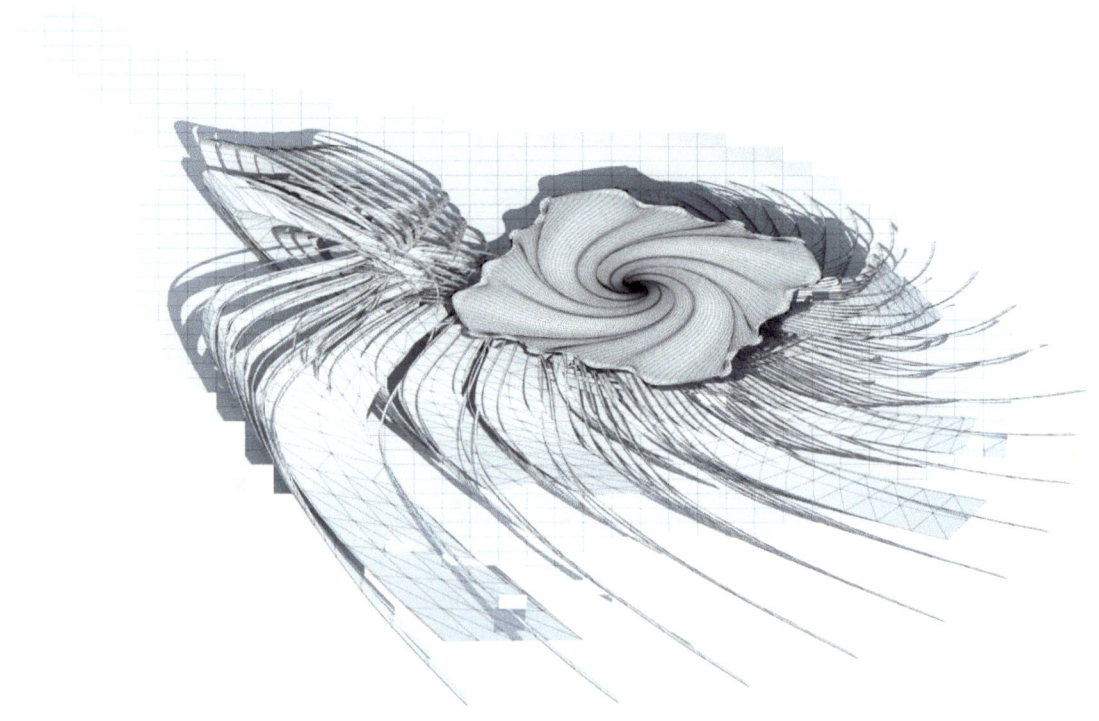

Site plan

Façade of pavilion

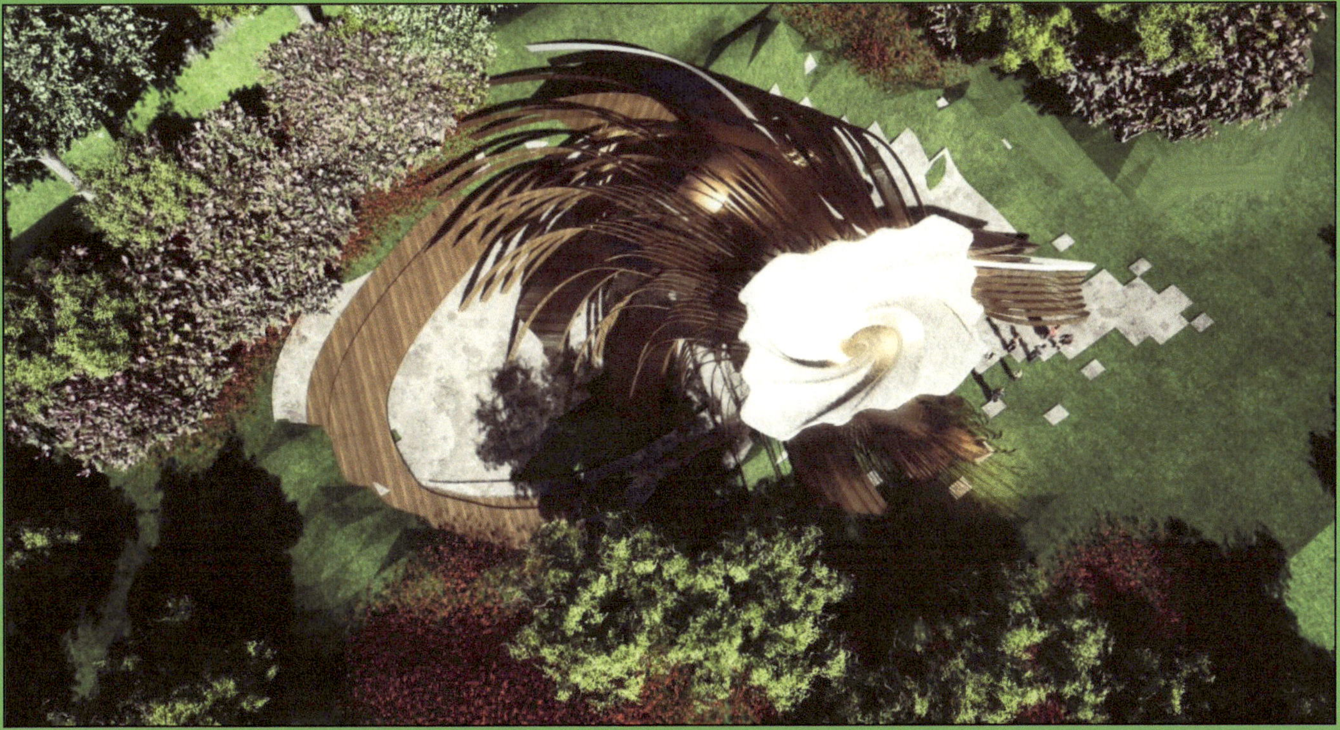

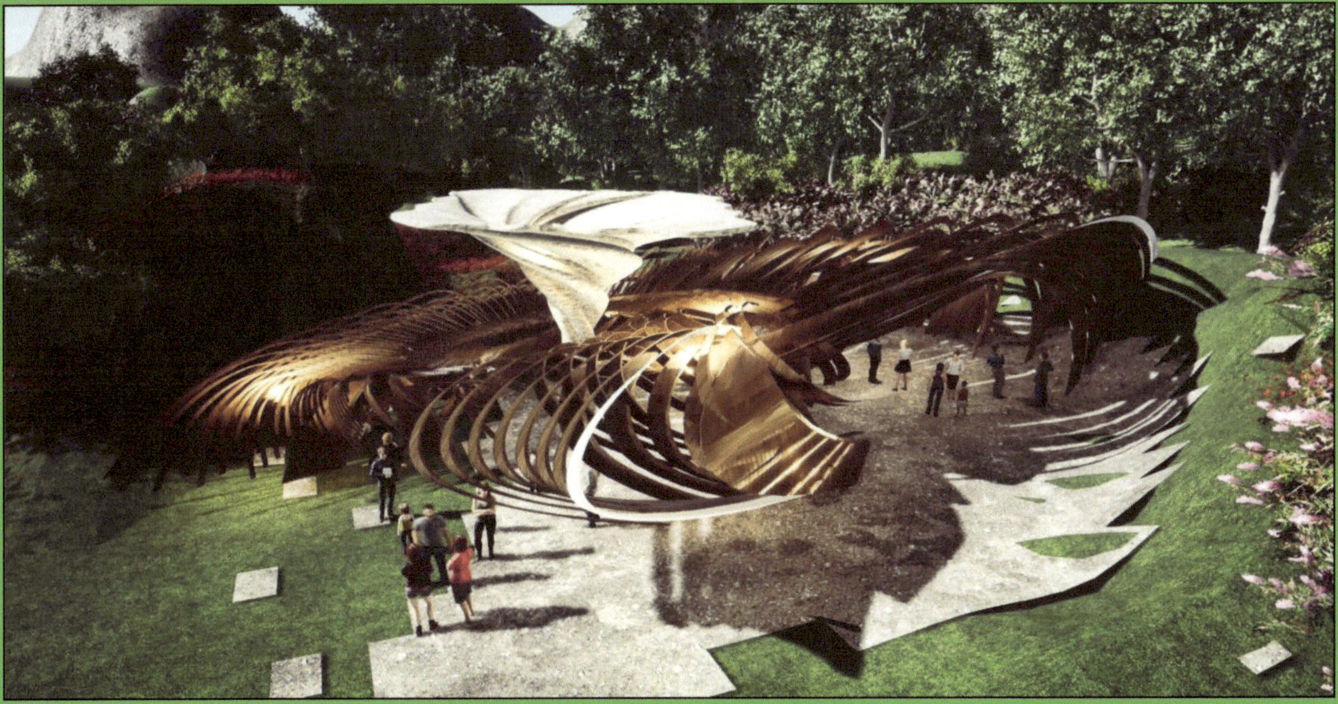

Land rise pavilion

Zahra Lotfi

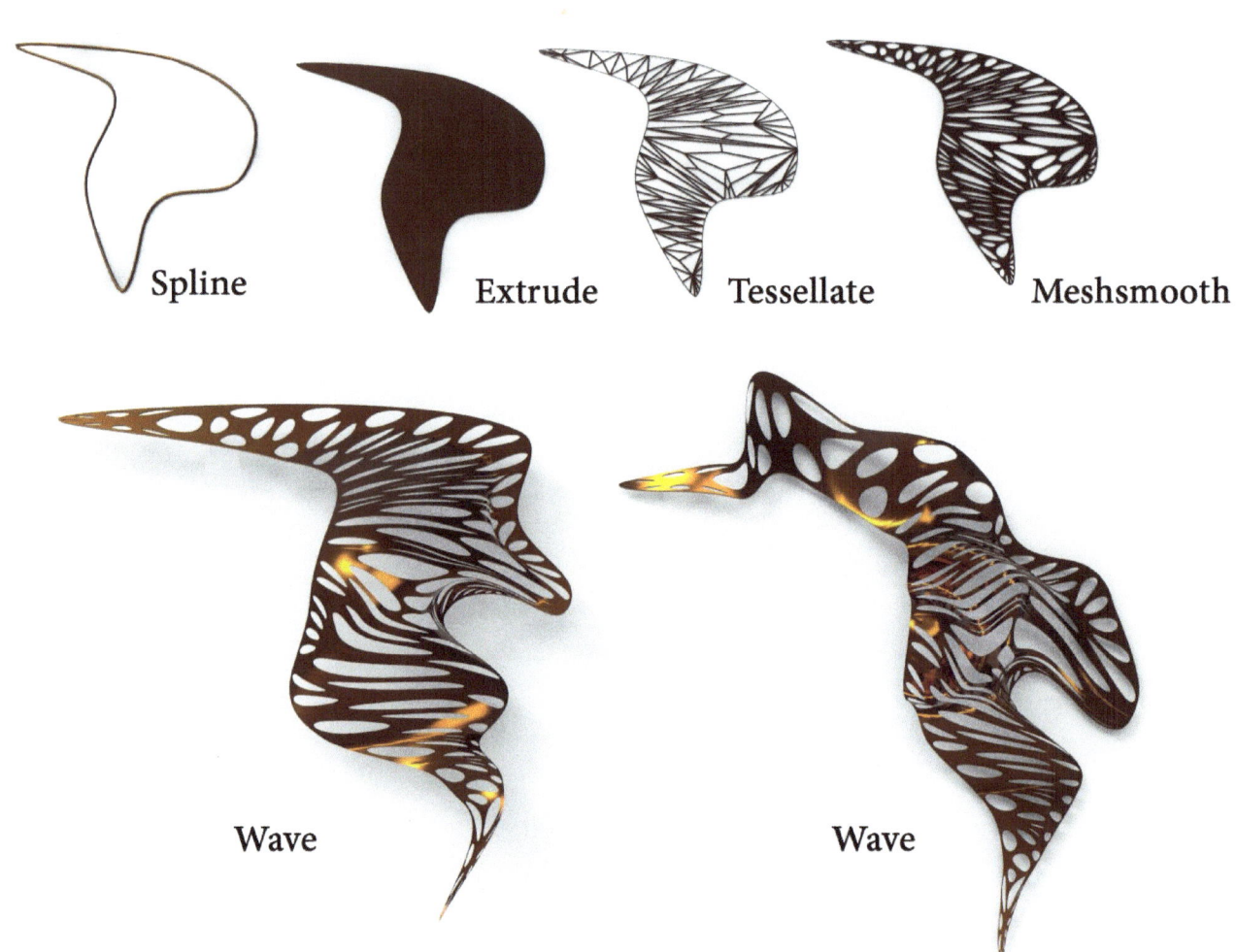

Design process

Siteplan design process

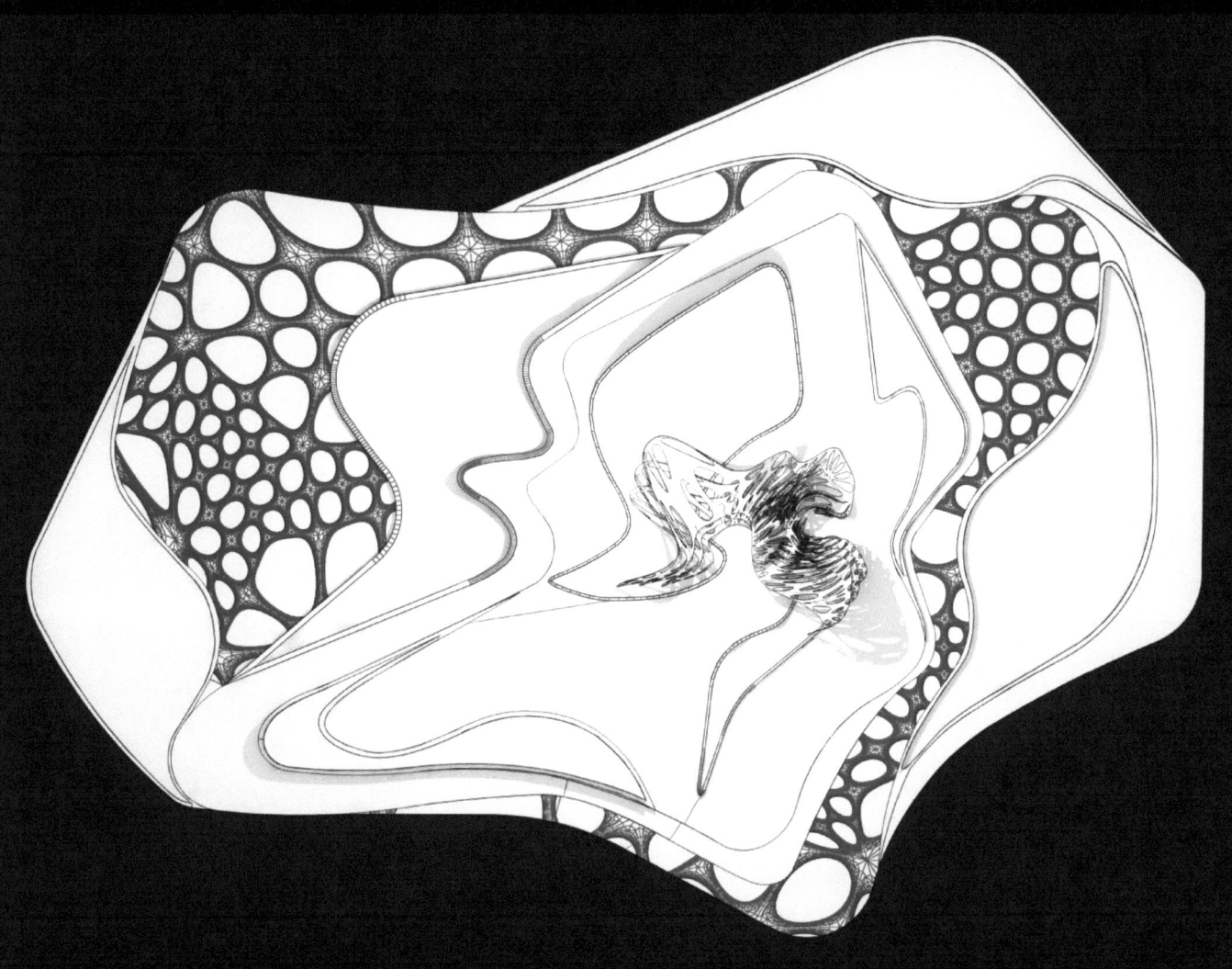

Site Plan

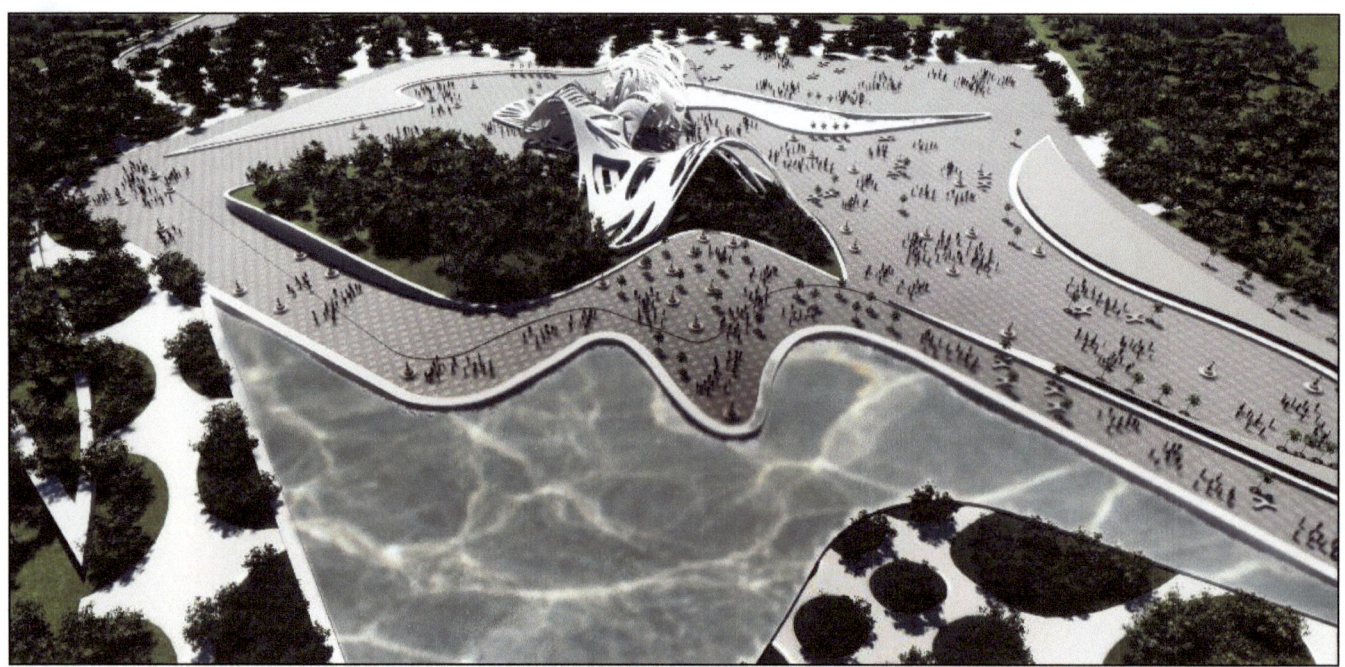

Haoma pavilion

Zahra Mohtadi

The design of the Pavilion has been in such a way that as a central point in the park, it can gather people around to use as art and theater exhibitions. It can also be used for photography and art workshops. The location of such spaces improves the use of parks and transforms them from a purely recreational place to places with multiple functions.

In the design of this pavilion, it is inspired by the Hume plant, which is the god of plants in ancient Persia and one of its properties is server and happiness.

Haoma Flowers - http://nature-bank.iranology.ir/

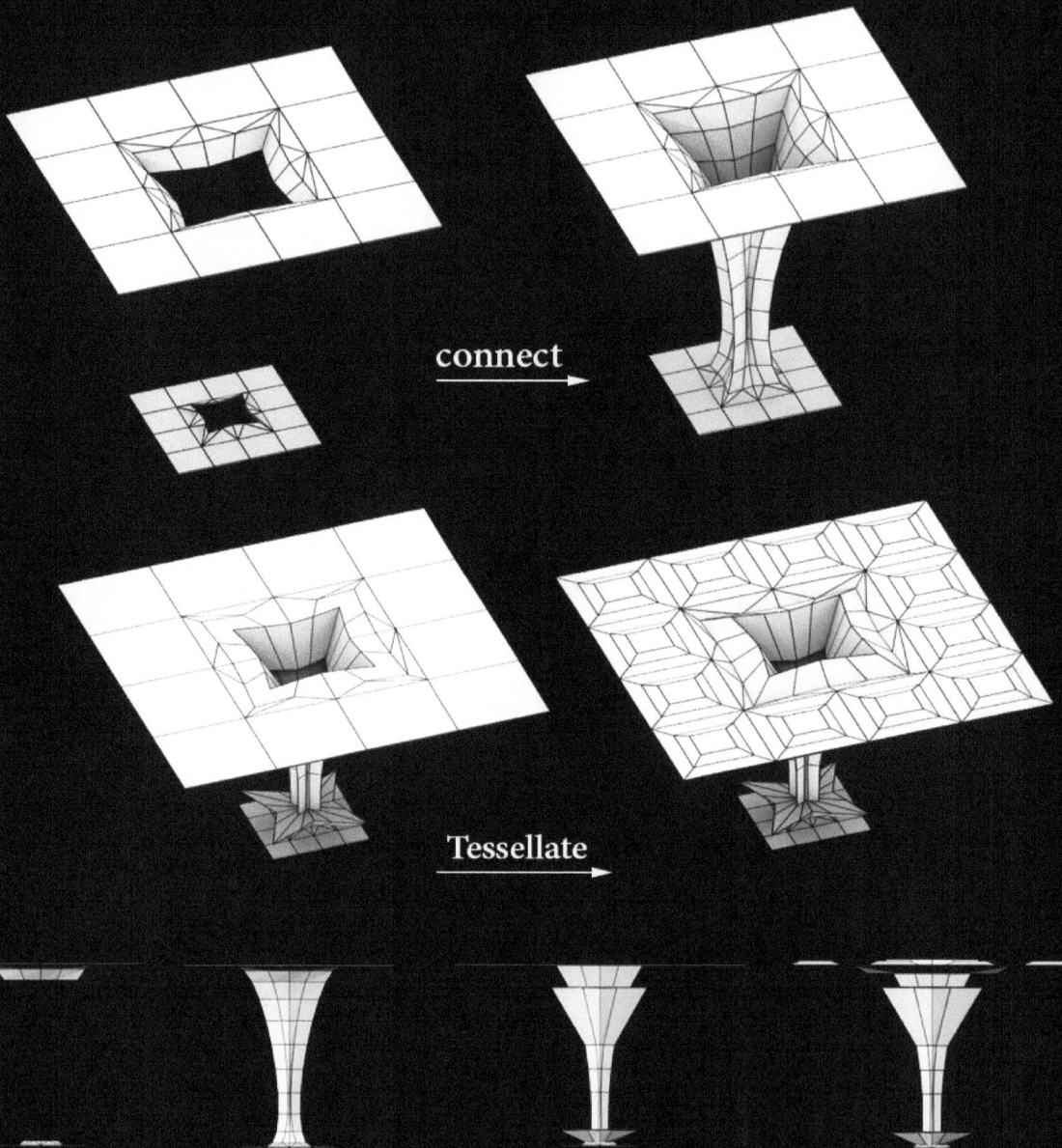

232

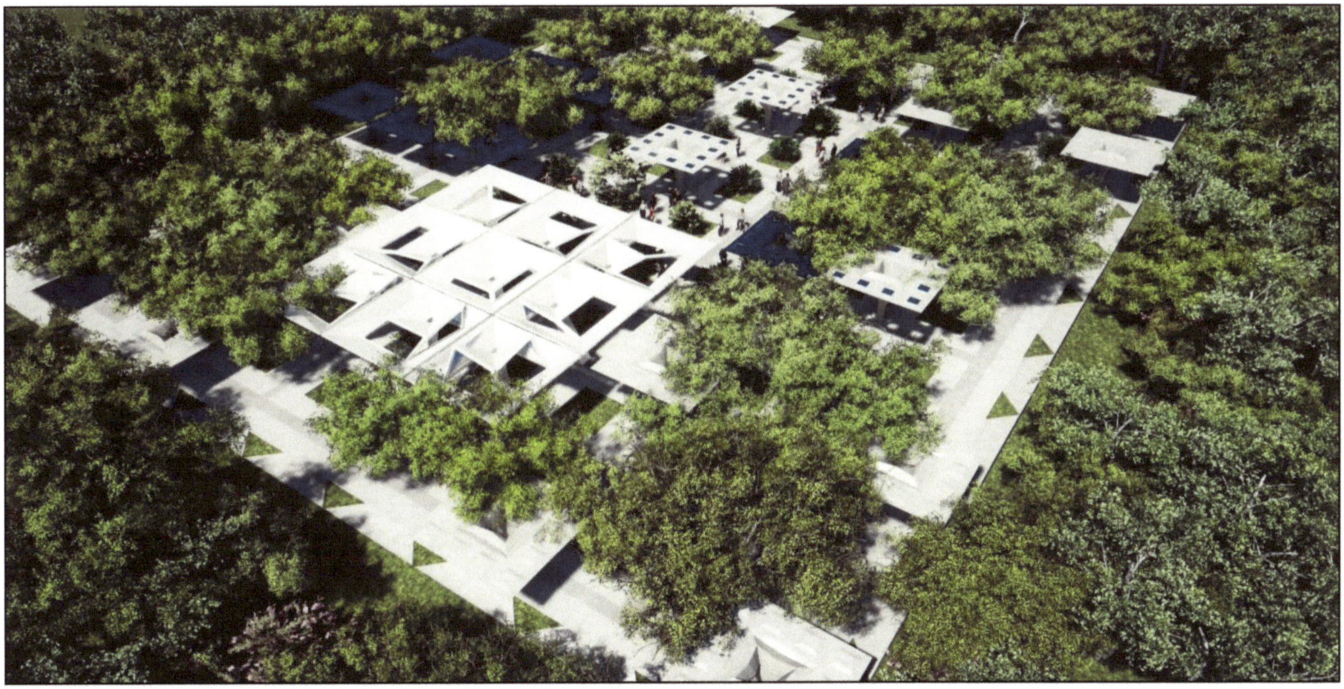

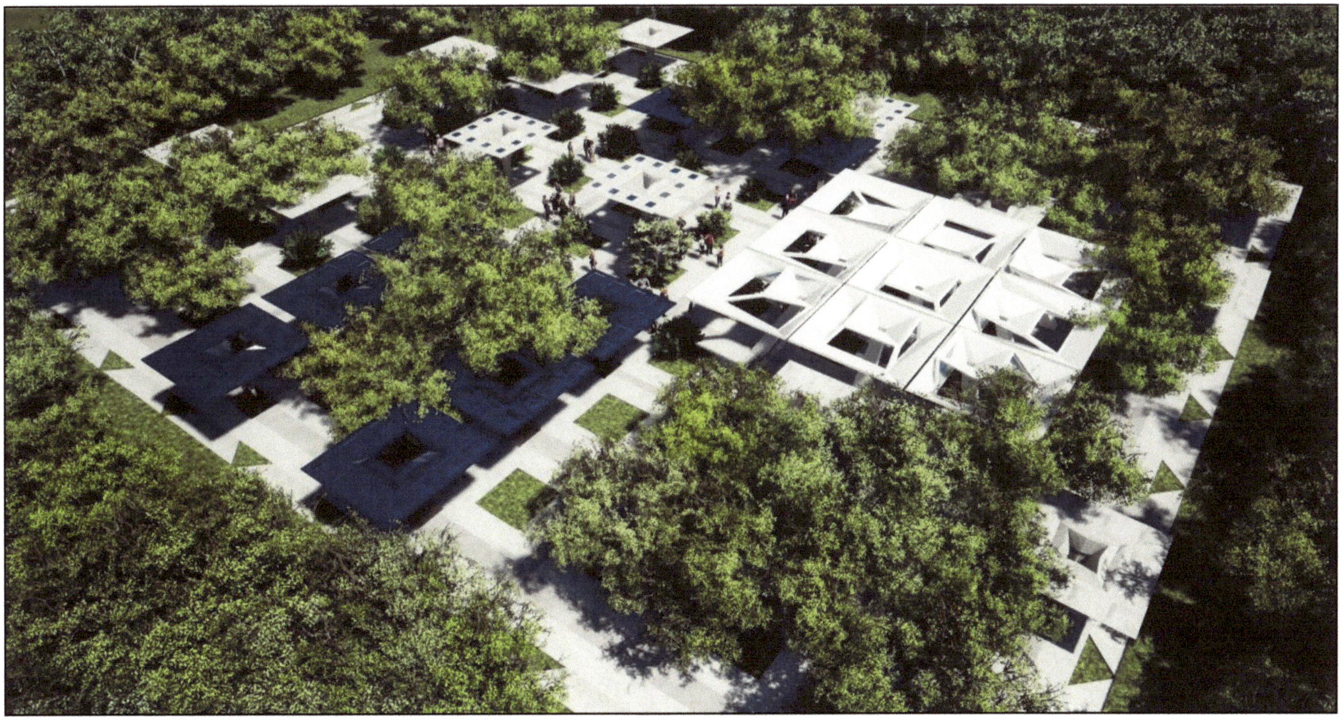

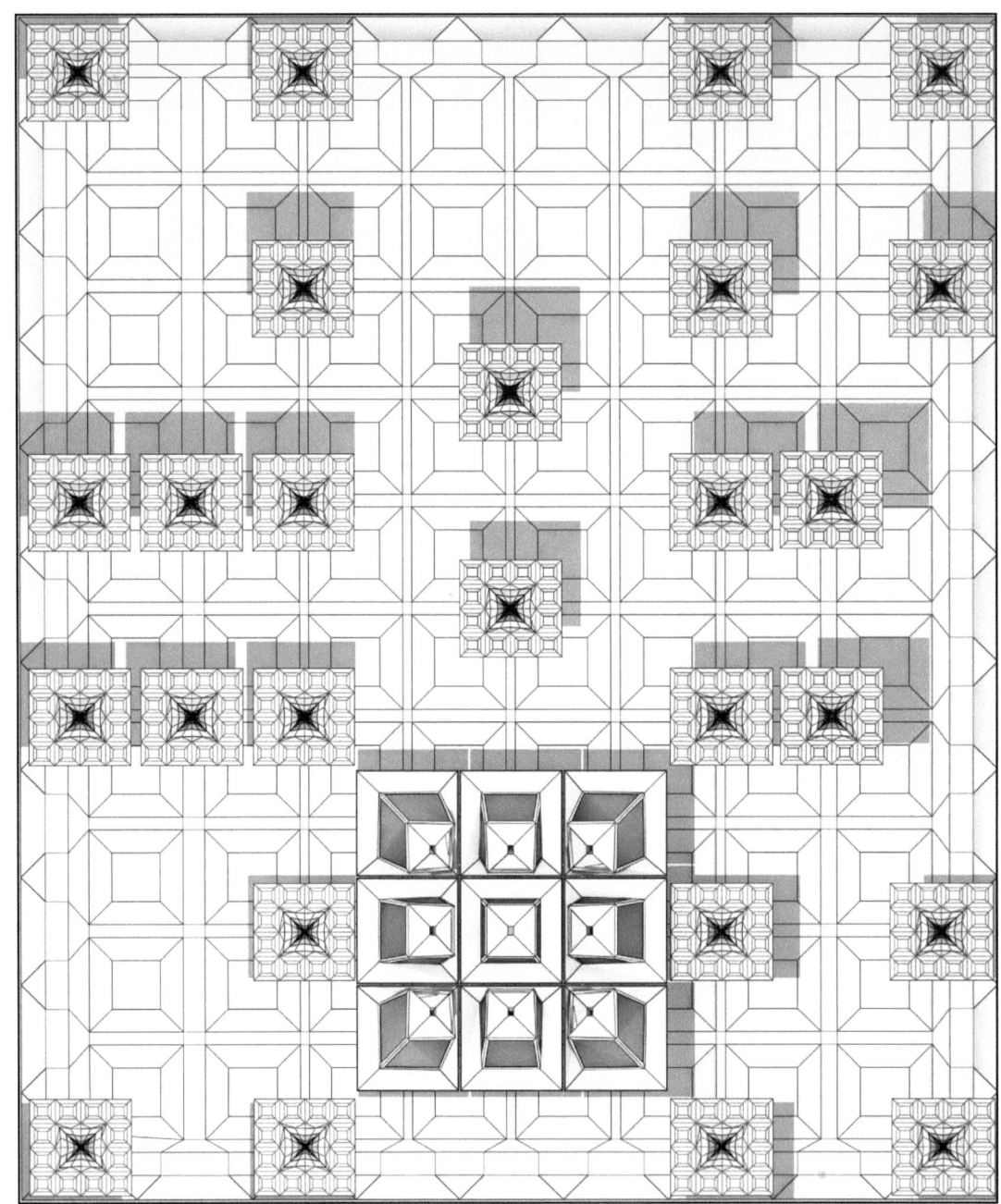

Site plan

234

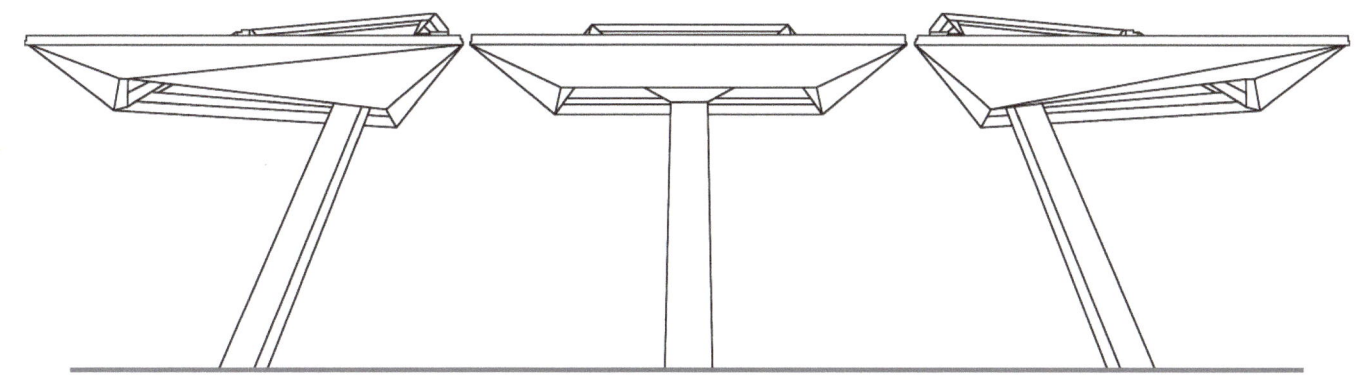

Pavilion facade

Project description

Maryam Torabi

Urban spaces are the center of urban and social life and the main element in identifying cities and promote the citizens' culture. The social content of the space such as humanistic spatial qualities including social interactions which are based on presence of the people in the urban spaces and their social communications and relations such that presence of the people and their social interactions have always been considered as one of the most important factors organizing peripheral quality of cities. In fact, success rate of urban spaces depends on the rate of using that space and presence of humans there. In other words, architecture and urban development should try to increase social interactions and correlation of humans instead of segregation. The main and important point in social interactions is to stay in space. To create interaction, the urban spaces should initially welcome people since presence and stay of people in the space creates automatically an interaction among them.

This project aims at designing a pavilion for rest, recreation, and public gatherings of the residents of Shahrak Marzdaran located at East Tabriz. In this regard, it is tried to provide a place for people using the elements being inspired from the nature, combining them with the nature of the park, inviting people to attend the park, continuous horizontal movement of the pavilion and building wings to sit, rest and stay there.

The main element of this pavilion is the shades with wide cover which is inspired from the nature and is a combination of butterfly wings and trees where the inner and outer spaces of the pavilion are connected to each other and it is tried to keep the visual relation of the visitor with the environment and each other. It is tried to lessen the view of the surrounding apartment in the spatial decoration of the pavilion and maintain the visual communication of the people with the garden and nature of the park to create possibility of more stay in the environment relying on the inherent attractiveness of the nature and the visitors have more time to stay the space and communicate with each other. In fact, designing a park to be together in Shahrak Marzdaran is a practice to design a float space with the concepts of relation between inner and outer spaces and open and closed spaces.

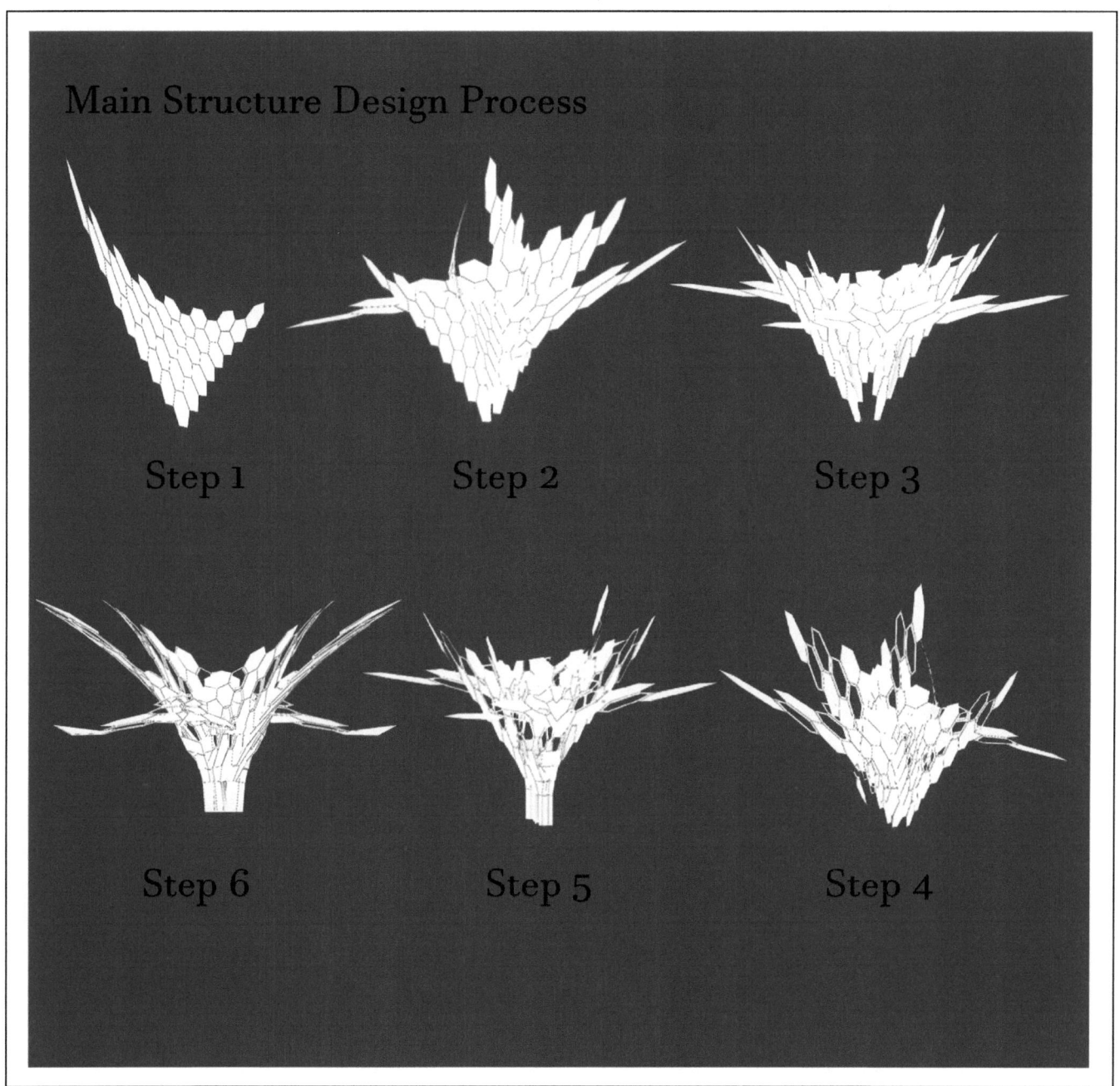

Design Process of the main pavilion

Main Structu[re]

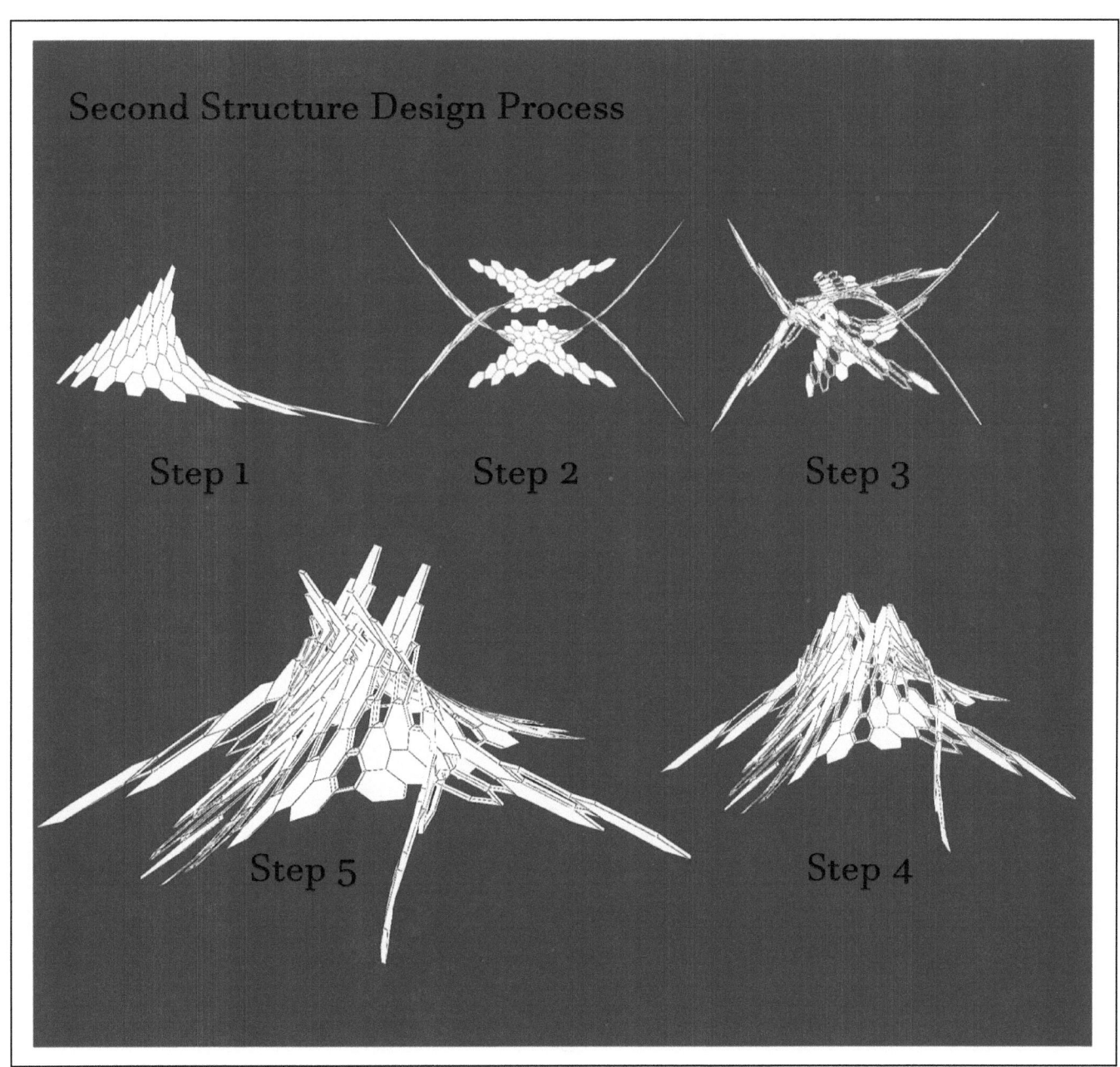

Design process of the second structure

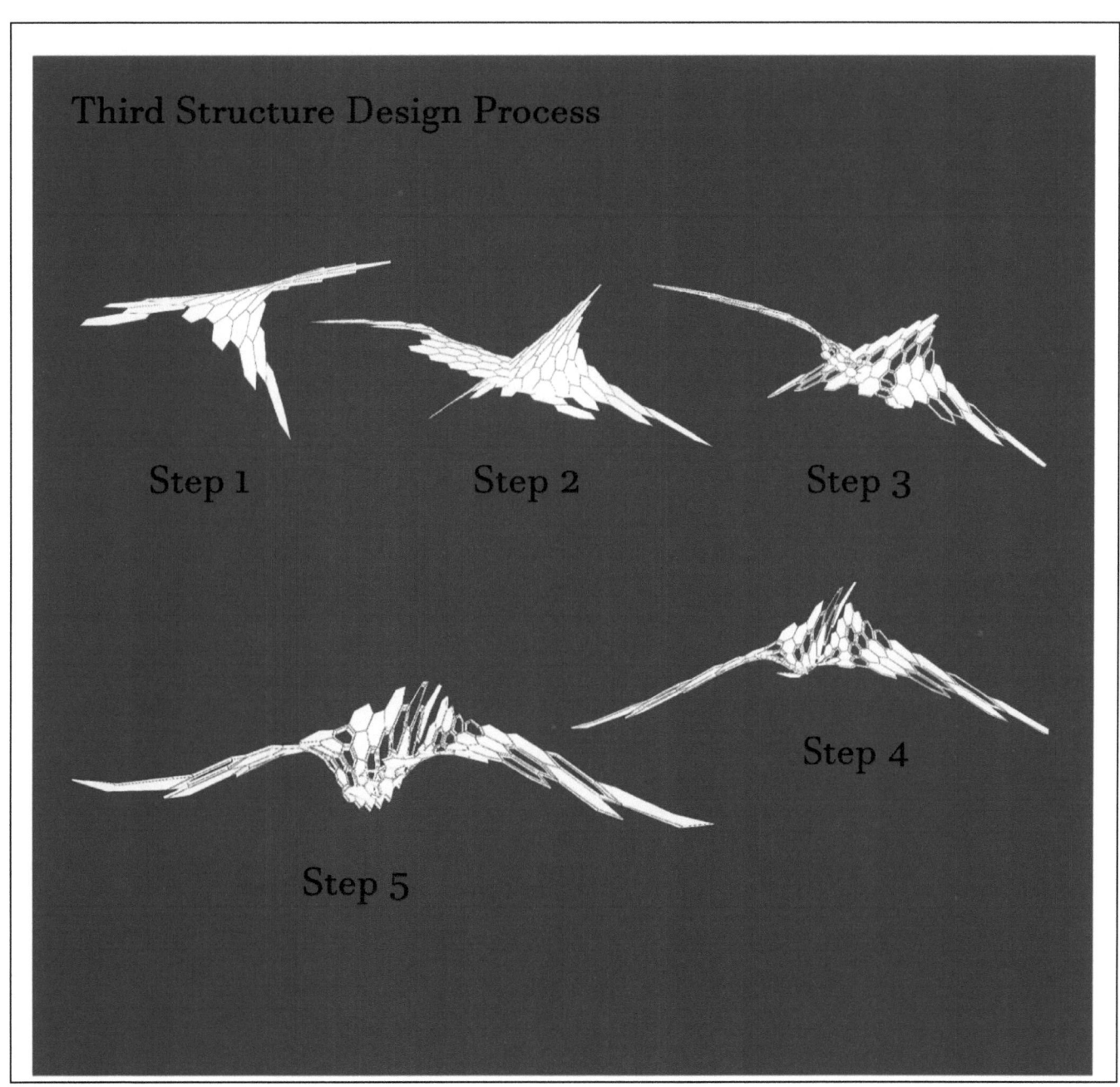

Design process of the third structure

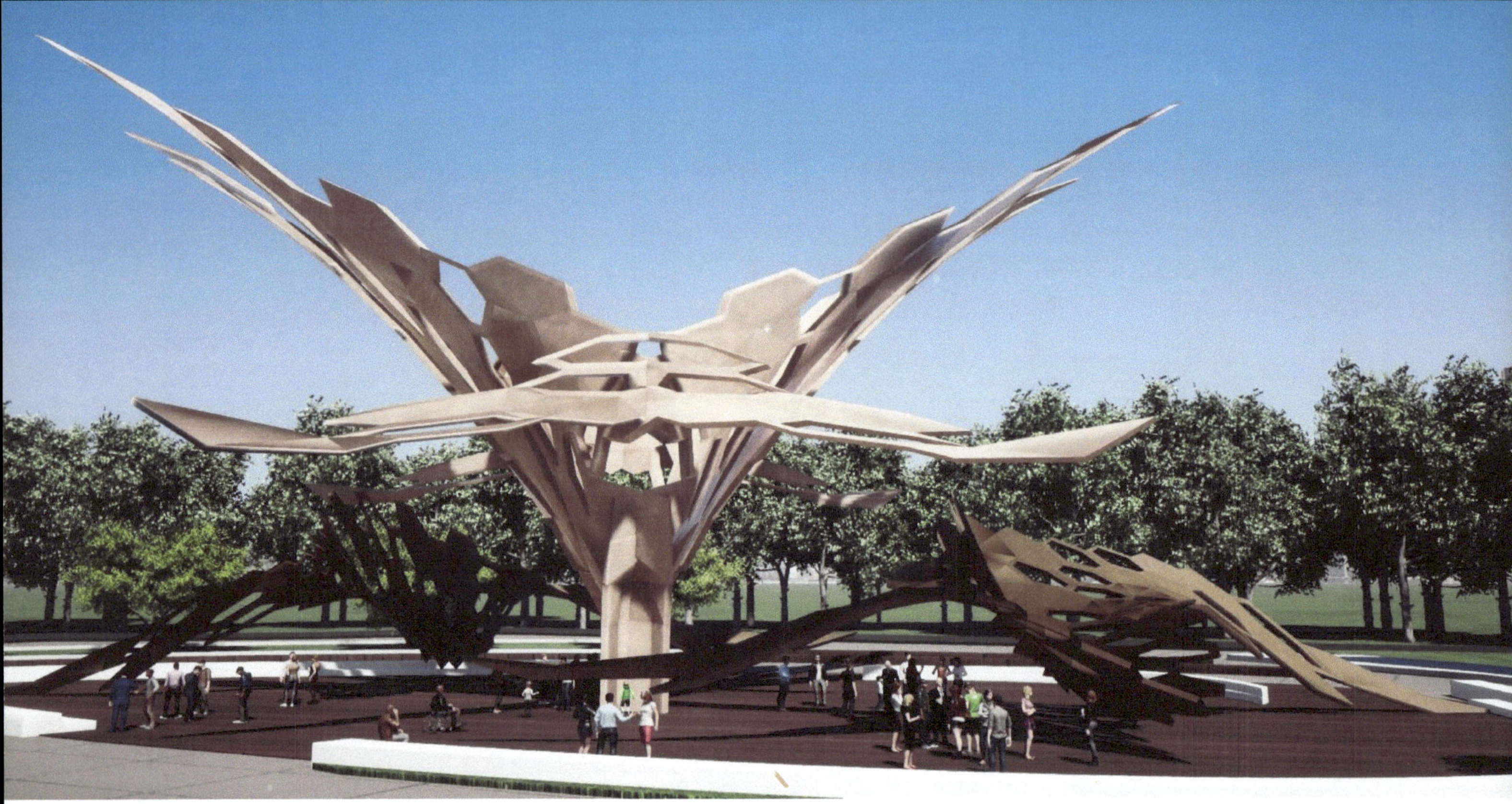

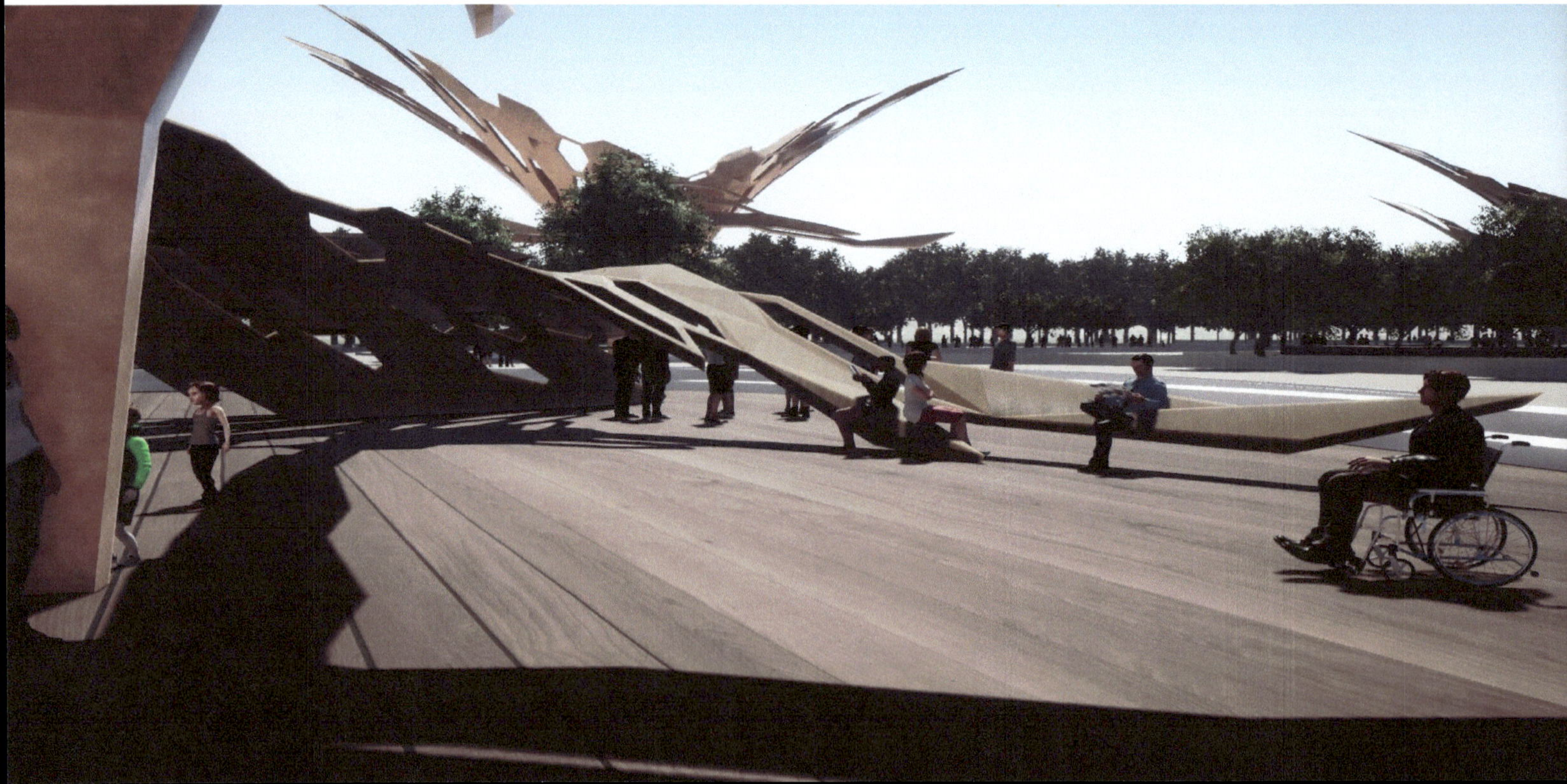

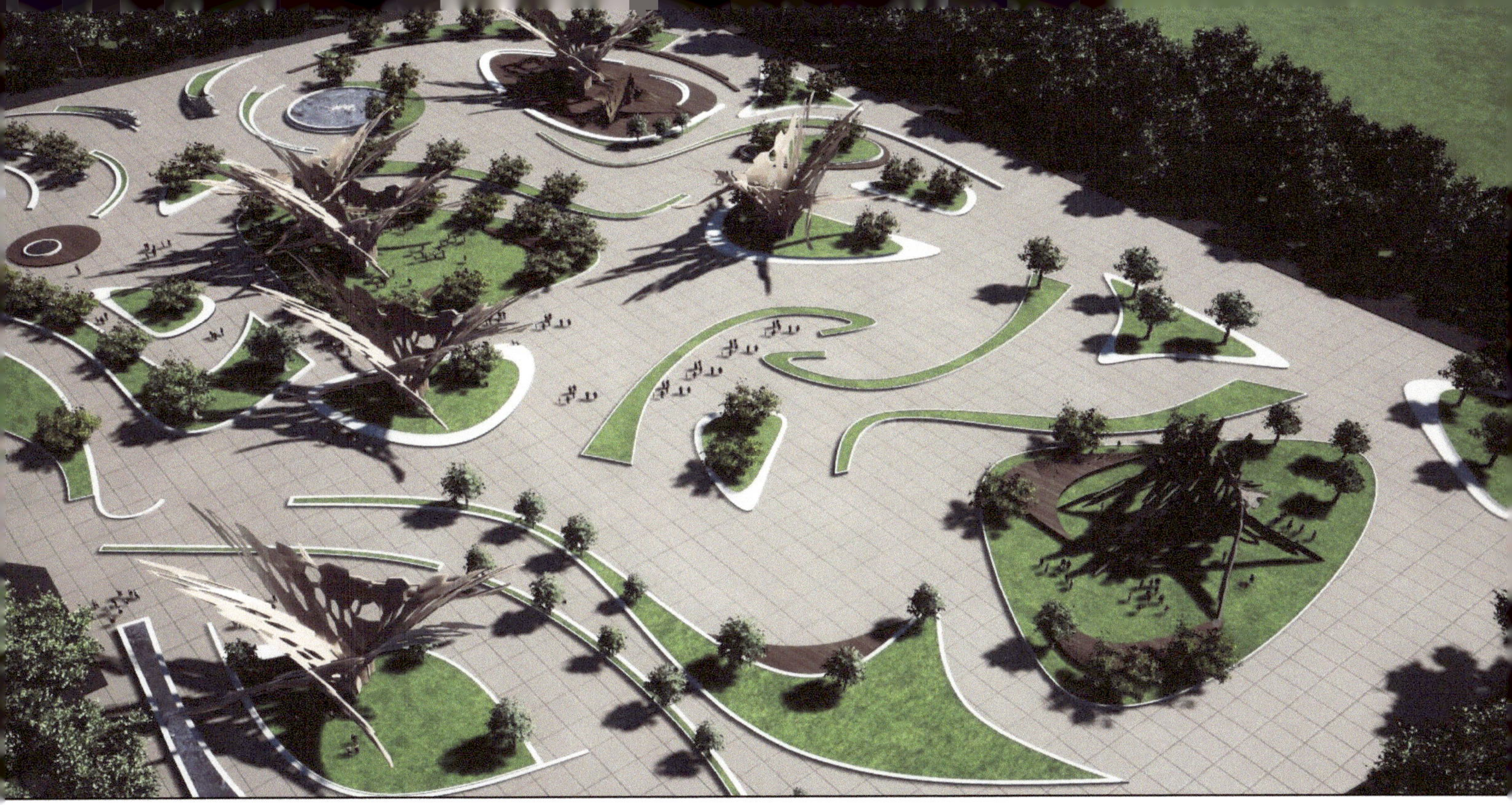

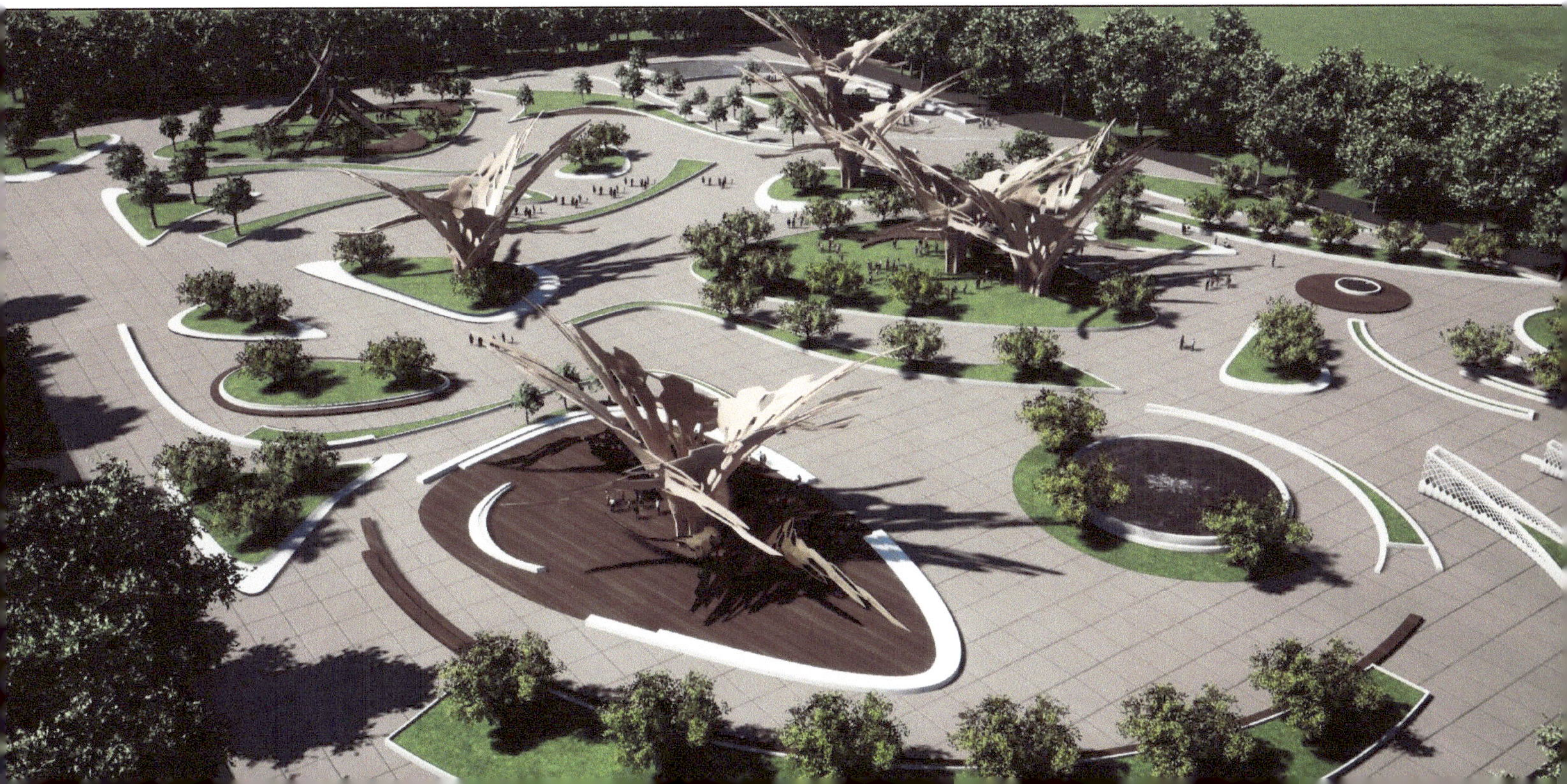

Lookout
Ali Ghorbani

Most projects designed in the workshop were developed horizontally. But, I decided to design my pavilion vertically. Its main idea roots from the high school period when there was a firefighting station where the first firefighting tower of Iran was built. I designed my pavilion based on this old 100- year tower with the height of 23 meters. I designed an 18-meter height tower in four stories connecting to each other with the spiral stairs.

Studying the design process, I concluded that the tower is not sufficient to attract people. Therefore, I designed a restaurant near the tower inspiring from its structure. The restaurant ceiling was made of wood and its projected structure was covered with grass and ivy. These two buildings are not tied to the site and may be built in different parks of Tabriz in line with the objectives of the workshop.

Firefighting tower- https://www.nabro.ir/

Design process of the main pavilion

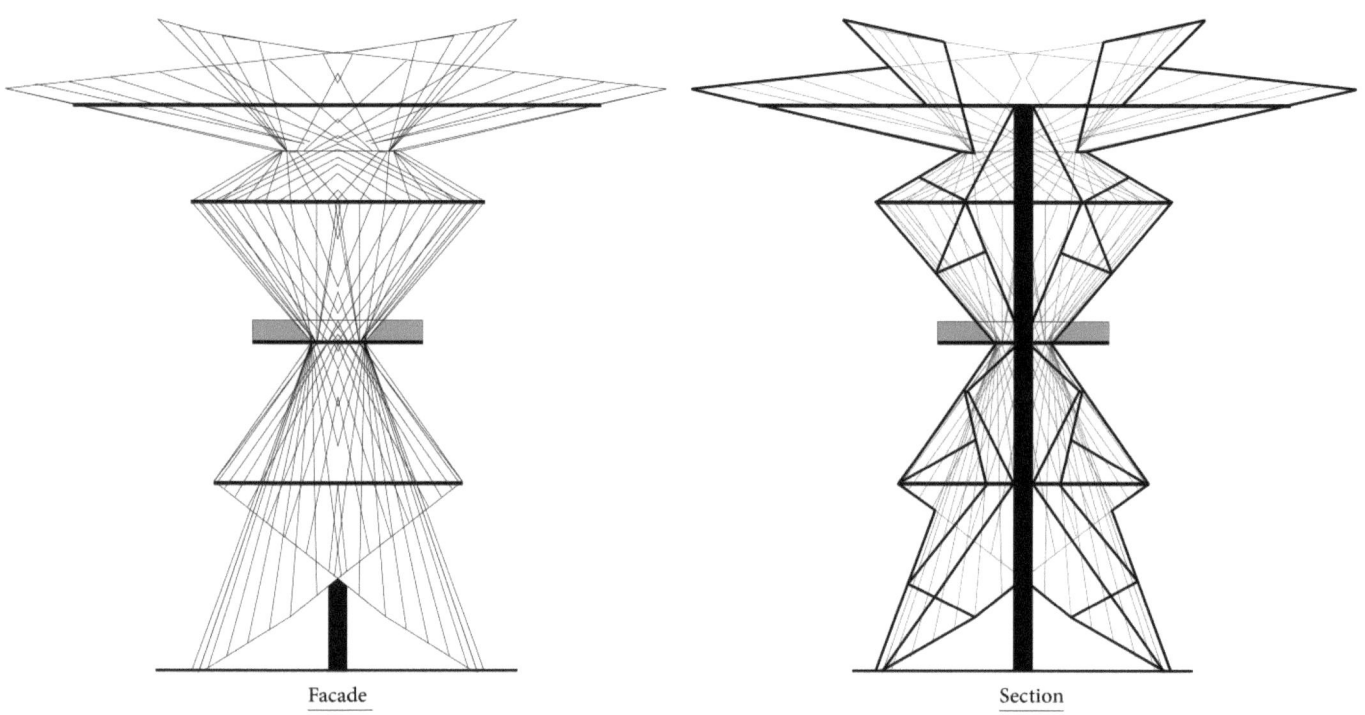

251

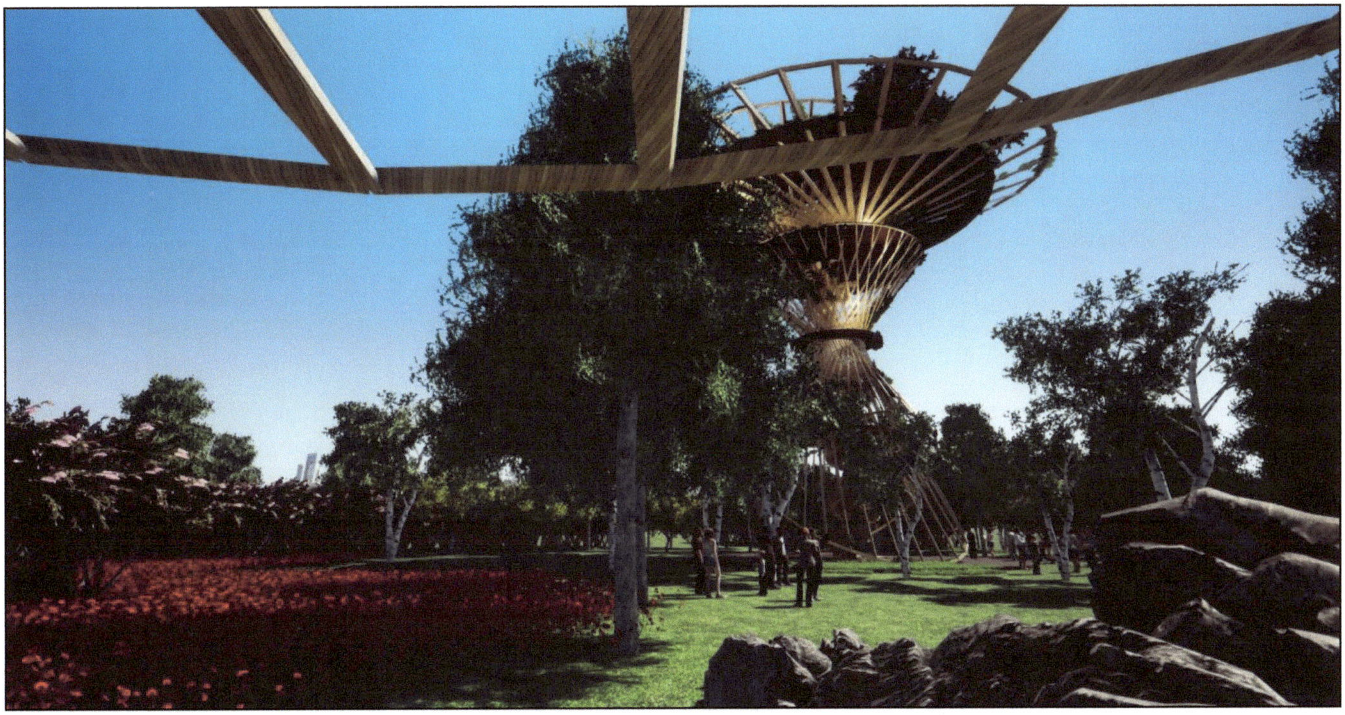

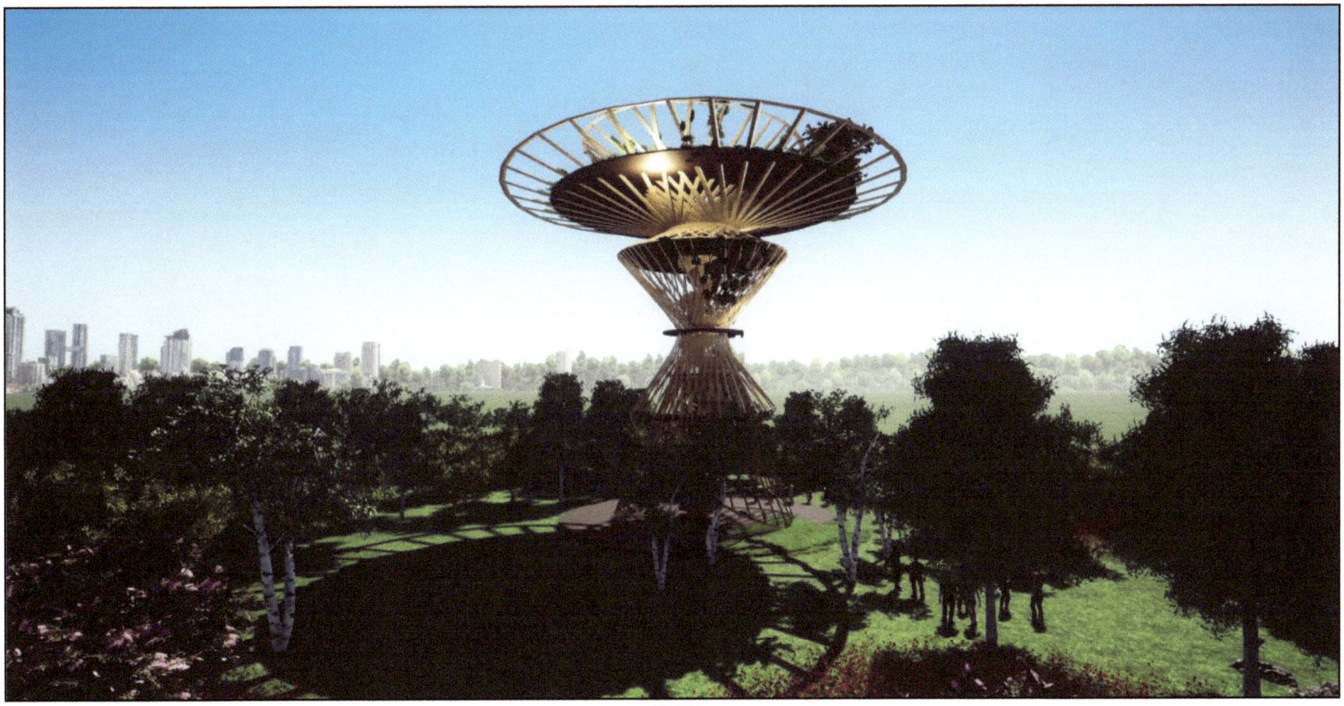

Bloom pavilion

Ali Ghorbani

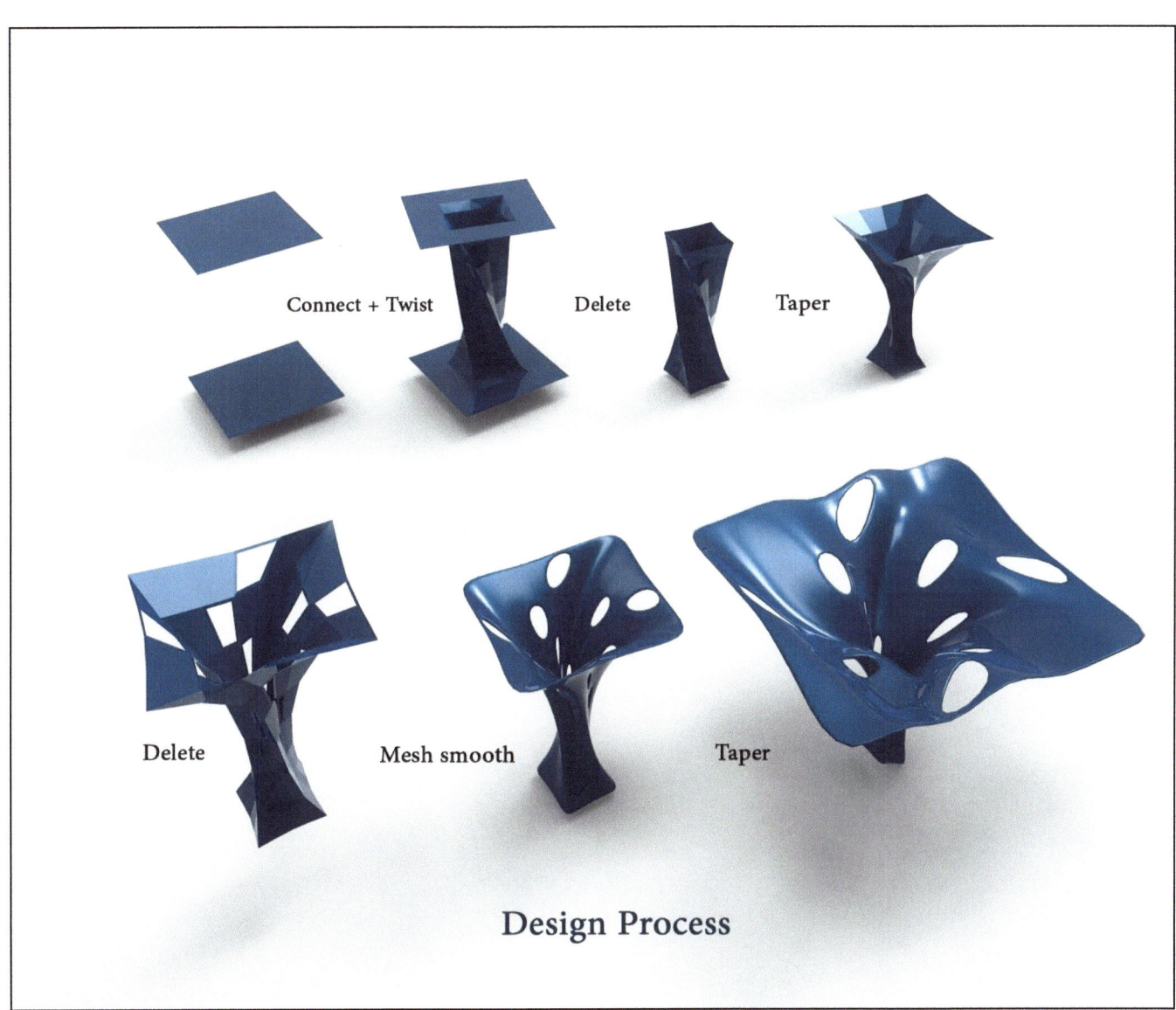

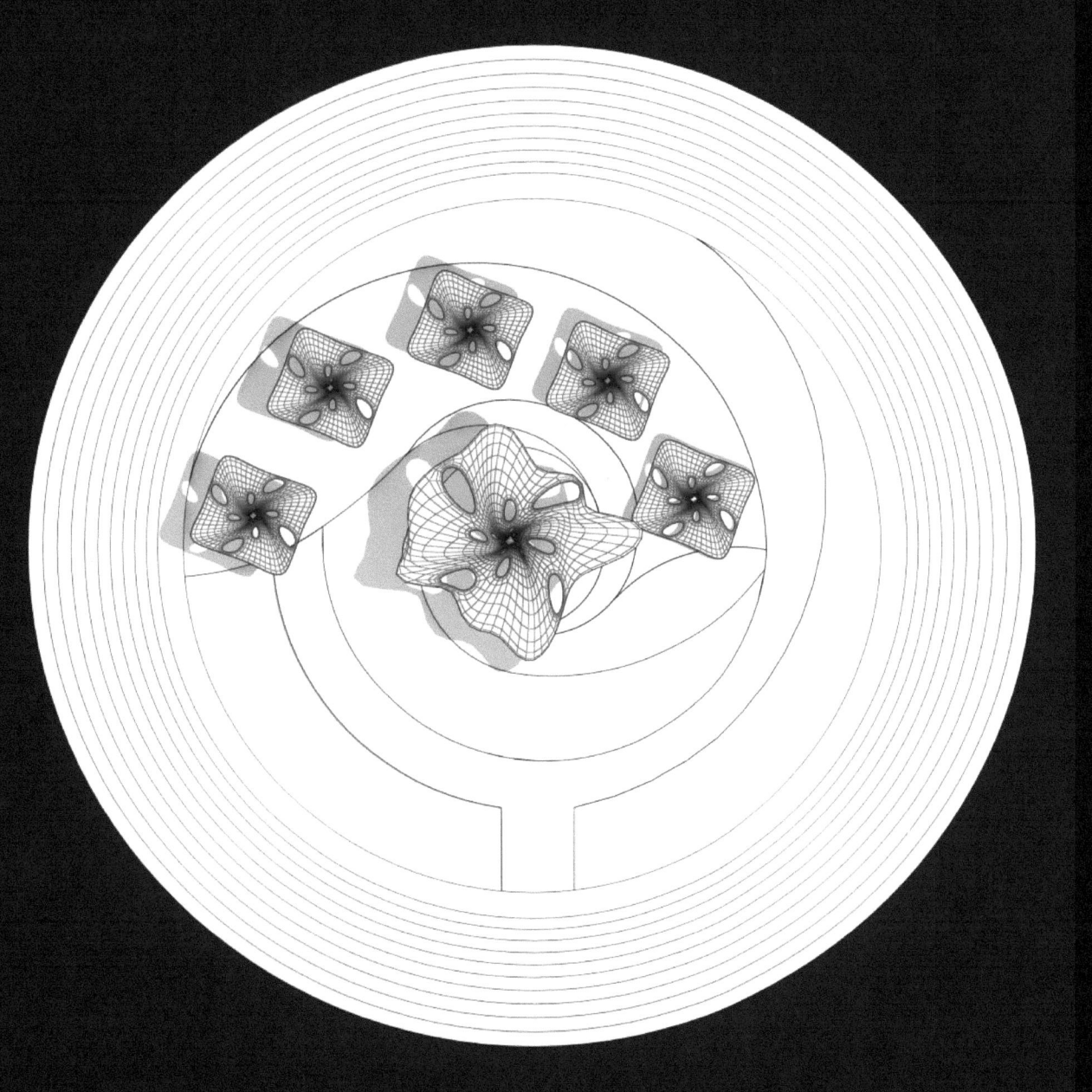

Site plan

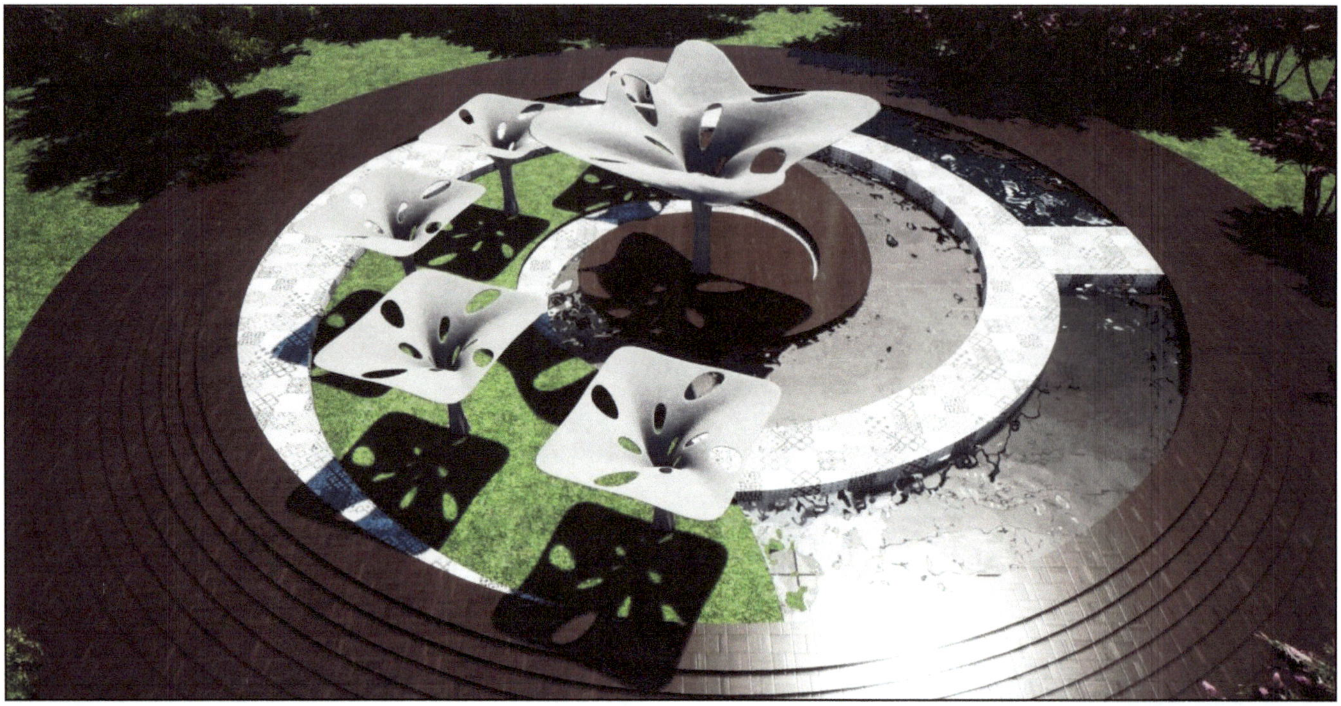

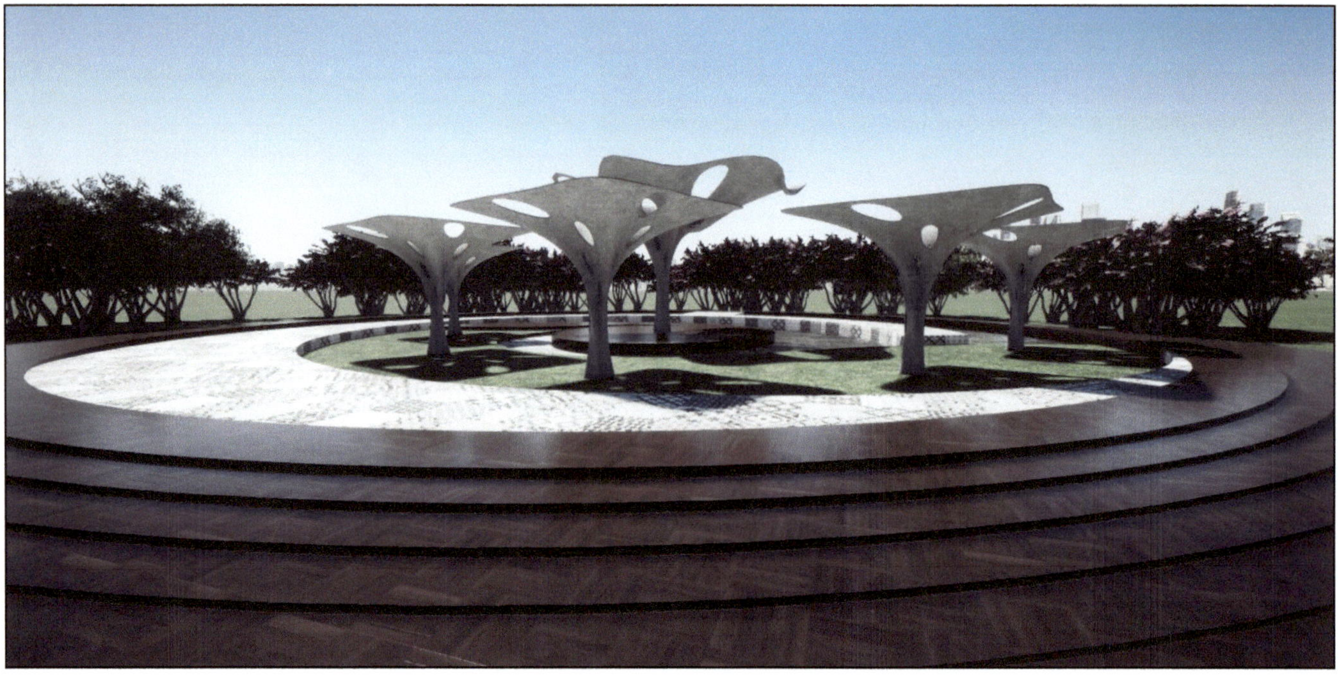

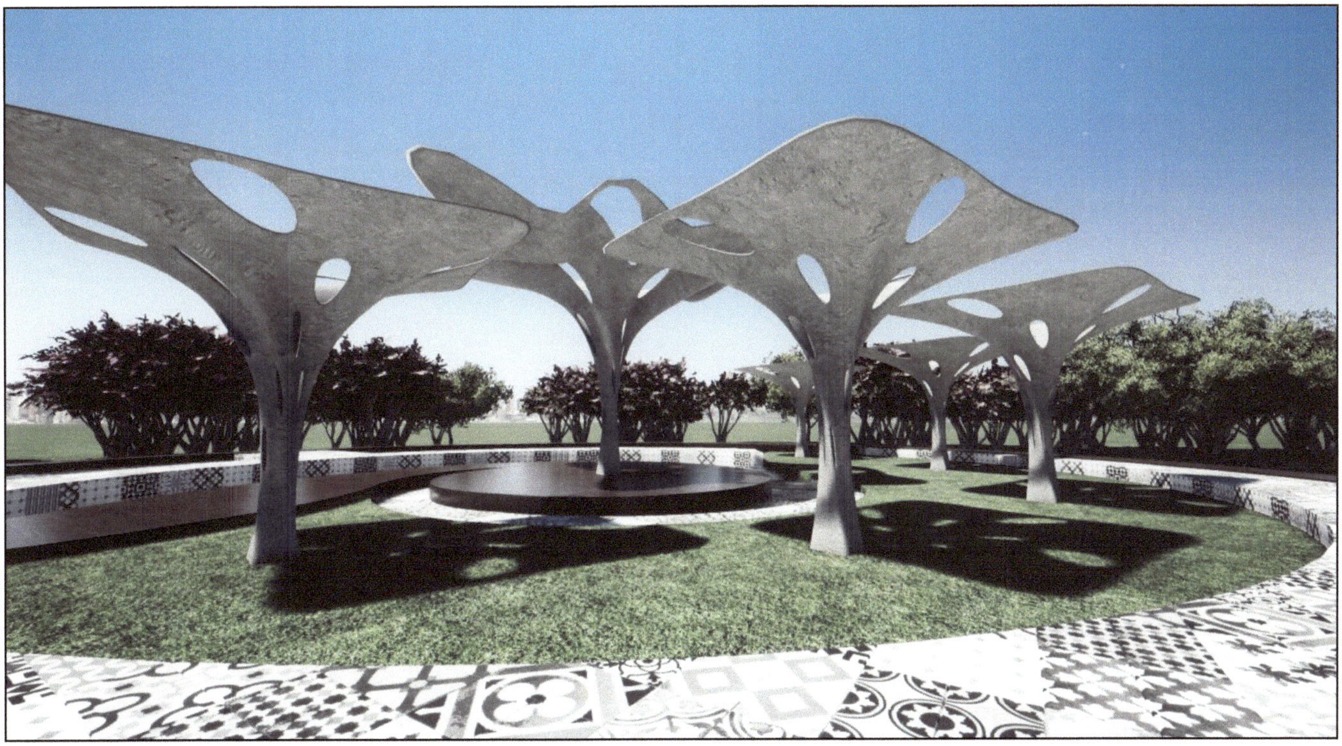

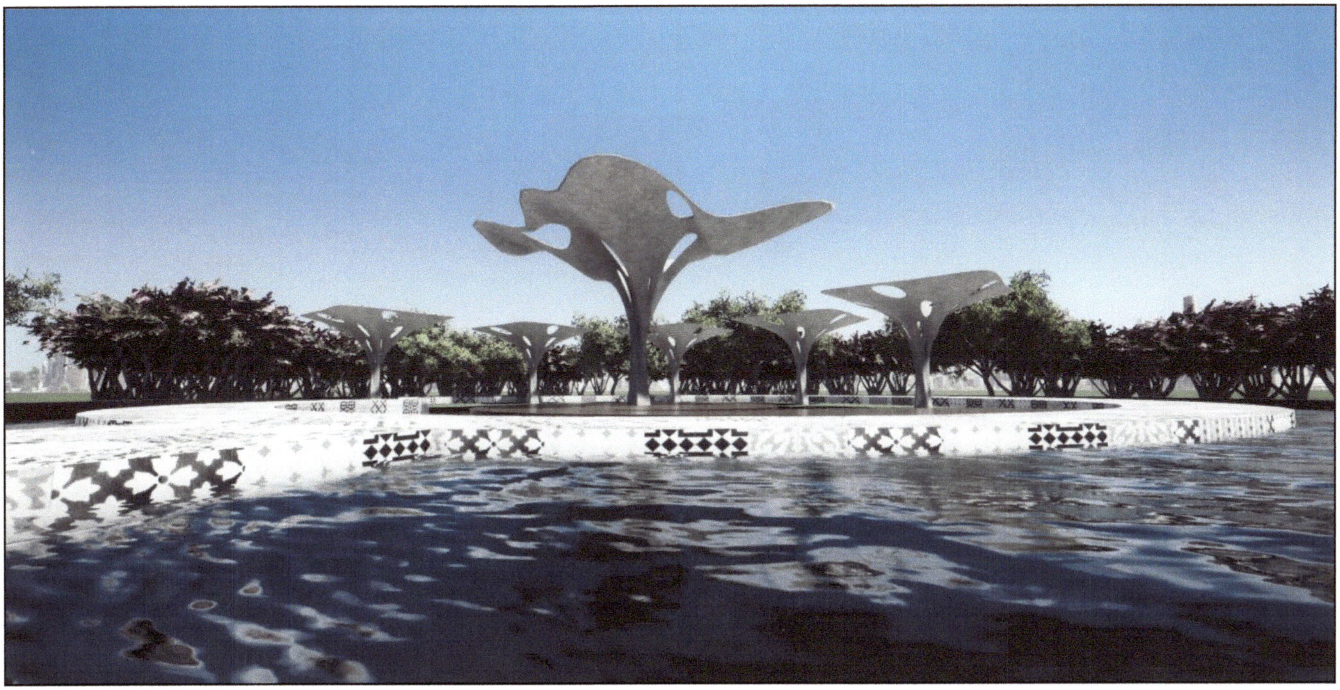

Books of Ali Khiabanian

Painting & Poetry:
– Dancing Shadows, Iran, winter 2004
– Leila & Rain man, Iran, summer 2008
– Song & Silence, USA, 2016

Architecture:
- The role of Creativity in Design Process1, Iran, 2009.
- The role of Creativity in Design Process2, Iran, 2010.
- Thoughts of the awake mind, Iran, 2011.
- The role of Creativity in Design Process3 (Parametric Architecture), Iran, 2012.
- Line & Color in Architecture (Collection of student's Sketches), Iran, 2013.
- Ideas of Facade Design, Iran, 2014
- Conceptual Sketches in Architectural Design, Supreme Century, USA, 2014
- The Role of Brain Hemispheres in Architectural Design, USA, 2015
- Impact of parametric design on young architects, USA, Supreme Art, 2016
- Tissues as a board for creative sketches "ideas for architectures, landscape, Pattern & textile design, Supreme Century, USA, 2016
- Animate Form, Animate Design, Animate Thinking, American Academic Research, USA, 2018
- Box in digital transformation, Supreme Century, USA, 2019

Amazon link for books:
https://www.amazon.com/Ali-Khiabanian/e/B00JY2UUEG%3Fref=dbs_a_mng_rwt_scns_share